Exam Ref 70-765 Provisioning SQL Databases

Joseph D'Antoni
Scott Klein

Exam Ref 70-765 Provisioning SQL Databases

Published with the authorization of Microsoft Corporation by: Pearson Education, Inc.

Copyright © 2018 by Pearson Education

ISBN-13: 978-1-5093-0381-6
ISBN-10: 1-5093-0381-2

Library of Congress Control Number: 2017953262

7 2019

Trademarks

Microsoft and the trademarks listed at *https://www.microsoft.com* on the "Trademarks" webpage are trademarks of the Microsoft group of companies. All other marks are property of their respective owners.

Warning and Disclaimer

Special Sales

For information about buying this title in bulk quantities, or for special sales opportunities (which may include electronic versions; custom cover designs; and content particular to your business, training goals, marketing focus, or branding interests), please contact our corporate sales department at corpsales@pearsoned.com or (800) 382-3419. For government sales inquiries, please contact governmentsales@pearsoned.com.
For questions about sales outside the U.S., please contact intlcs@pearson.com.

Editor-in-Chief	Greg Wiegand
Acquisitions Editor	Trina MacDonald
Development Editor	Troy Mott
Managing Editor	Sandra Schroeder
Senior Project Editor	Tracey Croom
Editorial Production	Backstop Media
Copy Editor	Christina Rudloff
Indexer	Julie Grady
Proofreader	Christina Rudloff
Technical Editor	Thomas LaRock
Cover Designer	Twist Creative, Seattle

Contents at a glance

Contents

What do you think of this book? We want to hear from you!

Microsoft is interested in hearing your feedback so we can continually improve our books and learning resources for you. To participate in a brief online survey, please visit:

https://aka.ms/tellpress

What do you think of this book? We want to hear from you!

Microsoft is interested in hearing your feedback so we can continually improve our
books and learning resources for you. To participate in a brief online survey, please visit:

https://aka.ms/tellpress

Introduction

This book contains three chapters to define and detail the objectives of the Microsoft 70-765 exam. The content contained in this publication covers what you should expect to see on the exam, but you should have a solid working knowledge of SQL Server and Azure skills. It is recommended to concentrate on one chapter at a time as you study the materials contained in this guide. At the end of each chapter you will find a thought experiment that you should complete. Complete the questions and review the answers for each experiment to test your knowledge of the subject material.

The exam reference series covers a high level of knowledge that you are expected to know in regards to the exam by covering why topics and "how to" processes with tasks allowing you to fully understand a topic and its use with the product in a working environment. The exam reference series makes the assumption you have some practical experience in the subject material through regular use of SQL Server, or possibly a previous version of the product. To be successful in taking the exam, you should be able to plan and architect Azure SQL Database, SQL Server in Azure IaaS, and SQL Server on-premises based solutions.

There are specific walkthroughs in different areas of the book, especially in new feature topic areas. There are numerous notes and links to external material so you can deep dive into additional subjects that will enable you to gain a more in depth understanding of features of SQL Server and allow you to obtain a better understanding of the subject material.

This book covers all of the objectives of the exam, however it may not cover every exam question. Only the Microsoft exam team knows the exam questions. Exam questions are regularly updated, so this book should be considered a supplement to real use experience of SQL Server, and not a complete comprehensive guide to every exam question. This edition of the book covers Azure and SQL Server as of mid-2017. As Azure SQL Database, SQL Server and Azure IaaS evolve, be sure to check the exam objectives to check for any changes or new version related information.

If you master the material in this book, coupled with the external links provided, and use the product to gain real world experience, you should have a recipe for success in your quest for Microsoft certification. Good luck on your goal!

Organization of this book

This book is organized by the "Skills measured" list published for the exam. The "Skills measured" list is available for each exam on the Microsoft Learning website: *https://aka.ms/examlist*. Each chapter in this book corresponds to a major topic area in the list, and the technical tasks in each topic area determine a chapter's organization. If an exam covers six major topic areas, for example, the book will contain six chapters.

Microsoft certifications

Microsoft certifications distinguish you by proving your command of a broad set of skills and experience with current Microsoft products and technologies. The exams and corresponding certifications are developed to validate your mastery of critical competencies as you design and develop, or implement and support, solutions with Microsoft products and technologies both on-premises and in the cloud. Certification brings a variety of benefits to the individual and to employers and organizations.

> **MORE INFO ALL MICROSOFT CERTIFICATIONS**
>
> For information about Microsoft certifications, including a full list of available certifications, go to *https://www.microsoft.com/learning*.

Acknowledgments

Joseph D'Antoni I would like to thank my wife Kelly and my team at Denny Cherry and Associates consulting (Denny, John, Kerry, and Monica) for their help and patience with this project.

Scott Klein When writing the acknowledgments, I always struggle with who to list first because there are a handful of people that have played a huge role in this and they all deserve to be at the top of the list. However, having said that, I would like to thank Joey D'Antoni for making the initial connection and getting this whole thing started for me.

A very close second (and third) are the two individuals who not only brought me on board for this project but were also very patient while I jumped in; Trina MacDonald and Troy Mott. Thank you both for this opportunity.

Next comes the always amazing Tom LaRock, a good friend of mine who provided amazing and very appreciated technical feedback. Tom has reviewed a couple of my other books so when I heard he was the technical reviewer for this, there was an element of both excitement and "oh crap," because I knew Tom would keep me honest, but at the same time he'd have a LOT of feedback, which I don't mind at all.

Lastly, my family. Thank you for letting me disappear for a few weeks.

Microsoft Virtual Academy

Build your knowledge of Microsoft technologies with free expert-led online training from Microsoft Virtual Academy (MVA). MVA offers a comprehensive library of videos, live events, and more to help you learn the latest technologies and prepare for certification exams. You'll find what you need here:

https://www.microsoftvirtualacademy.com

Quick access to online references

Throughout this book are addresses to webpages that the author has recommended you visit for more information. Some of these addresses (also known as URLs) can be painstaking to type into a web browser, so we've compiled all of them into a single list that readers of the print edition can refer to while they read.

Download the list at *https://aka.ms/exam765sqldatabases/downloads.*

The URLs are organized by chapter and heading. Every time you come across a URL in the book, find the hyperlink in the list to go directly to the webpage.

Errata, updates, & book support

We've made every effort to ensure the accuracy of this book and its companion content. You can access updates to this book—in the form of a list of submitted errata and their related corrections—at:

https://aka.ms/exam765sqldatabases/errata

If you discover an error that is not already listed, please submit it to us at the same page.

If you need additional support, email Microsoft Press Book Support at *mspinput@microsoft.com.*

Please note that product support for Microsoft software and hardware is not offered through the previous addresses. For help with Microsoft software or hardware, go to *https://support.microsoft.com.*

We want to hear from you

At Microsoft Press, your satisfaction is our top priority, and your feedback our most valuable asset. Please tell us what you think of this book at:

https://aka.ms/tellpress

We know you're busy, so we've kept it short with just a few questions. Your answers go directly to the editors at Microsoft Press. (No personal information will be requested.) Thanks in advance for your input!

Stay in touch

Let's keep the conversation going! We're on Twitter: *http://twitter.com/MicrosoftPress*.

Important: How to use this book to study for the exam

Certification exams validate your on-the-job experience and product knowledge. To gauge your readiness to take an exam, use this Exam Ref to help you check your understanding of the skills tested by the exam. Determine the topics you know well and the areas in which you need more experience. To help you refresh your skills in specific areas, we have also provided "Need more review?" pointers, which direct you to more in-depth information outside the book.

The Exam Ref is not a substitute for hands-on experience. This book is not designed to teach you new skills.

We recommend that you round out your exam preparation by using a combination of available study materials and courses. Learn more about available classroom training at *https://www.microsoft.com/learning*. Microsoft Official Practice Tests are available for many exams at *https://aka.ms/practicetests*. You can also find free online courses and live events from Microsoft Virtual Academy at *https://www.microsoftvirtualacademy.com*.

This book is organized by the "Skills measured" list published for the exam. The "Skills measured" list for each exam is available on the Microsoft Learning website: *https://aka.ms/examlist*.

Note that this Exam Ref is based on publicly available information and the author's experience. To safeguard the integrity of the exam, authors do not have access to the exam questions.

## CHAPTER 1

Implement SQL in Azure

Moving or provisioning new databases on the Azure platform requires a different set of skills than managing traditional on-premises installations. You need to have a broader understanding of cloud computing concepts and technologies like platform as a service, infrastructure as a service, and scripting.

Skills in this chapter:

- Skill 1.1: Deploy a Microsoft Azure SQL Database
- Skill 1.2: Plan for SQL Server installation
- Skill 1.3: Deploy SQL Server instances
- Skill 1.4: Deploy SQL Server databases to Azure virtual machines

> **IMPORTANT**
> *Have you read page xiii?*
> It contains valuable information regarding the skills you need to pass the exam.

Skill 1:1: Deploy a Microsoft Azure SQL Database

This skill deals with the process of setting up an Azure SQL Database. Azure SQL Database is a Platform as a Service (PaaS) offering that can be quite different from a traditional on-premises implementation of SQL Server.

> **This skill covers how to:**
> - Choose a service tier
> - Create servers and databases
> - Create a sysadmin account
> - Configure elastic pools

Choose a service tier

Unlike traditional on-premises architecture, or even Infrastructure as a Service (IaaS) architecture, Azure SQL Database is not configured by choosing CPU, RAM, and storage metrics. Microsoft has categorized several different service tiers:

- Basic
- Standard
- Premium
- Premium-RS

Your service tier affects several critical factors about your database including size, performance level, availability, and concurrency. Each tier of service has limits on sizing and performance capacity, which is measure in Database Transaction Units (DTUs). Let us examine each performance level in detail.

- **Basic**   The basic service tier is best suited for small databases that are in early stages of development. The size of this tier is limited to 2 gigabytes (GB) and computing resources are extremely limited.

- **Standard**   The standard tier offers a wide range of performance and is good for applications with moderate performance needs and tolerance for small amounts of latency. Your database can be up to 250 GB in size.

- **Premium**   The premium tier is designed for low latency, high throughput, mission critical databases. This service tier offers the broadest range of performance, high input/output (I/O) performance, and parallelism. This service tier offers databases up to 4 terabytes (TB) in size.

- **Premium RS**   The premium RS service tier is designed for databases that have I/O intensive workloads, but may not have the same availability requirements of premium databases. This could be used for performance testing of new applications, or analytical applications.

The fundamental concept of performance in Azure SQL Database is the Database Transaction Unit or DTU (you are introduced to this concept when you learn about elastic pools with the elastic Database Transaction Unit or eDTU). As mentioned earlier, when sizing an Azure SQL Database, you do not choose based on various hardware metrics, instead you choose a performance level based on DTUs.

There is one other significant feature difference as it relates to standard and basis tiers versus the premium performance tiers—in-memory features of SQL Server. Both columnstore and in-memory OLTP, which are features that are used for analytic and high throughput OLTP workloads are limited only to the premium and premium RS tiers. This is mainly due to resource limitations—at the lower service tiers there is simply not enough physical memory available to take advantage of these features, which are RAM intensive.

The basic performance level has a max DTU count as shown in Table 1-1.

TABLE 1-1 Basic performance level limits

Performance level	Basic
Max DTUs	5
Max database size	2 GB
Max in-memory OLTP storage	N/A
Max concurrent workers (requests)	30
Max concurrent logins	30
Max concurrent sessions	300

The standard performance level offers size increases, and increased DTU counts and supports increased concurrency (see Table 1-2).

TABLE 1-2 Standard performance tier limits

Performance level	S0	S1	S2	S3
Max DTUs	10	20	50	100
Max database size	250 GB	250 GB	250 GB	1024 GB
Max in-memory OLTP storage	N/A	N/A	N/A	N/A
Max concurrent workers (requests)	60	90	120	200
Max concurrent logins	60	90	120	200
Max concurrent sessions	600	900	1200	2400

Recently, Microsoft made several additions to the standard database performance offerings (Table 1-3), both increasing the size and performance limits of the standard tier.

TABLE 1-3 Extended Standard Performance Tier Limits

Performance level	S4	S6	S7	S9	S12
Max DTUs	200	400	800	1600	3000
Max Database Storage	1024 GB	1024 GB	1024 GB	1024 GB	1024 GB
Max in-memory OLTP storage (GB)	N/A	N/A	N/A	N/A	N/A
Max concurrent workers (requests)	400	800	1600	3200	6000
Max concurrent logins	400	800	1600	3200	6000
Max concurrent sessions	4800	9600	19200	30000	30000

The Premium performance tier (see Table 1-4) offers larger capacity, and greatly increased storage performance, making it ideal for I/O intensive workloads.

TABLE 1-4 Premium Performance Tier Limits

Performance level	P1	P2	P4	P6	P11	P15
Max DTUs	125	250	500	1000	1750	4000
Max database size	500 GB	500 GB	500 GB	500 GB	4096 GB	4096 GB
Max in-memory OLTP storage	1 GB	2 GB	4 GB	8 GB	14 GB	32 GB
Max concurrent workers (requests)	200	400	800	1600	2400	6400
Max concurrent logins	200	400	800	1600	2400	6400
Max concurrent sessions	30000	30000	30000	30000	30000	30000

The Premium RS tier (see Table 1-5) is similar to the Premium tier in terms of performance, but with lower availability guarantees, making it ideal for test environments.

TABLE 1-5 Premium RS performance tier limits

Performance level	PRS1	PRS2	PRS4	PRS6
Max DTUs	125	250	500	1000
Max database size	500 GB	500 GB	500 GB	500 GB
Max in-memory OLTP storage	1 GB	2 GB	4 GB	8 GB
Max concurrent workers (requests)	200	400	800	1600
Max concurrent logins	200	400	800	1600
Max concurrent sessions	30000	30000	30000	30000

EXAM TIP

It is important to understand the relative performance levels and costs of each service tier. You do not need to memorize the entire table, but you should have a decent understanding of relative performance and costs.

MORE INFO DATABASE TRANSACTION UNITS

For a single database at a given performance level, Microsoft offers a performance level based on a specific, predictable level of performance. This amount of resources is a blended measure of CPU, memory, data, and transaction log I/O. Microsoft built this metric based on an online transaction processing benchmark workload. When your application exceeds the amount of any of the allocated resources, your throughput around that resource is throttled, resulting in slower overall performance. For example, if your log writes exceed your DTU capacity, you may experience slower write speeds, and your application may begin to experience timeouts. In the Azure Portal you can see your current and recent DTU utilization, shown in Figure 1-1.

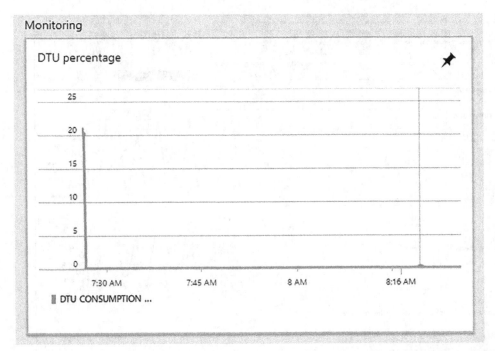

FIGURE 1-1 A screen shot of the DTU percentage screen for an Azure SQL Database from the Azure Portal

The Azure Portal offers a quick glance, but to better understand the components of your application's DTU consumption by taking advantage of Query Performance Insight feature in the Azure Portal, you can click Performance Overview from Support and Troubleshooting menu, which shows you the individual resource consumption of each query in terms of resources consumed (see Figure 1-2).

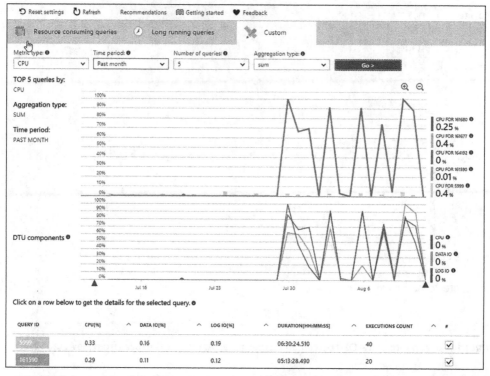

FIGURE 1-2 A screen shot of the DTU percentage screen for an Azure SQL Database from the Azure Portal

The graphic in Figure 1-2 is built on top of the data collected by the Query Store feature that is present in both Azure SQL Database and SQL Server. This feature collects both runtime data like execution time, parallelism, and execution plan information for your queries. The powerful part of the Query Store is combining these two sets of data to make intelligent decisions about query execution. This feature supports the Query Performance Insight blade on the Azure Portal. As part of this feature you can enable the performance recommendations feature, which creates and removes indexes based on the runtime information in your database's Query Store, and can changes query execution plans based on regression of a given query's execution time.

> **MORE INFO ABOUT QUERY PERFORMANCE INSIGHT**
>
> You can learn more about query performance insight at: *https://docs.microsoft.com/en-us/azure/sql-database/sql-database-query-performance*.

The concept of a DTU can be very confusing to a DBA or developer who is used to choosing hardware based on specific requirements like amount of RAM and number of CPU cores. Microsoft has built the DTU model to abstract those hardware decisions away from the user. It is important to understand that DTUs represent relative performance of your database—a database with 200 DTUs is twice as powerful as one with 100 DTUs. The DTUs are based on the

Azure SQL Database benchmark, which is a model that Microsoft has built to be a representative online transaction processing (OLTP) application, which also scales with service tier, and runs for at least one hour (see Table 1-6).

TABLE 1-6 Azure SQL Database Benchmark information

Class of Service	Throughput Measure	Response Time Requirement
Premium	Transactions per second	95th percentile at 0.5 seconds
Standard	Transactions per minute	90th percentile at 1.0 seconds
Basic	Transactions per hour	80th percentile at 2.0 seconds

> **MORE INFO ABOUT SQL DATABASE BENCHMARK**
>
> You can learn more about SQL Database Benchmark insight at: *https://docs.microsoft.com/en-us/azure/sql-database/sql-database-benchmark-overview*.

Performance tuning

Before the Query Store and Query Performance Insight was available, a database administrator would have had to either use a third-party monitoring tool or build their own repositories to store information about the runtime history of their database. With these features in conjunction with auto-tuning features that have been released, the administrator can focus efforts on deeper tuning, building more optimal data structures, and developing more robust applications.

Automatic tuning

This is a feature that is unique to Azure SQL Database, and is only possible because of the power of cloud computing and machine learning elements that support Microsoft Azure. Proper index design and management is the key to relational database performance, whether you are in an on-premises environment or a platform as a service one. By monitoring your workloads Azure SQL Database can teach itself to identify and create indexes that should be added to your database.

In a traditional environment, this process consisted of the database administrator trying to track many queries, write scripts that would periodically collect data from various system views, and then take a best guess effort at creating the right set of indexes. The Azure SQL Database automated tuning model analyzes the workload proactively, and identifies queries that could potentially be run faster with a new index, and identifies indexes that may be unused or duplicated.

Azure also continually monitors your database after it builds new indexes to ensure that the changes help the performance of your queries. Automatic tuning also reverts any changes that do not help system performance. This ensures that changes made by this tuning process have no negative impact against your workloads. One set of relatively new automatic tuning features came with the introduction of compatibility level 140 into Azure SQL Database.

Even though Azure SQL Database does not have versions, it does allow the administrator or developer to set the compatibility level of the database. It does also support older compatibility levels for legacy applications. Compatibility level does tie back to the level at which the database optimizer operates, and has control over what T-SQL syntax is allowed. It is considered a best practice to run at the current compatibility level.

Azure SQL Database currently supports compatibility levels from 100 (SQL Server 2008 equivalent) to 140 (SQL Server 2017 equivalent). It is important to note that if you are dependent on an older compatibility level, Microsoft could remove them as product versions go off support. You can check and change the compatibility level of your database by using SQL Server Management studio, or the T-SQL, as shown in Figure 1-3.

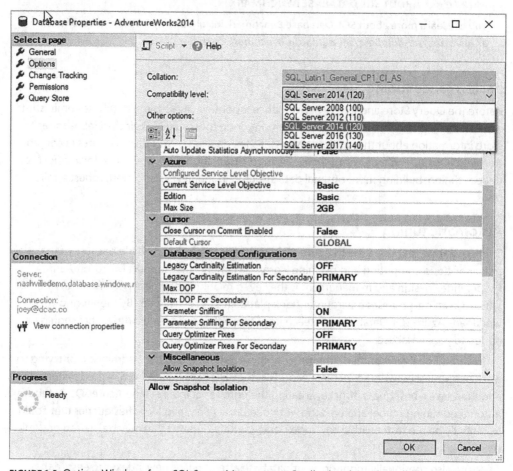

FIGURE 1-3 Options Windows from SQL Server Management Studio showing compatibility level options

To determine the current compatibility levels of the database in T-SQL, you can execute the following query:

```
SELECT compatibility_level
FROM   sys.databases
WHERE  [name] = 'Your Database Name';
```

To change the compatibility level of the database using T-SQL, you would execute the following command replacing "database_name" with the name of your database:

```
ALTER DATABASE database_name SET COMPATIBILITY_LEVEL =  140;
```

Performance enhancements in compatibility level 140

Compatibility level 140 introduces several new features into the query optimization process that further improve the automated tuning process. These features include:

- Batch mode memory grant feedback
- Batch mode adaptive join
- Interleaved query execution
- Plan change regression analysis

Let's look at each of these features in detail.

Batch mode memory grant feedback

Each query in SQL database gets a specific amount of memory allocated to it to manage operations like sorting and shuffling of pages to answer the query results. Sometimes the optimizer grants too much or too little memory to the query based on the current statistics it has on the data, which may affect the performance of the query or even impact overall system throughput. This feature monitors that allocation, and dynamically changes it based on improving future executions of the query.

Batch mode adaptive join

This is a new query operator, which allows dynamic selection to choose the most optimal join pattern based on the row counts for the queries at the time the query is executed.

Interleaved Execution

This is designed to improve the performance of statements that use multi-statement table valued functions (TVFs), which have traditionally had optimization issues (in the past the optimizer had no way of knowing how many rows were in one of these functions). This feature allows the optimizer to take count of the rows in the individual TVF to use an optimal join strategy.

Plan change regression analysis

This is probably the most interesting of these new features. As data changes, and perhaps the underlying column statistics have not been updated, the decisions the query optimizer makes may be based on bad information, and lead to less than optimal execution plans. Because the Query Store is maintaining runtime information for things like duration, it can monitor for queries that have suddenly had execution plan changes, and had regression in performance. If SQL Database determines that the plan has caused a performance problem, it reverts to using the previously used plan.

> **MORE INFO   ABOUT DATABASE COMPATIBILITY LEVELS**
>
> You can learn more about database compatibility levels at: *https://docs.microsoft.com/en-us/sql/t-sql/statements/alter-database-transact-sql-compatibility-level.*

Choosing an initial service tier

While Microsoft gives guidance for the type of application that should use each database, there is a wide range of potential performance tiers and costs associated with that decision. Given the importance of the database tier to overall application performance, it is important to choose correctly.

The first part of making this decision is understanding the nature of your application—is it an internet-facing application that will see large scale and requires the database to store session state? Or is it a batch processing application that needs to complete its work in an eight-hour window? The former application requires extremely low levels of latency and would mostly be placed in the premium storage tier, with adjustments to up the performance curve for peak times to optimize cost. An example of this might mean keeping the database at the P4 performance level during off-peak times, but using P11 for high loads like peak business hours, or holidays for retailers. For the batch processing application, an S2 or S3 may be a good starting point. The latency incurred does not matter so long as the batch processing occurs within its eight-hour window.

For most applications, the S2 or S3 tiers are a good starting point. For applications that rely on intensive CPU and I/O operations, the premium tier is a better fit, offering more CPU and starting at 10x I/O performance over the standard tier. The premium RS tier can be a good fit for performance testing your application because it offers the same performance levels as the premium tier, but with a reduced uptime service level agreement (SLA).

> **MORE INFO   ABOUT AZURE SQL DATABASE PERFORMANCE TIERS**
>
> You can learn more about Azure SQL Database service tiers at *https://docs.microsoft.com/en-us/azure/sql-database/sql-database-service-tiers.*

Changing service levels

Changing the service level of the database is always an option—you are not locked into the initial size you chose at the time of creation. You review elastic pools later in this chapter, which give more flexibility in terms of scale. However, scaling an individual database is still an option.

When you change the scale of an individual database, it requires the database to be copied on the Azure platform as a background operation. A new replica of your database is created, and no data is lost. The only outage that may occur is that in-flight transactions may be lost during the actual switchover (should be under four seconds, and is under 30 seconds 99 percent of the time). It is for this reason that it is important to build retry logic into applications that use Azure SQL Database. During the rest of the resizing process the original database is available. This change in service can last a few minutes to several hours depending on the size of the database. The duration of the process is dependent on the size of the database and its original and target service tiers. For example, if your database is approaching the max size for its service, the duration will be significantly longer than for an empty database. You can resize your database via the portal (Figure 1-4), T-SQL, or PowerShell. Additional options for making these changes include using the Azure Command Line Interface or the Rest API for Azure SQL Database.

EXAM TIP

Remember how to choose the right service tier based on the application workload and performance requirements.

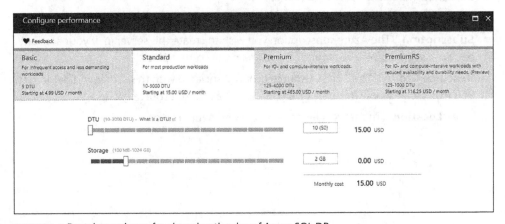

FIGURE 1-4 Portal experience for changing the size of Azure SQL DB

You can also execute this change in T-SQL.

```
ALTER DATABASE [db1] MODIFY (EDITION = 'Premium', MAXSIZE = 1024 GB, SERVICE_OBJECTIVE =
'P15');
```

The only major limitation around resizing individual databases is size. Performance level has some correlation with storage. For example, the database that is being resized in the above T-SQL example is now a P15, which supports up to 4 TB of data. If for example the database contained 2.5 TB of data, you would be limited to the P11 or P15 performance level because those support 4 TB, whereas the P1-P6 databases only supports 500 GB.

Create servers and databases

When talking about Platform as a Service offerings there are always many abstractions of things like hardware and operating systems. Remember, nearly everything in Microsoft Azure is virtualized or containerized. So, what does this mean for your Azure SQL Database? When you create a "server" with multiple databases on it, those databases could exist in different virtual machines than your "server." The server in this example is simply a logical container for your databases; it is not specific to any piece of hardware.

Now that you understand that your "server" is just a logical construct, you can better understand some of the concepts around building a server (see Figure 1-5). To create your server, you need a few things:

- **Server Name** Any globally unique name.
- **Server admin login** Any valid name.
- **Password** Any valid password.
- **Subscription** The Azure subscription you wish to create this server in. If your account has access to multiple subscriptions, you are in the correct place.
- **Resource Group** The Azure resource group associated with this server and databases. You may create a new resource group, or use an existing resource group.
    - **Location** The server can only exist in one Azure region.

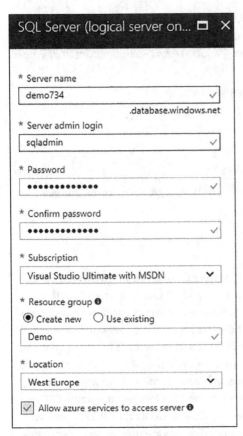

FIGURE 1-5 Creating an Azure SQL Database Server in the Azure Portal

In earlier editions of Azure SQL Database, you were required to use a system-generated name; this is no longer the case; however, your name must be globally unique. Remember, your server name will always be *servername.database.windows.net*.

Other Options for creating a logical server

Like most services in Azure, Azure SQL Database offers extensive options for scripting to allow for automated deployment. You can use the following PowerShell command to create a new server:

```
PS C:\>New-AzureSqlDatabaseServer -Location "East US" -AdministratorLogin "AdminLogin"
-AdministratorLoginPassword "Password1234!" -Version "12.0"
```

The Azure CLI is another option for creating your logical server. The syntax of that command is:

```
az sql server create --name YourServer--resource-group DemoRG --location $location \
    --admin-user "AdminLogin"  --admin-password "Password1234!"
```

To run these demos you need Azure PowerShell. If you are on an older version of Windows you may need to install Azure PowerShell. You can download the installer at: *https://www. microsoft.com/web/handlers/webpi.ashx/getinstaller/WindowsAzurePowershellGet.3f.3f.3fnew. appids.*

You can also install using the following PowerShell cmdlet:

```
# Install the Azure Resource Manager modules from the PowerShell Gallery
Install-Module AzureRM
```

> **MORE INFO** **ABOUT AZURE CLI AND SQL DATABASE**
>
> You can learn more the Azure CLI and database creation at: *https://docs.microsoft.com/en-us/azure/sql-database/sql-database-get-started-cli.*

Database and server firewall rules

One of the concepts of Azure SQL Database is that it is exposed over the Internet via a TCP endpoint over port 1433. This can sound a little bit scary—your database is open over the Internet? However, Microsoft provides you with multiple levels of security to secure your data and databases. Figure 1-6 provides an overview of how this security process works. There are two sets of firewall rules. The first is the database level firewall rule, which is the more granular of these two rules. The database level rule is set within the individual database where it can be viewed in the catalog view *sys.database_firewall_rules*. You can set these database rules using T-SQL within the database, however they may also be set using PowerShell, the Azure CLI, or the REST API interface. These rules as mentioned are specific to an individual database, if you need to replicate them across multiple databases you need to include that as part of your deployment scripts. You may also delete and update these firewall rules using all aforementioned methods. An example of the T-SQL to create a database level firewall rule is as follows:

```
EXECUTE sp_set_firewall_rule @name = N'ContosoFirewallRule',
    @start_ip_address = '192.168.1.1', @end_ip_address = '192.168.1.10'
```

Server level firewall rules on the other hand, can only be set through the Azure Portal, PowerShell, Azure CLI, the Rest API, or in the master database of the logical server. You can view server level firewall rules from within your Azure SQL Database by querying the catalog view *sys.firewall_rules.*

A server-level firewall rule is less granular than the database rule—an example of where you might use these two features in conjunction would be a Software as a Service application (SaaS) where you have a database for each of your customers in a single logical server. You might whitelist your corporate IP address with a server-level firewall rule so that you can easily manage all your customer databases, whereas you would have an individual database rule for each of your customers to gain access to their database.

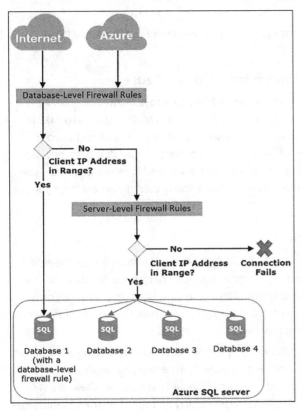

FIGURE 1-6 Azure SQL Database firewall schematic

As mentioned, there are several ways to set a firewall rule at the server level. Here is an example using PowerShell.

```
New-AzureRmSqlServerFirewallRule -ResourceGroupName "Group-8" '
-ServerName "servername" -FirewallRuleName "AllowSome" -StartIpAddress "192.168.1.0"
-EndIpAddress "192.168.1.4"
```

Here is an example using the Azure CLI

```
az sql server firewall-rule create --resource-group myResourceGroup \
    --server yourServer  -n AllowYourIp --start-ip-address 192.168.1.0 --end-ip-address
192.168.1.4
```

In both examples, a range of four IP addresses is getting created. All firewall rules can either be a range or a single IP address. Server level firewall rules are cached within Azure to improve connection performance. If you are having issues connecting to your Azure SQL Database after changing firewall rules consider executing the DBCC FLUSHAUTHCACHE command to remove any cached entries that may be causing problems, from a machine that can successfully connect to your database.

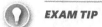

EXAM TIP

Remember how to configure firewall settings using both PowerShell and the Azure Portal.

Connecting to Azure SQL Database from inside of Azure

You may have noticed that in Figure 1-5 there was a check box that says, Allow Azure Services To Access This Server." This creates a server level firewall rule for the IP range of 0.0.0.0 to 0.0.0.0, which indicates internal Azure services (for example Azure App Services) to connect to your database server. Unfortunately, this means all of Azure can connect to your database, not just your subscription. When you select this option, which may be required for some use cases, you need to ensure that the security within your database(s) is properly configured, and that you are auditing traffic to look for anomalous logins.

Auditing in Azure SQL Database

One of the benefits of Azure SQL Database is its auditing functionality. In an on-premises SQL Server, auditing was commonly associated with large amounts of performance overhead, and was used rarely in heavily regulated organizations. With Azure SQL Database, auditing runs external to the database, and audit information is stored on your Azure Storage account, eliminating most concerns about space management and performance.

Auditing does not guarantee your regulatory compliance; however, it can help you maintain a record of what changes occurred in your environment, who accessed your environment, and from where, and allow you to have visibility into suspected security violations. There are two types of auditing using different types of Azure storage—blob and table. The use of table storage for auditing purposes has been deprecated, and blob should be used going forward. Blob storage offers greater performance and supports object-level auditing, so even without the deprecation, it is the better option.

> *MORE INFO* **ABOUT AZURE COMPLIANCE**
>
> You can learn more about Azure compliance practices at the Azure Trust Center: *https:// azure.microsoft.com/support/trust-center/compliance/.*

Much like with firewall rules, auditing can be configured at the server or the database level. There are some inheritance rules that apply here. An auditing policy that is created on the logical server level applies to all existing and newly created databases on the server. However, if you enable blob auditing on the database level, it **will not** override and change any of the settings of the server blob auditing. In this scenario, the database would be audited twice, in parallel (once by the server policy, and then again by the database policy). Your blob auditing logs are stored in your Azure Storage account in a container named "sqldbauditlogs."

MORE INFO **ABOUT AZURE SQL DB AUDIT FILE FORMATS**

You can learn more about Azure SQL Database Auditing here: *https://go.microsoft.com/ fwlink/?linkid=829599.*

You have several options for consuming these log files from Azure SQL Database. You can view them within the Azure Portal, as seen in Figure 1-7. Or you can consume them using the Sys.fn_get_audit_file system function within your database, which will return them in tabular format. Other options include using SSMS to save the audit logs into an XEL or CSV file, or even a SQL Database table, or using the Power BI template created by Microsoft to access your audit log files.

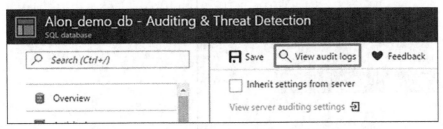

FIGURE 1-7 View Audit Log option in Azure SQL Database Blade in Azure Portal

Much like the rest of the Azure SQL Database platform, auditing can be configured using PowerShell or the Rest API, depending on your automation needs.

MORE INFO **ABOUT AZURE SQL DB AUDIT DATA ANALYSIS**

Learn more about auditing, and automation options for configuring auditing here: *https:// docs.microsoft.com/en-us/azure/sql-database/sql-database-auditing.*

SQL Database Threat Detection

Unlike auditing, which is mostly replicating the behavior of auditing in an on-premises SQL Server, Threat Detection is a feature that was born in Azure, and is very dependent on background Azure compute resources to provide higher levels of security for your databases and applications. SQL Threat Detection uses more advanced methodology to protect your database from common security threats like SQL Injection, suspicious database activities, and anomalous login patterns.

SQL Injection is one of the most common vulnerabilities among web applications. This occurs when a hacker determines that a website is passing unchecked SQL into its database, and takes advantage of this by generating URLs that would escalate the privileges of an account, or get a list of users, and then change one of their passwords.

Threat detection gives you several types of threats to monitor and alert on:

- All
- SQL Injection
- SQL Injection Vulnerability
- Anomalous client login

The best practice recommendation is just to enable all threat types for your threat detection so you are broadly protected. You can also supply an email address to notify in the event of a detected threat. A sample email from a SQL Injection vulnerability is in Figure 1-8.

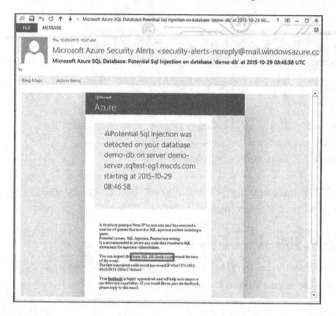

FIGURE 1-8 SQL Injection Vulnerability email

Microsoft will link to the event that triggered the alert to allow you to quickly assess the threat that is presented. Threat detection is an additional cost option to your Azure SQL Database, and integrates tightly with Azure Security Center. By taking advantage of machine learning in the Azure Platform, Threat Detection will become smarter and more reactive to threats over time.

Backup in Azure SQL Database

One of the benefits of Azure SQL Database is that your backup process is fully automated. As soon as your database is provisioned it is backed up, and the portal allows for easy point in time recovery with no manual intervention. Azure SQL Database also uses Azure read-access geo-redundant storage (RA-GRS) to provide redundancy across regions. Much like you might configure in an on-premises SQL Server environment Azure SQL Database takes full, differential, and transaction log backups of your database. The log backups take place based on the amount of activity in the database, or at a fixed time interval. You can restore a database to any point-in-time within its retention period. You may also restore a database that was deleted, if you are within the retention period for that database.

It is important to note that the service tier of your database determines your backup retention (the basic tier has a five-day retention period, standard and premium have 35 days). In many regulated industries backups are required to be retained for much longer periods—including up to seven years for some financial and medical systems. So, what is the solution? Microsoft has a solution that is used in conjunction with the Azure Recovery Services component that allows you to retain weekly copies of your Azure SQL Database backups for up to 10 years (see Figure 1-9).

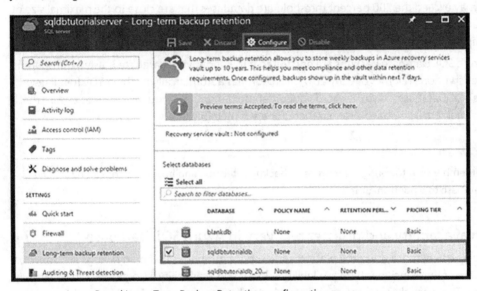

FIGURE 1-9 Azure Portal Long-Term Backup Retention configuration

To take advantage of the long-term retention feature, you need to create an Azure Recovery Vault in the same Azure region as your Azure SQL Database. You will then define a retention policy based on the number of years you need to retain your backups. Because this feature uses the Azure Backup services infrastructure, pricing is charged at those rates. There is a limit of 1000 databases per vault. Additionally, there is a limit of enabling 200 databases per vault in any 24-hour period. It is considered a best practice to use a separate vault for each Azure SQL Database server to simplify your management.

Restoring a database from long-term storage involves connecting to the backup vault where your database backups are retained and restoring the database to its server, much like the normal Azure SQL Database restore process.

Azure SQL Database pricing includes up to 200 percent of your maximum provisioned database storage for your backups. For example, a standard tier database would have 500 GB of backup associated with it. If your database exceeds that 200 percent threshold, you can either choose to have Microsoft support reduce your retention period, or pay extra for additional backup storage, which is priced at the standard RA-GRS pricing tier. Reasons why your database may exceed the 200 percent threshold are databases that are close to the maximal size of the service tier that have a lot of activity increasing the size of transaction log and differential backups.

Azure SQL Database backups are encrypted if the underlying database is using transparent data encryption (TDE). As of early 2017, Microsoft has automatically enabled TDE for all new Azure SQL Databases. If you created your database before then, you may want to ensure that TDE is enabled, if you have a requirement for encrypted backups.

EXAM TIP

Remember how to configure long-term backup retention and how to restore an Azure SQL Database to a point-in-time.

High availability and disaster recovery in Azure SQL Database

One of the benefits of using the platform as a service offering is that many things are done for you. One of those includes high availability—local high availability is configured automatically for you. There are always three copies of your database to manage things like patching and transient hardware failures. This protects you in the event of any failures that happen within a local Azure region. However, to protect your database and application against broader regional failures or to give your application global read-scale, you will want to take advantage of the Active Geo-Replication feature in Azure SQL Database.

Active geo-replication allows you to have up to four readable secondary replicas of your database in the region of your choosing (see Figure 1-10). These secondary replicas can be used strictly for disaster recovery or can be used for active querying. This protects your application against larger regional failures, and provides resiliency to allow you to perform operations like rolling application upgrades and schema changes. Azure makes recommendations as to the best region for your geo-replica—this is based on the paired region concept in Azure. This paired region concept is not a limiter—you can build your replicas in any supported region in Azure. Many organizations do this to provide global read-scale for applications that are distributed globally. You can put a replica of the database much closer to your users reducing latency and improving overall performance.

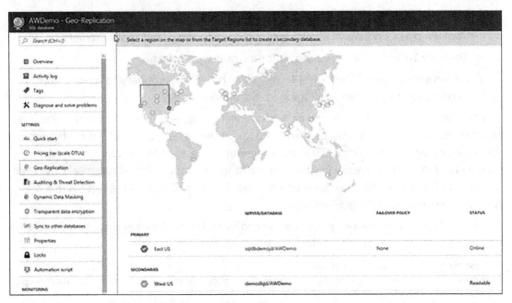

FIGURE 1-10 Geo-Replication for Azure SQL Database from Azure Portal

Configuring geo-replication requires you to have a logical server in each region you want to geo-replicate to. Configuring a second logical server is the only configuration that is required; no network or other infrastructure components are required. Your secondary database can run at a lower DTU level than your primary to reduce costs, however it is recommended to run with no less than half of the DTUs of the primary so that the replication process can keep up. The important metric to monitor for this is log IO percentage. For example if your primary database is an S3 (with 100 DTUs) and its log IO percentage was at 75 percent, your secondary would need to have at least 75 DTUs. Since there is no performance level with 75 DTUs, you would need an S3 as your secondary. Azure SQL Database requires that your secondary be on the same performance tier as the primary, for example it would not be supported to have a P1 primary and an S0 secondary, but you could have a S3 primary and an S0 secondary.

The administrator typically manages the failover process under normal circumstances, however in the event of an unplanned outage, Azure automatically moves the primary to one of the secondary copies. If after the failure, the administrator would like to be moved back to the preferred region, the administrator would need to perform a manual failover.

Automatic failover with failover groups

Failover groups increase the utility of geo-replicas by supporting group level replication for databases and automated failover processing. More importantly this feature allows applications to use a single connection string after failover. There are few key components to failover groups:

- **Failover Group** Unit of failover can be one or many databases per server, which are recovered as a single unit. A failover group must consist of two logical servers.
- **Primary Server** The logical server for the primary databases.
- **Secondary Server** The logical server, which hosts the secondary databases. This server cannot be in the same region as the primary server.

There are a few things to keep in mind with failover groups—because data replication is an asynchronous process, there may be some data loss at the time of failure. This is configurable using the GracePeriodWithDataLossHours parameter. There are also two types of listener endpoints: read-write and read-only to route traffic to either the primary (for write activity) or to a group of secondary replicas (for read activities). These are DNS CNAME records that are FailoverGroupName.database.windows.net.

Geo-replication and failover groups can be configured in the Azure Portal, using PowerShell (see below example), or the REST API.

```
# Establish Active Geo-Replication
$database = Get-AzureRmSqlDatabase -DatabaseName mydb -ResourceGroupName ResourceGroup1
 -ServerName server1
$database | New-AzureRmSqlDatabaseSecondary -PartnerResourceGroupName ResourceGroup2
-PartnerServerName server2 -AllowConnections "All"
```

Create a sysadmin account

Unlike SQL Server, where many users can be assigned the System Admin role, in Azure SQL Database there is only one account that can be assigned server admin. If your Azure subscription is configured with Azure Active Directory, this account can be an Azure Active Directory (AAD) group (not to be confused with on-premises Active Directory). Using an AAD group is the best practice for this admin account, because it allows multiple members of a team to share server admin access without having to use a shared password.

You can set the Active Directory admin for a logical server using the Azure Portal as seen in Figure 1-11. The only requirement for implementing this configuration is that an Azure Active Directory must be configured as part of the subscription.

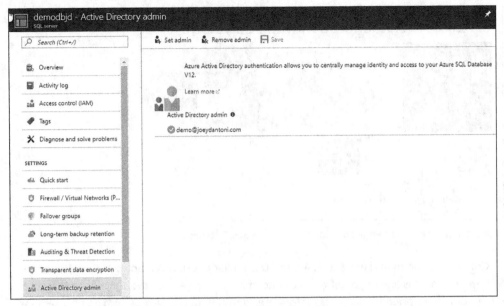

FIGURE 1-11 Azure Portal Azure Active Directory Admin configuration screen

Azure Active Directory and Azure SQL Database

Azure Active Directory gives a much more robust and complete security model for Azure SQL Database than merely using SQL logins for authentication. Azure AD allows you to stop the spread of identities across your database platform. The biggest benefit of this solution is the combination of your on-premises Active Directory being federated to your Azure Active Directory and offering your users a single-sign on experience.

In configurations with Active Directory Federation Services (ADFS), users can have a very similar pass-through authentication experience to using a Windows Authentication model with SQL Server. One important thing to note with ADFS versus non-ADFS implementations of hybrid Active Directory—in non-ADFS implementations the hashed values of on-premises user passwords are stored in the Azure AD because authentication is performed within Azure. In the example shown in Figure 1-12, where the customer is using ADFS, the authentication first routes to the nearest ADFS server, which is behind the customer's firewall. You may notice the ADALSQL in that diagram which is the Active Directory Authentication Library for SQL Server, which you can use to allow your custom applications to connect to Azure SQL Database using Azure Active Directory authentication.

Azure Active Directory offers additional benefits, including easy configuration for multi-factor authentication, which can allow verification using phone calls, text messages, or mobile application notification. Multi-factor authentication is part of the Azure Active Directory premium offering.

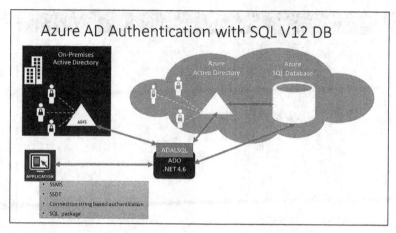

FIGURE 1-12 Azure AD Authentication Model for Azure SQL Database

Configuring logins and users with Azure AD is similar to using Windows Authentication in SQL Server. There is one major difference concerning groups—even though you can create a login from an on-premises Active Directory user, you cannot create one from an on-premises Active Directory group. Group logins must be created based on Azure Active Directory groups. In most cases, where you will want to replicate the on-premises group structure, you can just create holding groups in your Azure AD that have a single member, the on-premises Active Directory group. There are several options for authentication to your Azure SQL Database, as shown in Figure 1-13.

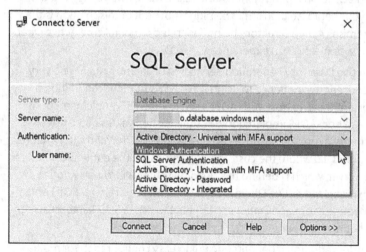

FIGURE 1-13 SQL Server Management Studio Options for Authentication

- **Windows Authentication**   Not supported for Azure SQL Database.
- **SQL Server Authentication**   Traditional authentication model where the hashed credentials are stored in the database.
- **Active Directory Universal Authentication**   This model is used when multi-factor authentication is in place, and generates a browser-based login experience that is similar to logging into the Azure Portal.
- **Active Directory Password Authentication**   This model has the user enter their username in user@domain.com format with their Azure Active Directory password. If MFA is enabled this will generate an error.
- **Active Directory Integrated**   This model is used when ADFS is in place, and the user is on a domain joined machine. If ADFS is not in place, connecting with this option will generate an error.

Some other recommendations from Microsoft for this include setting timeout values to 30 seconds because the initial authentication could be delayed. You also want to ensure that you are using newer versions of tools like SQL Server Management Studio, SQL Server Data Tools, and even bcp and sqlcmd command line tools because older versions do not support the Azure Active Directory authentication model.

EXAM TIP

Remember how to configure Azure Active Directory authentication for Azure SQL Database.

Configure elastic pools

All the topics you have read about so far refer to single database activities. Each database must be sized, tuned, and monitored individually. As you can imagine, in a larger organization or SaaS application that supports many customers it can be problematic to manage each database individually, and it may lead to overprovisioning of resources and additional costs associated with meeting performance needs. Elastic pools resolve this problem by provisioning a shared pool of resources that is shared by a group; like individual databases, elastic pools use a concept of eDTUs, which is simply the concept of DTUs applied to a group of databases. This concept allows databases to better share resources and manage peak processing loads. An easy thought comparison is that of a traditional SQL Server instance housing multiple databases from multiple applications.

Within a given pool a set eDTU is allocated and shared among all of the databases in the pool. The administrator can choose to set a minimum and maximum eDTU quota to prevent one database from consuming all the eDTUs in the pool and impacting overall system performance.

When to choose an elastic pool

Pools are a well suited to application patterns like Software as a Service (SaaS) where your application has many (more than 10) databases. The performance pattern that you are looking for is where DTU consumption Is relatively low with some spikes. This pattern can lead to cost savings even with as few as two S3 databases in a single pool. There are some common elements you want to analyze when deciding whether or not to put databases in a pool:

- **Size of the databases** Pools do not have a large amount of storage. If your databases are near the max size of their service tier, you may not get enough density to be cost effective.

- **Timing of peak workloads** Elastic pools are ideal for databases that have different peak workloads. If all of your databases have the same peak workload time, you may need to allocate too many eDTUs.

- **Average and peak utilization** For databases that have minimal difference between their average and peak workloads, pools may not be a good architectural fit. An ideal scenario is where the peak workload is 1.5x its average utilization.

Figure 1-14 shows an example of four databases that are a good fit for an elastic pool. While each database has a maximum utilization of 90 percent, the average utilization of the pool is quite low, and each of the databases has their peak workloads at different times.

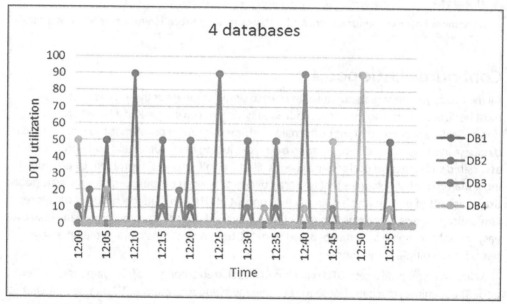

FIGURE 1-14 Image showing DTU workload for four databases

In Figure 1-15 you can see the workload utilization of 20 databases. The black line represents aggregate DTU usage for all databases; it never exceeds 100 DTUs. Cost and management are the key inputs into this decision—while eDTUs costs 1.5x more than DTUs used by single databases, they are shared across databases in the pool. In the scenario in Figure 1-15, the 20 databases could share 100 eDTUs versus each database having to be allocated 100 DTUs, which would reduce cost by 20x (this relies on S3 performance level for individual databases).

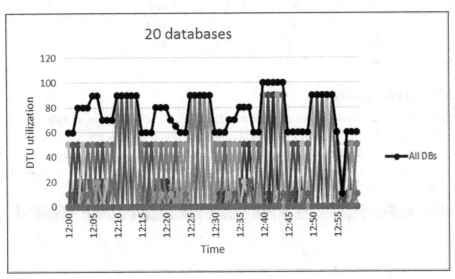

FIGURE 1-15 Chart showing the DTU workload for twenty databases

EXAM TIP

Understand when to choose an elastic pool versus a standalone database, both from the perspective of management and cost.

Sizing elastic pools

Sizing your elastic pool can be challenging, however elastic pools are flexible and can be changed dynamically. As a rule of thumb, you want a minimum of 10-15 databases in your pool, however in some scenarios, like the S3 databases mentioned earlier, it can be cost effective with as few as two databases. The formula for this is if the sum of the DTUs for the single databases is more than 1.5x the eDTUs needed for the pool, the elastic pool will be a cost benefit (this relating to the cost difference per eDTU versus DTUs). There is fixed upper limit to the number of databases you can include in a pool (shown in Table 1-7), based on the performance tier of the pool. This relates to the number of databases that reach peak utilization at the same time, which sets the eDTU number for your pool. For example, if you had a pool with four S3 databases (which would have a max of 100 DTUs as standalone) that all have a peak workload at the same time, you would need to allocate 400 eDTUs, as each database is consuming 100 eDTUs at exactly the same time. If as in Figure 1-14, they all had their peak at different times (each database was consuming 100 eDTUs, while the other 3 databases were idle), you could allocate 100 eDTUs and not experience throttled performance.

TABLE 1-7 Elastic Pool Limits

Tier	Max DBs	Max Storage Per Pool (GB)	Max DTUs per Pool
Basic	500	156	1600
Standard	500	1536	3000
Premium	100	4096	4000
Premium-RS	100	1024	1000

Configuring elastic pools

Building an elastic pool is easy—you allocate the number of eDTUs and storage, and then set a minimum and maximum eDTU count for each database. Depending on how many eDTUs you allocate, the number of databases you can place in the elastic pool will decrease (see Figure 1-16). Premium pools are less dense than standard pools, as shown by the maximum number of databases shown in Table 1-7.

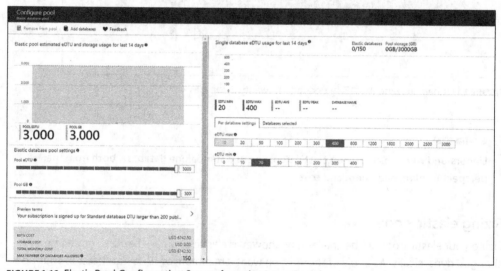

FIGURE 1-16 Elastic Pool Configuration Screen from the Azure Portal

You can also build elastic pools using PowerShell and the Azure CLI as shown in the next two examples.

```
Login-AzureRmAccount
New-AzureRmSqlElasticPool -ResourceGroupName "ResourceGroup01" -ServerName "Server01"
-ElasticPoolName "ElasticPool01" -Edition "Standard" -Dtu 400 -DatabaseDtuMin 10
-DatabaseDtuMax 100
```

```
az sql elastic-pool create ñname "ElasticPool01" --resource-group "RG01" \
      --server "Server01" --db-dtu-max 100 --db-dtu-min 100 --dtu 1000 --edition
"Standard" --max-size 2048
```

The process for creating an elastic pool is to create the pool on an existing logical server, then to either add existing databases to the pool, or create new databases within the pool (see Figure 1-17). You can only add databases to the pool that are in the same logical server. If you are working with existing databases the Azure Portal makes recommendations for service tier, pool eDTUs, minimum, and maximum eDTUs based on the telemetry data from your existing databases. You should note that these recommendations are based on the last 30 days of data. There is a requirement for a database to have existed for at least seven days to appear in these recommendations.

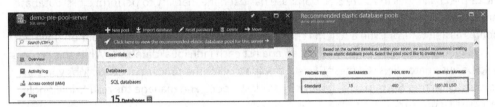

FIGURE 1-17 Elastic Pool Configuration Screen from the Azure Portal

Managing and monitoring an elastic pool is like managing an individual database. The best place to go for pool information is the Azure Portal, which shows pool eDTU utilization and enables you to identify databases that may be negatively impacting the performance of the pool. By default, the portal shows you storage and eDTU utilization for the last hour, but you can configure this to show more historical data. You can also use the portal to create alerts and notifications on various performance metrics. You may also move a database **out** of an elastic pool, if after monitoring it is not a good fit for the profile of the pool.

MORE INFO **ABOUT AZURE SQL DATABASE ELASTIC POOL LIMITS**

The elastic pool limits and resources are changing regularly. You can learn more about the limits and sizing of elastic pools here: *https://docs.microsoft.com/en-us/azure/sql-database/sql-database-elastic-pool*.

It is important to know that the limits of the pools are changing frequently as Microsoft makes updates to the Azure platform, so you should refer to books online and the portal before making decisions around designing your architecture.

If all the eDTUs in the elastic pool are consumed, performance in the pool is throttled. Each database receives an equal amount of resources for processing. The Azure SQL Database service ensures that each database has equal amounts of compute time. The easiest comparison to how this works is the use of the resource governor feature in an on-premises or IaaS SQL Server environment.

Changing pool sizing

There are two tiers of changing sizes in an elastic pool—one is changing the minimum and maximum eDTU settings for individual databases. These changes typically take less than five minutes. Changing the size of the elastic pool takes longer, and is dependent on the size of the databases in the pool, but in general a rule of thumb is that changing pool eDTUs takes around 90 minutes per 100 GB of data in your pool. It is important to keep this in mind if planning to dynamically alter the size of your pools for varying workloads—you may need to do this far in advance for larger pools.

Elastic jobs

One of the challenges to Azure SQL Database has been the inability to perform cross-database transactions. If we use the SaaS example, where each customer has a database, if you need to update master data, or issue a schema change across all customer databases, your deployment process would require a query to be issued against each individual database. While this process could be automated, it is still messy. Elastic pools allow for the concept of elastic jobs you can execute SQL across a group of databases in an elastic pool, and manage the results in a single place (see Figure 1-18).

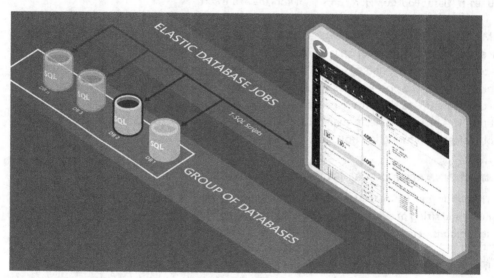

FIGURE 1-18 Elastic Database Jobs workflow

Running elastic jobs as a few requirements—you need to install elastic jobs components in your Azure environment, and your jobs must be *idempotent*, which means for the script to succeed and run again it must have the same result. For example, if you were creating a new stored procedure, you would want to use the CREATE OR ALTER PROCEDURE syntax versus simply using the CREATE PROCEDURE option, which would fail the second time the script was executed.

Elastic jobs do require an additional database, which is designated a control database to store all metadata and state data. In an elastic pool scenario, this database would have minimal additional cost. The job service talks to the control database and launches and tracks jobs. If you are using elastic pools, you can access the elastic jobs interface through the portal, however if you wish to use this feature for group of standalone databases, you need to use PowerShell or the Azure CLI.

Elastic pools and geo-replication

Databases that are in an Elastic pools do have the same architecture as standalone databases, so features like backup and high availability are already in place. Just like standalone databases, you have the option to configure active geo-replication for databases in an elastic pool. The geo-replication is quite flexible because you do not have to include every database in the pool in your geo-replication set, and you may geo-replicate either to a standalone database, or an elastic pool. The only hard requirement is that the service tiers of the pools be the same.

Skill 1:2: Plan for SQL Server installation

This skill deals with planning for SQL Server installation. This includes choosing the right infrastructure, whether you are on-premises or in the cloud, configuring storage to meet your performance needs, and understanding best practices for installation.

> **This skill covers how to:**
> - Plan for an IaaS or on-premises SQL Server deployment
> - Select the appropriate size for a virtual machine
> - Plan storage pools based on performance requirements
> - Evaluate best practices for installation
> - Design a storage layout for a virtual machine

Plan for an IaaS or on-premises SQL Server deployment

Planning is needed for any SQL Server deployment, whether it is in the cloud or on-premises. It can be quite a challenge to gather the information you need to properly size and build out your environment. There are many questions you want to ask before beginning any deployment project:

- What is your licensing situation?
  - What edition are you licensed for, and for how many cores?
  - If Azure, are you renting the license or bringing your own?
  - Do you have Software Assurance?

- Are you migrating an existing application?
  - Are you upgrading versions of SQL Server?
  - Are you able to capture workload from the existing application?
- What are the availability needs of the application?
  - Do you need a multiple data center solution?
  - Do you need high availability?
  - How long can the application be down?
  - What are the performance needs of the application?
  - Is this a customer facing latency-sensitive application?
- Or is it a batch processing application that only needs to complete its jobs in a large time window?
  - How much data are you going to have to store?
  - How much data is accessed regularly?
  - How many concurrent sessions are you expecting?

Licensing

Licensing is not the most interesting topic; however, it is very important to many architectural discussions. You do not need to be a licensing expert; however, you do need to understand the basic rules and how they work. An important change Microsoft made with SQL Server 2016 is that all non-production environments (development, QA, test) only need to be licensed with developer edition. They also made developer edition free—this combination can greatly reduce license costs. Express Edition is also free for production use, but is limited to database sizes of 10 GB.

Standard Edition is licensed by either a Server/Client Access License (CAL) model or a core based licensing model. The server/CAL model is best suited for smaller organizations who do not have a lot of users (the "users" here refer to users of the application and not database users), where the core model is best suited for Internet facing applications that effectively have an unlimited number of users. One important thing to note is as of Service Pack 1 of SQL Server 2016, Standard Edition has the same programming surface area as Enterprise Edition.

Enterprise Edition is licensed in the core model only. Enterprise Edition is designed for applications that need scaling. It supports unlimited memory, larger scale-out farms, and the support needed for tier-1 workloads.

Software Assurance is effectively an annual support contract with Microsoft that entitles you to upgrades and more importantly grants you the right to have a second idle server for either high availability or disaster recovery. For example, if you have a license of Enterprise Edition for 16 cores, and you ran your production application with that, you would be entitled to have a second server (as part of an Availability Groups, Log Shipping Partner, Failover Cluster Instance, etc.) with no additional licensing charge. You may not use that server for any operations like backups, integrity checks, or restores, otherwise a license is required.

Azure VMs have two options for licensing SQL Server—you can rent the license as part of your monthly Azure cost, or you can bring your own license (BYOL), which lowers your monthly cost (see Figure 1-19).

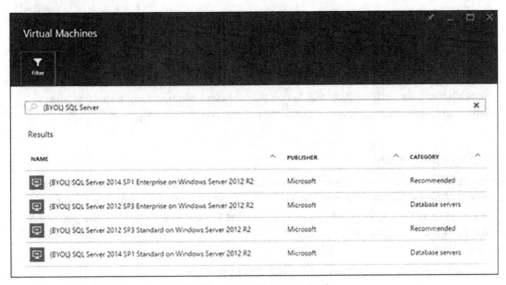

FIGURE 1-19 Bring Your Own License SQL Server VMs in Azure Portal

You do need to have Software Assurance to choose this option.

It is important to choose a BYOL image if you are using an existing license; otherwise, you will be charged for the cost of the SQL Server licensing and a support ticket will be required to switch to your own license. Additionally, you can bring your own Windows license; this is a different process that you can see in Figure 1-20 that happens at VM deployment. Similarly, this option must be configured at deployment, or you will be charged the cost of the Windows license as part of your monthly bill. A support ticket can also resolve this issue, if you need to change after the fact.

EXAM TIP

Have a good understanding of the comparative costs associated with running SQL Server on Azure including infrastructure (compute and storage) and licensing. Understand the licensing rules as they relate to high availability and disaster recovery.

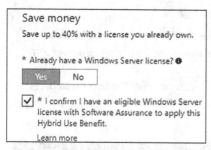

FIGURE 1-20 Bring Your Own License for WINDOWS VMs in Azure Portal

MORE INFO **ABOUT SQL SERVER LICENSING**

To learn more about the costs of SQL Server licensing by edition and software assurance visit: *https://www.microsoft.com/en-us/sql-server/sql-server-2016-pricing*.

Existing application

If you are migrating an existing application to a new SQL Server, you can bypass a lot of assessment. Whether as part of a migration to an Azure VM or a new on-premises server, you have access to all the working data you need. The first thing you want to do is use performance monitor to gather a performance profile of the source system. To do that, you can execute the following steps:

1. Launch Performance Monitor from the Windows menu.

2. If you are running this remotely, select Action > Connect To Another Computer and enter the name of the server in the Select Compute dialog box. (Note: you will need permission to run Perfmon on a remote server)

3. Click Data Collector Sets.

4. Right click User Defined and select New > Data Collector Set as shown in Figure 1-21.

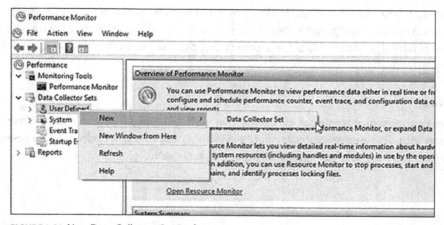

FIGURE 1-21 New Data Collector Set Performance Monitor

5. Name your collection set SQL Server Baseline and click the radio button to create manually.

6. On the screen that says, What Kind Of Data Do You Want To Include? click the radio button next to Performance Counters.

7. On the next screen click, Add, and you should then see the screen in Figure 1-22.

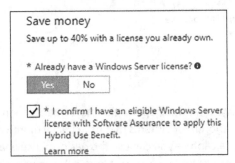

FIGURE 1-22 Performance Monitor counter add screen

8. Add the following counters:

Processor Information

```
Processor(*)% Processor Time
Process(sqlservr)% Processor Time
Processor(*)% Privileged Time
Process(sqlservr)% Privileged Time
```

Memory

```
Available Mbytes
Memory Pages/sec
Process(sqlservr)Private Bytes
Process(sqlservr)Working Set
SQLServer: Memory Manager Total Server Memory
SQLServer: Memory Manager Target Server Memory
```

Physical Disk

```
PhysicalDisk(*)Avg. Disk sec/Read
PhysicalDisk(*)Avg. Disk sec/Write
PhysicalDisk Avg. Disk Queue Length
Disk Bytes/sec
Avg Disk Bytes/Transfer
Process(sqlservr)IO Data Operations/sec
```

Network

```
Network InterfaceBytes Received/sec
Network InterfaceBytes Sent/sec
Network Interface(*)Output Queue Length

SQL Server: SQL Statistics Batch Requests/sec
SQL Server: SQL Statistics SQL Compilations/sec
SQL Server: SQL Statistics SQL Recompilations/sec

SQL Server: Wait Statistics
Latch Waits > 15 sec
Locks > 30 sec
IO Latch Timeouts
```

Typically, when assessing a server workload you want to capture this performance monitor data over a period of at least a week, or even a month for systems that have heavy month end processing. Once you have completed your data capture you can use the performance analysis of logs (PAL) tool, an open-source project to analyze and format your logs. You can use this analysis to help you design your target environment.

> **MORE INFO ABOUT PAL TOOL**
>
> The Performance Analysis of Logs tool is a Microsoft created open-source tool which allows for easier analysis of Performance Monitor input: *https://github.com/clinthuffman/PAL*.

Managing availability

You need to plan your SQL Server deployment for high availability and disaster recovery. If your application is critical to the business you need to design your underlying infrastructure to reflect that criticality. SQL Server offers many features for that high availability and disaster recovery in the form of AlwaysOn Availability Groups and Failover Cluster Instances. Or you can choose to deploy a more manual solution like log shipping either by itself or in conjunction with another option. Both of these options are dependent on Windows Server Failover Cluster (WSFC), though starting with SQL Server 2017, Availability Groups may be deployed for migration purposes only, without an underlying WSFC. These techniques all protect against machine and operating system failure, and allow you to minimize downtime during maintenance operations like patching Windows and SQL Server.

Failover Cluster Instances are an option that provides local high availability. This option depends on shared storage, where a single copy of your instance floats between two or more nodes running SQL Server. Failover cluster instances require a dedicated cluster installation of SQL Server. Most installations of failover cluster instance are in one location; however, they may be combined with storage replication to provide disaster recovery. To implement failover cluster instances in Azure, you need Windows Server 2016 Storage Spaces Direct to provide shared storage. A failover cluster instance has a single point of failure at the shared storage layer, so you need to use an additional technique like Availability Groups if you need additional data protection.

A failover cluster instance encompasses your while instance. This means things like logins and SQL Agent jobs are always on all nodes where your instance is installed. There is no process required to sync because the instance contains a single copy of that master data. The unit of failover is at the instance level.

Availability Groups are an option that can provide a level of high availability locally and disaster recovery in a remote data center. Like Failover Cluster Instances, Availability Groups (AGs) are built on top of a WSFC. However, AGs use standalone instances of SQL Server, and do not encompass the entire instance. The AG is a group of databases that are organized together to send transaction data to one or more secondary replicas. An AG can have up to eight replicas for a total of nine nodes. These replicas can be used for reading and backups to offload work from the primary replica. An AG provides an additional measure of protection over a failover cluster instance because there are inherently multiple copies of the data in the environment. Additionally, there is automatic page repair for any data page that is deemed corrupt from the primary replica.

Each AG has its own listener, which serves as a virtual IP address for the group. By default, the listener always routes a connection to the primary instance, however if used in conjunction with read-only routing and the *application intent* flag in a SQL Server connection string, connections can be routed to a secondary for read offload. An AG offers two types of replicas, synchronous and asynchronous, which are typically used for local and remote copies respectively. If you are using synchronous mode, you should be aware that a write transaction will not complete on the primary replica until it reaches the transaction log on the secondary replica, so it is important to ensure that there is minimal latency between the replicas. Additionally, you can only have automatic failover between nodes that are synchronous. Asynchronous replicas require manual failover due to the potential data loss of in-flight transactions.

One challenge with AGs is keeping users and jobs in sync between replicas—because the feature uses standalone instances there is nothing to keep the jobs or users in sync. For users, the solution is relatively straightforward—you can use contained database users, which are local to the database in question, rather than stored in the master database.

> **MORE INFO CONTAINED DATABASE USERS**
>
> You can learn about creating contained database users and the security requirements around them here: *https://docs.microsoft.com/en-us/sql/relational-databases/security/contained-database-users-making-your-database-portable*.

Agent jobs are a little bit more challenging because you would need to build some intelligence into the job to determine which node is currently primary. One solution is to regularly copy the agent jobs from the primary to the secondary server(s), and to add logic to the job to ensure that it only operates on the primary replica.

As shown in Figure 1-23, these two technologies (FCIs and AGs) can be combined to provide higher levels of data protection. The one caveat to combining the techniques is that automatic failover can no longer be used within the AG due to the presence of the FCI. It should be noted that the WSFC is using a file share for quorum. This is common configuration for multi-subnet distributed clusters. Another option if you are using Windows Server 2016 is to use Azure Blob Storage for your cloud quorum option. You should always try to use the latest supported version of Windows for your SQL Server installations because enhancements to the failover clustering software stack have been numerous in recent releases.

Choosing the right high availability solution comes down to budget and the needs of your business for your application. You should have an understanding from your business of what the availability needs for each application are, and design your architecture appropriately.

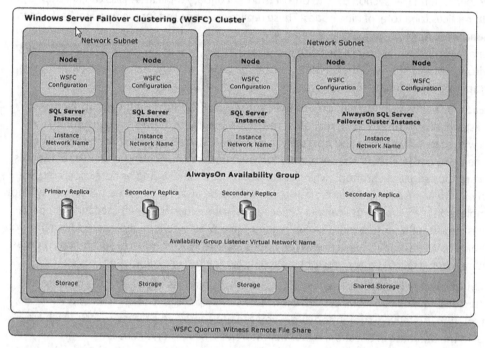

FIGURE 1-23 Availability Group and Failover Cluster Instance Combined Architecture

Managing performance

Performance is one of the more challenging components in developing new deployments. Whether you are in Azure or on-premises, or on physical hardware or virtual hardware, all database systems have differing performance requirements, based on both available hardware resources, workload of the application, and business requirements of the application.

For example, a database that paints web pages for a customer facing application needs to have extremely low latency, whereas an application that does overnight back office processing typically just needs to have enough resources to finish its batch within an eight-hour time-frame.

The official requirements for installing SQL Server are as follows.

TABLE 1-8 SQL Server Installation Requirements

Component	Requirement
MEMORY	Minimum:
	Express Editions: 512 MB
	All other editions: 1 GB
	Recommended:
	Express Editions: 1 GB
	All other editions: At least 4 GB and should be increased as database size increases to ensure optimal performance.
PROCESSOR SPEED	Minimum: x64 Processor: 1.4 GHz
PROCESSOR TYPE	Recommended: 2.0 GHz or faster x64 Processor: AMD Opteron, AMD Athlon 64, Intel Xeon with Intel EM64T support, Intel Pentium IV with EM64T support
STORAGE	A minimum of 6 GB is required to install SQL Server

Table 1-8 shows the minimum hardware requirements as specified by Microsoft for SQL Server 2016. It is important to note that these are absolute minimum supported values, especially when talking about memory—4 GB is required just to get SQL Server up and running. In a production environment, you should use at least 16 GB, and adjust depending on your workload.

Storage

You will notice the only disk requirement is the 6 GB required to install SQL Server. You learn more about proper disk layout for SQL Server on Azure later in this section, however there are two other important metrics around disk to know about—I/O Operations Per Second (IOPs) and latency. IOPs are a measure of how fast your disk can read and write data, while latency is a measure of how long it takes the data to be read from disk. Latency will be reduced greatly when using solid state drives—in fact in Azure, it is effectively a requirement to use Premium Storage (which is SSD based) with SQL Server workloads. More and more on-premises SQL Server workloads are using SSD based storage due to the reduced latency and higher IOPs that the SSDs offer. Storage performance is critical to database performance, so it is important to properly design your storage subsystem.

> **MORE INFO ABOUT SQL SERVER STORAGE CONFIGURATION**
>
> You can learn more about SQL Server storage performance at: *https://technet.microsoft.com/en-us/library/cc298801.aspx*.

Storage architecture is complex, especially given the number of different storage options on the market. The important thing is to perform testing of your storage configuration to ensure that it meets the expected needs of your application. Microsoft supplies a tool named Disk-Speed, which is a benchmarking tool to help you understand the performance of your storage subsystem, and lets you assess any changes. If you are migrating an existing application, you can use the following Performance Monitor (Performance Monitor) counters from SQL Server to get an assessment of your current IOPs:

- SQL Server Resource Pool Stats: Disk Read IO/Sec
- SQL Server Resource Pool Stats: Disk Write IO/Sec

Those two counters will get the number of IOPs performed by your SQL Server instance. If you want latency metrics you can also use Performance Monitor to get that data:

- Physical Disk/Logical Disk->Avg. Disk Sec/Read
- Physical Disk/Logical Disk->Avg. Disk Sec/Write

You can also get this data from the SQL Server dynamic management views and functions (DMVs and DMFs) including sys.dm_io_virtual_file_stats, however, that DMF is not resettable (its stats exist for the life of the instance) so using Performance Monitor gives you more real-time information.

Memory

One of the biggest keys to database performance is having enough available memory so that the working set of data does not have to be read from disk. As fast as modern disk is, it is still orders of magnitude slower than reading and writing from memory. It is a common myth that database servers are memory hogs, while a SQL Server instance will use all the memory allocated to it, which is by design as opposed to any runaway processing. Memory does tend to be a little bit of a black box, however there is a Performance Monitor metric from SQL Server that can give you a good idea of memory utilization.

So how do you decide how much memory to include in your SQL Server? If you are running in Azure, this is relatively straightforward. Choose what you think is best and then adjust the size of your server up or down to better suit the needs of your application. If you are running the standard edition of SQL Server you are limited to 128 GB, however, with Enterprise Edition having unlimited memory, this can be a tough decision. There are a few inputs you can use to guide this:

- What is your largest table?
- Are you using in-memory features like OLTP and columnstore?
- Are you using data compression?

There is no hard and fast rule for how much memory your SQL Server instance needs. There are a couple things you will want to monitor: disk usage and page life expectancy (PLE) in SQL Server (how long a page is expected to last in the buffer pool). If you do not have enough RAM, you will see significantly more disk activity as the database needs to reach out to the storage to bring pages into memory. Additionally, you will see PLE decease rapidly when you do not have enough memory. If you are using data compression, that can give you better utilization of RAM, by allowing your largest tables in indexes to fit into fewer data pages. If you are using features like in-memory OLTP or columnstore, you need to account for that in your calculation.

Sizing your system's memory is challenging and does require changing over time, however, buying additional RAM tends to be cheaper than buying additional storage IOPs, and can mask a lot of bad development practice, so it is best to err on the high side of RAM.

> **MORE INFO** **ABOUT SQL SERVER MEMORY UTILIZATION**
>
> SQL Server memory utilization can be complicated; here are some examples of how to monitor SQL Server's memory internals: *https://docs.microsoft.com/en-us/sql/relational-databases/performance-monitor/monitor-memory-usage*.

CPU

Like memory, CPU for a new application tends to be a black box. Unlike memory, due to the way SQL Server is licensed, increasing the amount of CPU allocated to your SQL Server can carry a very expensive cost beyond the hardware involved. If you are migrating an existing workload, you can look at the output from your Performance Monitor around processor utilization, and adjust up or down based on current processor utilization. As a rule of thumb for adequate throughput, you would like to see your database servers running at under 70-80 percent processor utilization during normal operation. There will be spikes during heavy processing, but if your server is constantly running at 80-90 percent, your throughput will be limited and latency may increase.

If helps to understand the nature of your application as well—most online analytical processing databases (OLAP) benefit from a higher CPU count, due to the parallel nature of reporting. On the other hand, OLTP systems benefit from pure CPU speed, so when building your servers, you may want to go with a lower core count, but with faster individual cores. Also, on some virtual platforms over allocating CPU can lead to poorer performance because of scheduling operations. So, do not needlessly over allocate CPU in virtualized environments.

Select the appropriate size for a virtual machine

One of the differences between using a cloud platform like Azure, and working in a traditional on-premises model, is that the cost for cloud platform is right in front you, giving a clear indication on spend for a given a system. This tends to make administrators conservative because they have an opportunity to save their organization money by choosing the right size VM. A very undersized VM can lead to a very poor user experience, however, so it is important to find a proper balance between cost and performance.

Table 1-9 shows the guidance for VMs running SQL Server. Microsoft recommends using a DS2 or higher VM for Standard Edition, and a DS3 or higher for Enterprise Edition. You may also notice that in the disks section, P30 disks are mentioned. It is implied that premium storage should be used for SQL Server production workloads. You learn more about properly configuring storage later in this section.

TABLE 1-9 Microsoft Guidance for SQL Server on Azure VMs

Area	Optimizations
VM SIZE	DS3 or higher for SQL Enterprise edition.
	DS2 or higher for SQL Standard and Web editions.
STORAGE	Use Premium Storage. Standard storage is only recommended for dev/test.
	Keep the storage account and SQL Server VM in the same region.
	Disable Azure geo-redundant storage (geo-replication) on the storage account.
DISKS	Use a minimum of 2 P30 disks (1 for log files; 1 for data files and TempDB).
	Avoid using operating system or temporary disks for database storage or logging.
	Enable read caching on the disk(s) hosting the data files and TempDB.
	Do not enable caching on disk(s) hosting the log file.
	Important: Stop the SQL Server service when changing the cache settings for an Azure VM disk.
	Stripe multiple Azure data disks to get increased IO throughput.
	Format with documented allocation sizes.

Types of Azure VMs

Azure offers several types of VM including general purpose, compute optimized, storage optimized, GPU (graphic processing unit optimized), and memory optimized. Given the memory intensive nature of database servers, we will focus on the memory optimized VMs here. However, it helps to be aware of the other types of VMs that may meet the needs of unusual workloads. Also, the range of VMs offered by Microsoft is constantly changing and evolving, so it helps to stay up to date on the offerings that are available in the Azure marketplace.

> **MORE INFO MICROSOFT AZURE VM SIZES AND TYPES**
>
> The sizes of Azure Virtual Machine offerings are constantly changing, visit books online to see what is current: *https://docs.microsoft.com/en-us/azure/virtual-machines/windows/sizes.*

Memory optimized VMs have a high memory to CPU ratio, which is a good fit for the nature of relational databases and their needs for large amounts of RAM to buffer data. Let's talk about the components that make up a given Azure VM:

- **vCPU** The number of cores or hyperthreads that are available to a VM. Hyperthreads are a recently added concept and are not in all VM types. They offer slightly lower performance at a lower cost versus dedicated cores.

- **Memory** This is simply the amount of RAM allocated to your virtual machine. This memory is fully allocated, there is no oversubscription in Azure.

- **Temp Storage (SSD)** This is local SSD storage that is directly attached to the physical host running your VM. It has extremely low latency for writes, but in most cases, is temporary. When the VM reboots, whatever is on the volume is lost. It can still have use cases for transient data like tempdb and caches.

- **Max Data Disks**   Depending on the size of your VM, you can have a maximum number of data disks. If you have a particularly large database, this can lead you to choosing a larger VM than you may otherwise need. It may also limit your options for down scaling during idle times.

- **IOPs/Storage Throughput**   In addition to limiting the number of disks, the amount of bandwidth to them is also controlled. This means your latency and IOPs should be predictable.

- **Network Bandwidth**   The network bandwidth is correlated to the size of the VM.

Azure Compute Units

Like DTUs in Azure SQL Database, Azure VMs have a measurement to compare system performance based on CPU and relative performance. This number is called the Azure Compute Unit or ACU (see Table 1-10). ACUs allow you to easily compare CPU performance across the various tiers of compute within Azure. The ACU is standardized on the standard A1 VM being 100 ACUs. The ACUs are per CPU, so a machine with 32 vCPUs and an ACU of 100 would have a total of 3200 ACUs.

TABLE 1-10 ACU Chart for Azure VM families

SKU Family	ACU \ vCPU
A0	50
A1-A4	100
	100
	100
	100
	225*
	160
	210 - 250*
	160
	210-250*
	160-190* **
	160-190* **
	160-190* **
	160-190* **
	210-250*
	210-250*
	180 - 240*
	180 - 240*
	290 - 300*
	180 - 240*
	160-180**

Use Intel® Turbo technology to increase CPU frequency and provide a performance boost. The amount of the boost can vary based on the VM size, workload, and other workloads running on the same host.
*** Indicate virtual cores that are hyperthreaded.*

Azure VMs for SQL Server

As mentioned, you should focus on the memory optimized VMs for SQL Server, but you should also focus on the VMs that have "S" in the name (DS_v3, GS5) because they support premium storage. If you do not choose an S VM, you cannot change to a premium storage VM without a migration. In this section, you learn about all the premium storage VM options.

ES_V3 series

The ES_v3 instances use the 2.3 GHZ Intel XEON E5-2673 v4 processor, which is in the Broadwell family and can achieve up to 3.5 Ghz with Intel Turbo Boost (see Table 1-11).

TABLE 1-11 Es-V3 Series VMs

Size	vCPU	Memory	Temp storage (SSD) GiB	Max data disks	Max cached and temp storage throughput: IOPS / MBps (cache size in GiB)	Max uncached disk through-put: IOPS / MBps	Max NICs / Expected network perfor-mance (Mbps)
Standard_E2s_v3	2	16	32	4	4,000 / 32 (50)	3,200 / 48	2 / moder-ate
Standard_E4s_v3	4	32	64	8	8,000 / 64 (100)	6,400 / 96	2 / moder-ate
Standard_E8s_v3	8	64	128	16	16,000 / 128 (200)	12,800 / 192	4 / high
Standard_E16s_v3	16	128	256	32	32,000 / 256 (400)	25,600 / 384	8 / high
Standard_E32s_v3	32	256	512	32	64,000 / 512 (800)	51,200 / 768	8 / ex-tremely high
Standard_E64s_v3	64	432	864	32	128,000/1024 (1600)	80,000 / 1200	8 / ex-tremely high

The Es-V3 VM series is relatively new, but offers some of the largest memory and the highest amounts of CPU in all of Azure. It can handle your largest workloads. The Es-V3 series has an ACU of 160-190.

DS Series

Before the introduction of the DSv2 and EsV3 series of VMs, these VMs were the core VMs for running mid-tier SQL Server workloads, which made up the bulk of Azure workloads (see Table 1-12).

TABLE 1-12 DS Series VMs

Size	vCPU	Memory	Temp storage (SSD) GiB	Max data disks	Max cached and temp storage throughput: IOPS / MBps (cache size in GiB)	Max un-cached disk throughput: IOPS / MBps	Max NICs / Expected network performance (Mbps)
Standard_DS11	2	14	28	4	8,000 / 64 (72)	6,400 / 64	2 / 1000
Standard_DS12	4	28	56	8	16,000 / 128 (144)	12,800 / 128	4/2000
Standard_DS13	8	56	112	16	32,000 / 256 (288)	25,600 / 256	8/2000
Standard_DS14	16	112	224	32	64,000 / 512 (576)	51,200 / 512	8 / 6000 - 8000

The DS series has an ACU of 160, and while it was the core of SQL Server VMs, going forward workloads should move DSv2 and newer VM types with faster vCPUs.

DS_V2 series

The DS_V2 series is now the current core of VMs for SQL Server workloads. These VMs have a good memory to CPU ratio, and range from 14 to 140 GB of memory, which is extremely well suited to most mid-tier SQL Server workloads. These VMs have a good amount of temp SSD storage, which can be used for tempdb or buffer pool extensions to improve performance without added cost (see Table 1-13). The VMs can also support storage up to 40 TB with 80,000 IOPs offering the high levels of I/O performance required at an affordable cost.

TABLE 1-13 DS_V2 VM Sizes

Size	vCPU	Memory	Temp storage (SSD) GiB	Max data disks	Max cached and temp storage throughput: IOPS / MBps (cache size in GiB)*	Max un-cached disk throughput: IOPS / MBps	Max NICs / Ex-pected network performance (Mbps)
Standard_DS11_v2	2	14	28	4	8,000 / 64 (72)	6,400 / 96	2 / 1500
Standard_DS12_v2	4	28	56	8	16,000 / 128 (144)	12,800 / 192	4 / 3000
Standard_DS13_v2	8	56	112	16	32,000 / 256 (288)	25,600 / 384	8 / 6000
Standard_DS14_v2	16	112	224	32	64,000 / 512 (576)	51,200 / 768	8 / 6000 - 12000 **
Standard DS15_v2	20	140	290	40	80,000/ 640 (720)	64,000/ 960	8/20000***

The maximum disk throughput (IOPS or MBps) possible with a DSv2 series VM may be limited by the number, size, and striping of the attached disk(s).
**Instance is an isolated node that guarantees that your VM is the only VM on our Intel Haswell node.*
***25000 Mbps with Accelerated Networking.*

The DS_V2 VMs have an ACU of 210-250, and the largest VM the DS15_V2 offers dedicated hardware so that there is no chance of any other workloads causing contention.

GS Series

While the DS and DS_V2 series of VMs are the bulk of SQL Server workloads, the largest workloads require the memory and dedicated processing power of the GS series of VMs (see Table 1-14).

TABLE 1-14 GS Series VM Sizes

Size	vCPU	Memory	Temp storage (SSD) GiB	Max data disks	Max cached and temp storage throughput: IOPS / MBps (cache size in GiB)	Max un-cached disk throughput: IOPS / MBps	Max NICs / Expected network performance (Mbps)
Standard_GS1	2	28	56	4	10,000 / 100 (264)	5,000 / 125	2 / 2000
Standard_GS2	4	56	112	8	20,000 / 200 (528)	10,000 / 250	2 / 4000
Standard_GS3	8	112	224	16	40,000 / 400 (1,056)	20,000 / 500	4 / 8000
Standard_GS4	16	224	448	32	80,000 / 800 (2,112)	40,000 / 1,000	8 / 6000 - 16000
Standard_GS5*	32	448	896	64	160,000 / 1,600 (4,224)	80,000 / 2,000	8 / 20000

*Instance is isolated to hardware dedicated to a single customer.

The GS series of VMs has an ACU 180-240. While the lower end VMs in the GS series are comparable to some of the other tiers, the CPU and memory in the GS4 and GS5 represent some of the largest VMs in all of Azure and in all the public cloud. The GS5 is a dedicated machine that can perform 160,000 IOPs with the maximum disk configuration.

Choosing your VM size in Azure is a little bit easier than buying physical hardware on-premises because it is possible to change after the fact. The first decision you want to make is how much data you need to store, followed by how much memory you need. This should narrow down your selection to two to three VM options, and you can pick what matches your workload best from there.

EXAM TIP

It is not a requirement to have the individual VM's sizes memorized, however you should know the families and their relative sizes in case you are asked to size a solution on the exam. You should also know which VMs support premium storage.

Plan storage pools based on performance requirements

When Azure began many years ago, there were two things that administrators working in Azure managed quite differently—storage and networking. As classic Azure was replaced by Azure Resource Manager (ARM) networking became relatively close to what exists in most on-premises environments. However, storage is still managed differently mainly due to the Azure Infrastructure and the way storage is deployed. Azure uses what is known as *Object Based Storage*, which means that all storage objects are managed as files. When you attach "disks" to a virtual machine they are simple VHD (Hyper-V file format) files that are presented to the guest virtual machine. This is different from the traditional on-premises approach of using *block-based storage*, which manages data as sectors and tracks of data. Some newer on-premises storage subsystems are built using object based storage as well, so some of these concepts are common across Azure and on-premises.

What this object-based storage model does is abstract the physical layer away from the actual disks and allow them to be managed by the virtualization hypervisor, which allows more flexibility in management. One of the other elements that is built into the Azure storage infrastructure is RAID (Redundant Array of Independent Disks)—RAID is typically used on-premises to provide data protection amongst disk. The general assumption is that disks will always fail so they must use striping or mirroring to protect against data loss. Azure takes a similar approach, but it maintains three copies of all data within the same region using its own software defined RAID. In the event of disk failure, one of the secondary copies of storage is promoted to the new primary. What does this mean for you? It means your data is protected on the back end, so when you present disks to your VM you can pool them without introducing any RAID that would limit your performance and your capacity. In the view of your VM, you are using RAID 0, because the Azure storage infrastructure is protecting your data. This is executed by using Storage Spaces in Windows Server with simple recovery.

In Figure 1-24 you can see a representation of what RAID 0 would like if we were writing directly to disk. The values are split across the three disks, and the loss of any one disk would result in complete data loss. However, because in Azure our data is protected by the infrastructure, you can use RAID Windows Storage Space in your VMs.

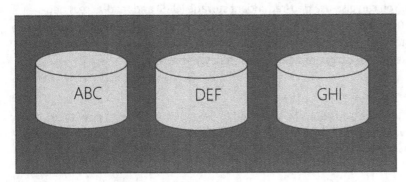

FIGURE 1-24 RAID 0 Example

Disks in Azure

There is a focus in premium storage for SQL Server VMs, however we also discuss standard storage because it can be used for backups and perhaps the O/S drive on your systems.

TABLE 1-15 Premium Storage Disk Options

Premium Disks Type	P4	P6	P10	P20	P30	P40	P50
DISK SIZE	32 GB	64 GB	128 GB	512 GB	1024 GB (1 TB)	2048 GB (2 TB)	4096 GB (4 TB)
IOPS PER DISK	120	240	500	2300	5000	7500	7500
THROUGHPUT PER DISK	25 MB per second	50 MB per second	100 MB per second	150 MB per second	200 MB per second	250 MB per second	250 MB per second

There is no service level agreement (SLA) for standard storage, however disks on basic VMs can have up to 300 IOPs and disks on standard VMs can have up to 500 IOPs per disk. As you can see from Table 13, the P30 disk balances performance and capacity (and cost) nicely, offering 5000 IOPs per disk. To get more IOPs for your SQL Server workloads, you need to pool disks together. To do this in Windows you need to use the Storage Spaces feature to pool the disks to get the total IOPs and capacity of the disks.

It is also recommended that you use managed disks for your SQL Server workloads; managed disks have higher levels of availability, and removes the limits on IOPs to a given storage account that were present with unmanaged disks in Azure.

> **MORE INFO** **MICROSOFT AZURE PREMIUM STORAGE**
>
> You can learn more about the differences between managed and unmanaged storage and the different types of premium storage options here: *https://docs.microsoft.com/en-us/azure/storage/common/storage-premium-storage*.

Premium storage only offers resiliency within a single data center by providing its three copies of your data. You can also use geo-redundant storage (GRS) and read-access geo-redundant storage (RA-GRS) to store your backup files. GRS and RA-GRS use standard storage, which is replicated to a paired region; however, this model is not supported for database data and log files because there is no guarantee of consistency across regions.

Storage spaces

After you have allocated disks to your VM, you need to use storage spaces to pool them. If you are using a SQL Server template (which you learn more about in the next section) this may be done for you, however these guidelines presume that you are doing this manually.

To begin, go to the Azure Portal and add disks to your VM:

1. Click Disks on the Blade for your VM (Figure 1-25).

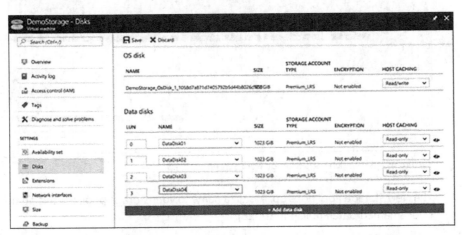

FIGURE 1-25 Add Disk to VM Screen in Azure Portal

2. In the data disks area, click the pull down under Name and click Create Disk. You need to assign a name to each disk. If you are not using managed disks, you may need to assign a storage account. You repeat this process for each disk that you want to assign to your VM. For this example, there are four disks. Click Save in the disk screen and wait until the operation completes (this could take up to a couple of minutes).

3. Log into your VM using Remote Desktop.

4. Open Server Manager and click File And Storage Services (Figure 1-26).

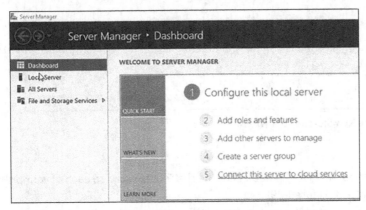

FIGURE 1-26 The Server Manager Screen from Windows Server 2016

5. From there, click Storage Pools. In the bottom right, you should see the four physical disks you created that are ready for assignment.

6. In the top right of the screen, click Tasks and select New Storage Pool (Figure 1-27).

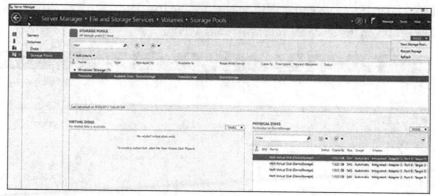

FIGURE 1-27 Server Manage Storage Pool Screen

7. The New Storage Pool pops up. Assign a name to your storage pool. For this demo, the pool is named Data Pool (Figure 1-28).

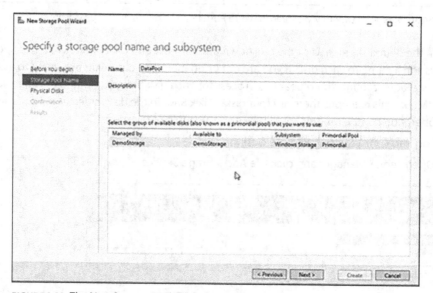

FIGURE 1-28 The New Storage Pool Wizard

8. Click next to continue.

9. Next you add your disks to the pool. Click the check boxes next to each of your disks, and then click Next (Figure 1-29).

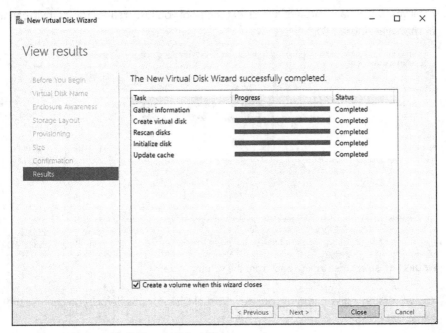

FIGURE 1-29 Storage Pool Wizard - Select Disks

10. On the Confirmation screen, click Create.

11. On the Progress screen check the box next to Create A Virtual Disk When This Wizard Closes, and click Close after the storage pool is completed (Figure 1-30).

You have successfully completed the New Storage Pool Wizard.

Task	Progress	Status
Gather information		Completed
Create storage pool		Completed
Update cache		Completed

☑ Create a virtual disk when this wizard closes

FIGURE 1-30 Completed Storage Pool Wizard

12. After the wizard launches you will select the pool you just created for your virtual disk, as shown in Figure 1-31.

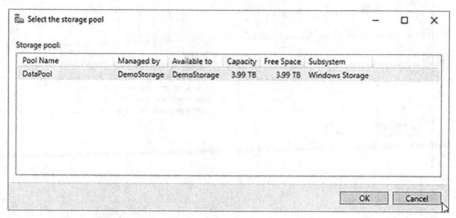

FIGURE 1-31 Select the storage pool from the Volume Wizard

13. You will assign a disk name to your new Virtual Disk, for this demo, you can use the name Data Disk.

14. You will then select a storage layout. Because you are using Azure storage, you can use the simple layout (Figure 1-32).

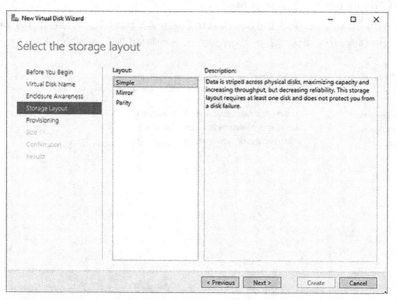

FIGURE 1-32 Storage Layout screen from the Virtual Disk Wizard

15. Click Next. On the next screen, you can choose a size for your disk. Click the button next to Maximum Size, and Click Next.

16. On the Confirmation screen click Create, and click the check box next to Create A Volume When This Wizard Closes.

17. The new Volume Wizard will launch. Click Next on the first two screens for server and disk, and size (Figure 1-33). You then choose a drive letter. Please note that you cannot use the letter E: in Azure because it is reserved.

FIGURE 1-33 The The Assign To A Drive Letter Or Folder screen from the New Volume Wizard

18. Click Next. On the File System Settings screen (Figure 1-34), accept the default for NTFS, change the allocation unit size to 64k (which is best practice recommendation for SQL Server), and assign a label to your volume. The label used here is a DataVolume.

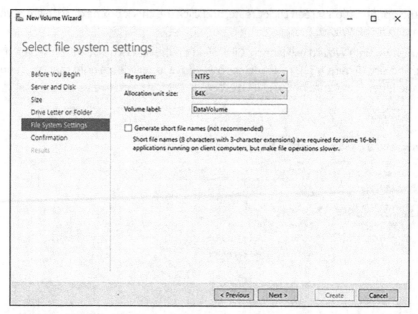

FIGURE 1-34 The Select File System Settings screen... Screen in the New Volume Wizard

Your process of creating a storage pool is now complete. If you open Windows Explorer (see Figure 1-35) you should see your new disk with its full storage allocation.

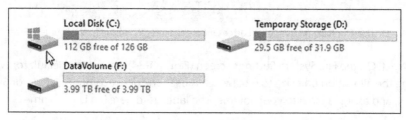

FIGURE 1-35 Screen shot of Windows Explorer after disk creation

In this example, you created a storage pool that can perform 20,000 IOPs and has a capacity of 4 TB. There are two major inputs into creating a storage system for your SQL Server the first being the total amount of data, and second being the number of IOPs. You can adjust both capacity and IOPs by adding more disks to an existing pool, however be warned that when adding new disks to the pool your data will not automatically be balanced across all the disks. You need to run the optimize-storagepool PowerShell cmdlet to rebalance your data. This command may take a long time to complete. This is an I/O intensive operation, so performance may be degraded during the process, however your disks are available during the process.

One other thing to note is that you should set the interleave (stripe size) to 64 KB (65536 bytes) for OLTP workloads and 256 KB (262144 bytes) for data warehousing workloads to avoid performance impact due to partition misalignment. You will learn more about optimal storage configuration for SQL Server later in this section.

MORE INFO **ABOUT OPTIMIZING STORAGE SPACES POOLS**

Storage pools are the key to designing proper storage solutions in Azure VMs. It is important to understand them. Learn more here: *https://technet.microsoft.com/en-us/itpro/pow-ershell/windows/storage/optimize-storagepool.*

Evaluate best practices for installation

A default SQL Server installation does not necessarily contain all the best practices for all workloads. Microsoft has worked to improve this particularly with the releases of SQL Server 2016 and 2017, which have some of the settings that many SQL Server experts used to apply after installation, built into the product. There are still many settings that should be changed before releasing your database server into production. Some settings are workload dependent, and some of the settings you learn about are specific to running in Azure VMs.

SQL Server settings

While SQL Server is the same product whether you install on-premises or in Azure VM there are some recommendations, due to the nature of Azure, to optimize your installation. It is recommended to install your binary files to C drive—there is no real benefit to installing them anywhere else. You should also only install the SQL Server components you need for your installation. If you are installing Analysis Services, Reporting Services, or Integration Services alongside your database engine, you should be aware that those processes running can take memory and resources away from the database engine, impacting your overall performance. For production configurations, it is a best practice to install one component per VM.

- **Disk Caching** The default caching policy on your operating system (C:\ drive) disk is read/write. It is not recommended to put database or transaction log files on the C:\ drive. It is recommended to use read caching on the disks hosting your data files and TempDB files, but not your transaction logs. Do not use read/write caching on any SQL Server data disk, as it can potentially lead to data loss. Additionally, stop your SQL Server service before changing any cache settings to avoid the possibility of database corruption.

- **NTFS Allocation Unit Size** The best practice for all SQL Server databases is to use the 64-KB allocation unit size.

- **Data Compression** It is recommended to use data compression (page) on your larger indexes and tables in SQL Server when running on Azure. There is no fixed guideline fr what size tables to compress, however a good way to evaluate is to review your largest 10 tables, and start from there. While it may increase CPU consumption, it will greatly reduce the number of I/Os required to service a query. For workloads that are analytic in nature you should consider using clustered columnstore indexes, which offer an even bigger reduction in I/O.

- **Instant File Initialization** This option is part of the SQL Server 2016 installer, and is a check box, which should be checked. If you are running an older version of SQL Server, you can enable this by granting the service account running SQL Server the Perform Volume Maintenance Tasks permission in Windows security policy. This feature enables SQL Server to grow data (but not transaction log) files without zeroing them out, making data file growth less costly to your I/O performance.

- **Data File Management** Proactively grow your database and transaction log files to what you expect them to be. Do not rely on autogrowth, because growing those files (especially transaction logs) will be detrimental to performance.

- **Shrink** You should almost never shrink a database. This is an I/O intensive operation, and fragments the database extensively. It is ok to shrink a transaction log, after runaway growth, but you should use backups and proper transaction management to manage the size of your transaction log.

- **Log and Trace Files** You should move the errorlog and trace files for SQL Server to one of your data drives. This can be performed by editing the startup parameters of SQL Server using configuration manager, as seen in Figure 1-36.

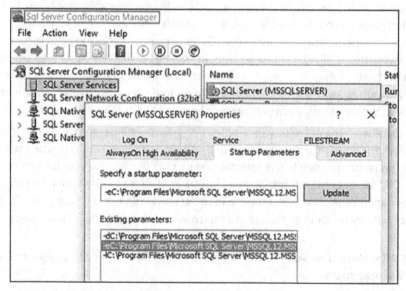

FIGURE 1-36 SQL Server Configuration Manager Log and Trace File Settings

- **Set Default Backup and Database File Location** These should be set to one of your data file volumes. It is important that your backup volume exist, even if you are backing up to an Azure URL. The SQL Server service may not start after patching if the backup location does not exist.

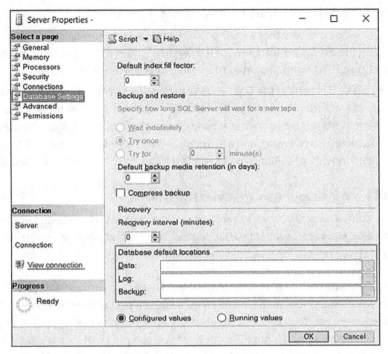

FIGURE 1-37 Server Properties screen

- **Patching** It is important to apply all Service Packs and Cumulative updates to your SQL Server instance. In addition to security patches, there are performance enhancements and new management features that are frequently built-in to these patches.

- **Locked Pages in Memory** Enable locked pages in memory to reduce I/O and paging activities. This is a Windows level setting.

MORE INFO **ABOUT LOCKED PAGES IN MEMORY**

The locked pages in memory setting is somewhat complicated to configure, learn more about it here: *https://docs.microsoft.com/en-us/sql/database-engine/configure-windows/enable-the-lock-pages-in-memory-option-windows*.

You learn more about other database configuration options in Chapter 2, "*Manage databases and instances*."

Design a storage layout for a SQL Server virtual machine

In the previous section, you learned how to create a disk pool using Storage Spaces to aggregate IOPs and storage capacity. Now you are going to learn about the best practices for configuring storage for SQL Server running on an Azure VM. Given the important of I/O performance to overall database performance you should follow these guidelines closely.

First let's examine the disks that come with an Azure VM:

- **O/S Disk**   This disk can be either a HDD or SSD because its performance will have minimal impact on the overall performance of the server. If you are trying to reduce cost, consider using an HDD for this volume. You should enable read/write caching.

- **Temporary Disk**   This will be the D drive on your Windows VMs. Data is not persisted on this drive, so you should never store data files or transaction log files there. For D, Dv2, Ev3, and G series VMs this disk is solid state and direct attached. This disk can be used for very write intensive TempDB workloads, as TempDB is recreated every time SQL Server starts. You need to write a startup script to create a folder to put TempDB on the D drive.

> **MORE INFO** **USING THE D DRIVE ON AZURE VMS FOR TEMPDB**
>
> Configuring the D drive for SQL Server use, requires some startup scripts and configuration: *https://blogs.technet.microsoft.com/dataplatforminsider/2014/09/25/using-ssds-in-azure-vms-to-store-sql-server-tempdb-and-buffer-pool-extensions/.*

- **Data and Log Volumes**   At a minimum you should use two premium storage P30 disks where one disk contains the   data and log files. If you have a good understanding of your IOPs required, you should pool as many disks as required to reach your IOPs requirements. If your workload is not IOPs intensive you can put both logs and data in the same storage pool. Otherwise create one storage pool for the data files and one storage pool for the transaction log files. You can include TempDB on the data file pool, if your TempDB workload is not write intensive, otherwise consider placing it on the D drive.

- **Caching Policy**   You should enable read caching for the data disks hosting your data files. This is performed at the portal under Disks. Before changing cache settings stop your SQL Server service to avoid any possible disk corruption.

- **Backup to Azure Storage**   Because the number of volumes that are assigned to a given VM are limited based on your VM size, one of the ways you can reduce space utilized in those volumes is by backing up directly to Azure Blob storage. Starting with SQL Server 2012 SP1 CU2 this feature has been available and allows for native SQL Server backups to blob storage. This storage account can be running in standard storage. Many customers use RA-GRS storage for their backups to provide some level of disaster recovery.

> **MORE INFO** **BACKUP TO URL IN SQL SERVER**
>
> Setting backup to Azure storage requires some information from your Azure storage account. Learn more here: *https://msdn.microsoft.com/library/dn435916.aspx.*

- **SQL Server Data Files in Azure**   This is another option to potentially reduce the number of disks associated with your Azure VM running SQL Server. This feature allows you to attach your data and transaction log files as Azure blobs and offers comparable performance to that of regular storage. However, your data files are limited in size to 1 TB when using this model.

Skill 1:3: Deploy SQL Server instances

This skill deals with deployment of your SQL Server instances and databases, you learn about how to perform command line installation, strategies for deployment, and the use of ARM templates to deploy new SQL Server VMs.

> **This skill covers how to:**
> - Deploy a SQL Server instance in IaaS and on-premises
> - Manually install SQL Server on an Azure Virtual Machine
> - Provision an Azure Virtual Machine to host a SQL Server instance
> - Automate the deployment of SQL Server databases
> - Deploy SQL Server by using templates

Deploy a SQL Server instance in IaaS and on-premises

There are several approaches you can take to deploying SQL Server instances either in Azure on IaaS or in your own on-premises environments. Many organizations have moved to a private cloud model where machines are templated and cloned to rapidly deploy new environments to development teams and business units. Azure can simplify this process by providing templates and the Azure Resource Manager (ARM) framework for automation and deployment. However, many organizations like to manage their own templates to manage custom settings and configurations.

Building your own SQL Server template

There is a basic process to creating a SQL Server VM template for deployment. While the specific operations depend on which toolset you are using, there are some common patterns that apply. The first is that you will want the SQL Server binaries installed as part of your template. This may seem counterintuitive, however trying to install SQL Server at deployment time delays your deployments and may lead to network timeouts.

There is no harm in having SQL Server installed on your template. At deployment time your Windows administrator needs to execute sysprep.

> **MORE INFO** **USING SYSPREP IN VM DEPLOYMENTS AND CREATING VM TEMPLATES WITH SYSTEM CENTER**
>
> Sysprep is used to remove the server name from the registry and other places. Learn more here: *https://technet.microsoft.com/en-us/library/hh427282(v=sc.12).aspx*.

The minor issue you will encounter is that SQL Server will initially have the wrong name listed in the *sys.servers* catalog view. You learn how to address this later in this section.

When you deploy your template, there are many other settings based on the server name and physical setting you may want to configure, as showing in the following SQL script. This code sets best practices on a SQL Server installation based on the current hardware, which means it should be run as a post deployment task in your environment.

```
/******  BEST PRACTICES  ******/
    --Trace Flag 3226    Suppress the backup transaction log entries from the SQL
Server Log
    USE MASTER
    GO
    CREATE OR ALTER PROCEDURE dbo.enable_trace_flags
    AS
        DBCC TRACEON (3226, -1);
        DBCC TRACEON (1222, -1);
    GO
EXEC sp_procoption @ProcName = 'enable_trace_flags', @OptionName = 'startup',
        @OptionValue = 'true';
    EXEC enable_trace_flags;
    /* Disable SA Login */
    ALTER LOGIN [sa] DISABLE;
GO
    --modify model database
    ALTER DATABASE model SET RECOVERY SIMPLE;
    GO
    ALTER DATABASE model MODIFY FILE (NAME = modeldev, FILEGROWTH = 100MB);
    GO
    ALTER DATABASE model MODIFY FILE (NAME = modellog, FILEGROWTH = 100MB);
    GO
    --modify msdb database
    ALTER DATABASE msdb SET RECOVERY SIMPLE;
    GO
    ALTER DATABASE msdb MODIFY FILE (NAME = msdbdata, FILEGROWTH = 100MB);
    GO

    ALTER DATABASE msdb MODIFY FILE (NAME = msdblog, FILEGROWTH = 100MB);
    GO
    --modify master database
    ALTER DATABASE master SET RECOVERY SIMPLE;
    GO
    ALTER DATABASE master MODIFY FILE (NAME = master, FILEGROWTH = 100MB);
    GO
    ALTER DATABASE master MODIFY FILE (NAME = mastlog, FILEGROWTH = 100MB);
    GO
    sp_configure 'set advanced options', 1
    GO
    RECONFIGURE WITH OVERRIDE
    GO
    /******  CONFIGURE TEMPDB  DATA FILES ******/
    DECLARE @sql_statement NVARCHAR(4000) ,
        @data_file_path NVARCHAR(100) ,
        @drive_size_gb INT ,
        @individ_file_size INT ,
        @number_of_files INT
    SELECT  @data_file_path = ( SELECT DISTINCT
```

```
                              ( LEFT(physical_name,
                                     LEN(physical_name) - CHARINDEX('\',
                                                           REVERSE(physical_
name))

                                     + 1) )
                         FROM    sys.master_files mf
                                 INNER JOIN sys.[databases] d ON mf.[database_
id] = d.[database_id]
                         WHERE   d.name = 'tempdb'
                                 AND type = 0
                     );
     --Input size of drive holding temp DB files here

     SELECT @DRIVE_SIZE_GB=total_bytes/1024/1024/1024 from sys.dm_os_volume_stats (2,1)
     SELECT  @number_of_files = COUNT(*)
     FROM    sys.master_files
     WHERE   database_id = 2
             AND type = 0;
     SELECT  @individ_file_size = ( @drive_size_gb * 1024 * .2 )
             / ( @number_of_files );
     /*
     PRINT '-- TEMP DB Configuration --'
     PRINT 'Temp DB Data Path: ' + @data_file_path
     PRINT 'File Size in MB: ' +convert(nvarchar(25),@individ_file_size)
     PRINT 'Number of files: '+convert(nvarchar(25), @number_of_files)
     */
     WHILE @number_of_files > 0
         BEGIN
             IF @number_of_files = 1 -- main tempdb file, move and re-size
                 BEGIN
                     SELECT  @sql_statement = 'ALTER DATABASE tempdb MODIFY FILE (NAME =
tempdev, SIZE = '
                             + CONVERT(NVARCHAR(25), @individ_file_size)
                             + ', filename = ' + NCHAR(39) + @data_file_path
                             + 'tempdb.mdf' + NCHAR(39)
                             + ', FILEGROWTH = 100MB);';
                 END;
             ELSE -- numbered tempdb file, add and re-size
                 BEGIN
                     SELECT  @sql_statement = 'ALTER DATABASE tempdb MODIFY FILE (NAME =
temp'
                             + CONVERT(NVARCHAR(25), @number_of_files)
                             + ',filename = ' + NCHAR(39) + @data_file_path
                             + 'tempdb_mssql_'
                             + CONVERT(NVARCHAR(25), @number_of_files) + '.ndf'
                             + NCHAR(39) + ', SIZE = '
                             + CONVERT(VARCHAR(25), @individ_file_size)

                             + ', FILEGROWTH = 100MB);';
                 END;

             EXEC sp_executesql @statement = @sql_statement;
             PRINT @sql_statement;
             SELECT  @number_of_files = @number_of_files - 1;
         END;
```

```
-- TODO: Consider type
DECLARE @sqlmemory INT
;with physical_mem (physical_memory_mb) as
(
 select physical_memory_kb / 1024
 from sys.dm_os_sys_info
)
select @sqlmemory =
-- Reserve 1 GB for OS
-- TODO: Handling of < 1 GB RAM
physical_memory_mb - 1024 -
(
case
-- If 16 GB or more, reserve an additional 4 GB
when physical_memory_mb >= 16384 then 4092
-- If between 4 and 16 GB, reserve 1 GB for every 4 GB
-- TODO: Clarify if 4 GB is inclusive or exclusive minimum. This is exclusive.
-- TODO: Clarify if 16 GB is inclusive or exclusive maximum. This is inclusive.
when physical_memory_mb > 4092 and physical_memory_mb < 16384 then physical_
memory_mb / 4
    else 0 end
)
-
(
case
-- Reserve 1 GB for every 8 GB above 16 GB
-- TODO: Clarify if 16 GB is inclusive or exclusive minimum. This is exclusive.
when physical_memory_mb > 16384 then ( physical_memory_mb - 16384 )/ 8
else 0
end
)
from physical_mem
 EXEC sp_configure 'max server memory', @sqlmemory;
 -- change to #GB * 1024, leave 2 GB per system for OS, 4GB if over 16GB RAM
RECONFIGURE WITH OVERRIDE;
/*SELECT MaxDOP for Server Based on CPU Count */
BEGIN
    DECLARE @cpu_Countdop INT;
    SELECT  @cpu_Countdop = cpu_count
    FROM    sys.dm_os_sys_info dosi;
    EXEC sp_configure 'max degree of parallelism', @cpu_Countdop;
    RECONFIGURE WITH OVERRIDE;
END;

EXEC sp_configure 'xp_cmdshell', 0;
GO
RECONFIGURE;
GO
EXEC sp_configure 'remote admin connections', 1;
GO
RECONFIGURE;
GO
EXEC sp_configure 'backup compression default', 1;
RECONFIGURE WITH OVERRIDE;
```

```
GO
RECONFIGURE WITH OVERRIDE;
GO
sp_configure 'Database Mail XPs', 1;
GO
RECONFIGURE;
GO
RECONFIGURE;
GO
EXEC sp_configure 'cost threshold for parallelism', 35;
GO
RECONFIGURE;
GO
```

You may wish to customize some of these settings. You learn about their proper configuration values in Chapter 2.

Changing your SQL Server name

If your server admin has changed the name of your Windows Server in template deployment, you may need to change the name of your SQL Server instance. Having the wrong name for your server will not stop SQL Server from running, however you will experience connection failures and features such as replication will not function properly. Fortunately, you can include the following T-SQL in your post deployment scripts to rename SQL Server.

```
use master
declare @old varchar(50)
declare @oldsql nvarchar(4000)
select @old=@@servername;
select @oldsql='exec sp_dropserver '''+@old+''';'
exec sp_executesql @oldsql
declare @new varchar(50)
declare @newsql nvarchar(4000)
select @new=convert(sysname,serverproperty('servername'));
select @newsql='exec sp_addserver '''+@new+''',local;'
exec sp_executesql @newsql
```

This code uses dynamic SQL to reset your server name. You also need to restart the SQL Server service to complete the renaming process. You can verify that you have the correct server name by executing the select @@Servername *T-SQL command.*

Manually install SQL Server on an Azure Virtual Machine

The process of installing SQL Server on an Azure IaaS is the same as you would do on-premises. You can use the setup GUI, however many organizations use a command line installation process with a configuration file, and a post-installation configuration script as shown earlier in this section. This allows the installation process to be automated, and more importantly to be done consistently and with best practices across your SQL Server environments. In the following steps, you learn how to generate a configuration file (and see a sample configuration) using the GUI, and then how to install SQL Server from the command line.

1. Launch setup.exe from the SQL Server installation media. Click New SQL Server stand-alone installation or add features to an existing installation.

2. SQL Server will run a rules check, and check the box for Microsoft updates.

3. Select Perform a New Installation and choose the edition you will be using. Click Next

4. Accept the License Terms and click next.

5. You should be on the feature selection screen as shown in Figure 1-40. Carefully select only the features you want to include in your installation to limit the surface area installed.

It is important to note that if you are installing R or Python as part of your installation, your server either needs to be on the Internet, or you will need follow the installation directions at: *https://docs.microsoft.com/en-us/sql/advanced-analytics/r/installing-ml-components-without-internet-access.*

Another note about this setup screen—starting with SQL Server 2017, SQL Server Reporting Services has been decoupled from the SQL Server installation, so you need to download and install it separately from the Database Engine and Analysis Services.

1. After selecting your features and clicking Next twice, you should be on the Instance configuration screen. Accept the default setting of a default instance, and click next.

2. On the next screen, you can either change your service accounts or accept the defaults. Many customers choose to use Active Directory accounts for their service accounts Additionally, you should click the check box next to Grant Perform Volume Maintenance Task Privilege To SQL Server Service, as seen in Figure 1-38.

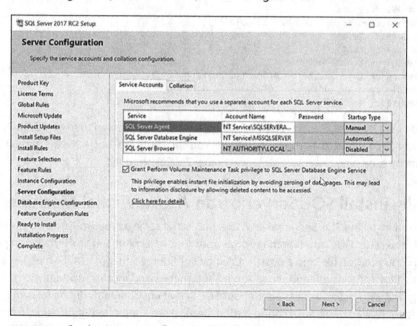

FIGURE 1-38 Service Account configuration SQL Server setup

3. On the Server Configuration screen, click the Add Current User button to make your account an admin. You may wish to add other users or groups here, and if you wish to enable Mixed Mode authentication, set the SA password here.

4. On the Server Configuration screen click the TempDB tab. You will note that SQL Server has configured multiple files based on the number of CPUs in your server. You can choose to adjust the size and location of your TempDB files in this screen, in accordance with best practices and your preferred configuration. Click next after this configuration. You can also change the location of TempDB (such as locating it on the D: drive) on this screen (Figure 1-39).

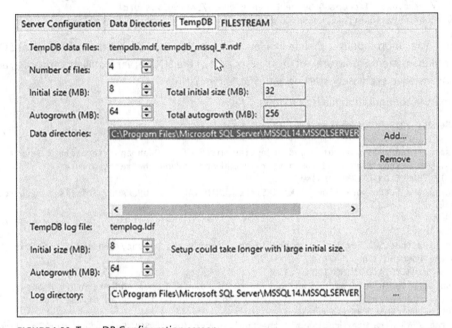

FIGURE 1-39 TempDB Configuration screen

5. The feature configuration rules will run and you will be on the Ready to Install screen.

6. On the Ready To Install screen you see, on the bottom, a configuration file location (Figure 1-40).

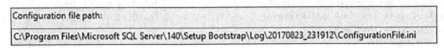

FIGURE 1-40 Configuration File Location

7. Navigate to that file location and make a copy of the configuration file. In Figure 1-43 it has been copied to C:\temp. Cancel out of SQL Server Setup. You can only run one copy of setup.exe at a time, so your command line install will fail if both are running.

8. Open your configuration file in notepad. Remove the line that begins with UIMODE and change the value of QUIETSIMPLE from False to True.

9. Launch a PowerShell window in Administrative mode.

10. Change to the drive where your SQL Server iso is located and issue the following command:

```
./setup.exe /IacceptSQLServerLicenseTerms /SAPwd=P@ssw0rd!
/ConfigurationFile=C:\temp\ConfigurationFile.ini /Action=Install
```

Your installation should complete in a few minutes. You should note that tools such as SQL Server Management Studio are not installed as part of the SQL Server installation process, and must be installed separately, starting with SQL Server 2016.

A sample configuration file is as follows:

```
;SQL Server 2017 RC2 Configuration File
[OPTIONS]
; By specifying this parameter and accepting Microsoft R Open and Microsoft R Server
 terms, you acknowledge that you have read and understood the terms of use.
IACCEPTPYTHONLICENSETERMS="False"
; Specifies a Setup work flow, like INSTALL, UNINSTALL, or UPGRADE. This is a required
 parameter.

ACTION="Install"
; Specifies that SQL Server Setup should not display the privacy statement when ran
 from the command line.
SUPPRESSPRIVACYSTATEMENTNOTICE="False"
; By specifying this parameter and accepting Microsoft R Open and Microsoft R Server
 terms, you acknowledge that you have read and understood the terms of use.
IACCEPTROPENLICENSETERMS="False"
; Use the /ENU parameter to install the English version of SQL Server on your localized
 Windows operating system.
ENU="True"
; Setup will not display any user interface.
QUIET="False"
; Setup will display progress only, without any user interaction.
QUIETSIMPLE="True"
; Specify whether SQL Server Setup should discover and include product updates.
The valid values are True and False or 1 and 0. By default SQL Server Setup will
 include updates that are found.
UpdateEnabled="True"
; If this parameter is provided, then this computer will use Microsoft Update
to check for updates.
USEMICROSOFTUPDATE="True"

; Specify the location where SQL Server Setup will obtain product updates. The
valid values are "MU" to search Microsoft Update, a valid folder path, a relative
 path such as .\MyUpdates or a UNC share. By default SQL Server Setup will search
 Microsoft Update or a Windows Update service through the Window Server Update Services.
```

UpdateSource="MU"
; Specifies features to install, uninstall, or upgrade. The list of top-level
 features include SQL, AS, IS, MDS, and Tools. The SQL feature will install the
Database Engine, Replication, Full-Text, and Data Quality Services (DQS) server.
The Tools feature will install shared components.
FEATURES=SQLENGINE,REPLICATION,CONN,BC,SDK
; Displays the command line parameters usage
HELP="False"
; Specifies that the detailed Setup log should be piped to the console.
INDICATEPROGRESS="False"
; Specifies that Setup should install into WOW64. This command line argument is not
 supported on an IA64 or a 32-bit system.
X86="False"
; Specify a default or named instance. MSSQLSERVER is the default instance for
non-Express editions and SQLExpress for Express editions. This parameter is required
 when installing the SQL Server Database Engine (SQL), or Analysis Services (AS).
INSTANCENAME="MSSQLSERVER"
; Specify the root installation directory for shared components. This directory remains
 unchanged after shared components are already installed.
INSTALLSHAREDDIR="C:\Program Files\Microsoft SQL Server"

; Specify the root installation directory for the WOW64 shared components. This
 directory remains unchanged after WOW64 shared components are already installed.
INSTALLSHAREDWOWDIR="C:\Program Files (x86)\Microsoft SQL Server"
; Specify the Instance ID for the SQL Server features you have specified. SQL Server
 directory structure, registry structure, and service names will incorporate the
 instance ID of the SQL Server instance.
INSTANCEID="MSSQLSERVER"
; TelemetryUserNameConfigDescription
SQLTELSVCACCT="NT Service\SQLTELEMETRY"
; TelemetryStartupConfigDescription
SQLTELSVCSTARTUPTYPE="Automatic"
; Specify the installation directory.
INSTANCEDIR="C:\Program Files\Microsoft SQL Server"
; Agent account name
AGTSVCACCOUNT="NT Service\SQLSERVERAGENT"
; Auto-start service after installation.
AGTSVCSTARTUPTYPE="Manual"
; CM brick TCP communication port
COMMFABRICPORT="0"
; How matrix will use private networks
COMMFABRICNETWORKLEVEL="0"
; How inter brick communication will be protected

COMMFABRICENCRYPTION="0"
; TCP port used by the CM brick
MATRIXCMBRICKCOMMPORT="0"
; Startup type for the SQL Server service.
SQLSVCSTARTUPTYPE="Automatic"
; Level to enable FILESTREAM feature at (0, 1, 2 or 3).
FILESTREAMLEVEL="0"
; Set to "1" to enable RANU for SQL Server Express.
ENABLERANU="False"
; Specifies a Windows collation or an SQL collation to use for the Database Engine.
SQLCOLLATION="SQL_Latin1_General_CP1_CI_AS"

```
; Account for SQL Server service: Domain\User or system account.
SQLSVCACCOUNT="NT Service\MSSQLSERVER"
; Set to "True" to enable instant file initialization for SQL Server service. If
 enabled, Setup will grant Perform Volume Maintenance Task privilege to the Database
 Engine Service SID. This may lead to information disclosure as it could allow
deleted content to be accessed by an unauthorized principal.
SQLSVCINSTANTFILEINIT="True"
; Windows account(s) to provision as SQL Server system administrators.
SQLSYSADMINACCOUNTS="DOMAIN\joey"
; The default is Windows Authentication. Use "SQL" for Mixed Mode Authentication.
SECURITYMODE="SQL"
; The number of Database Engine TempDB files.
SQLTEMPDBFILECOUNT="4"
; Specifies the initial size of a Database Engine TempDB data file in MB.
SQLTEMPDBFILESIZE="8"
; Specifies the automatic growth increment of each Database Engine TempDB data
file in MB.
SQLTEMPDBFILEGROWTH="64"
; Specifies the initial size of the Database Engine TempDB log file in MB.
SQLTEMPDBLOGFILESIZE="8"
; Specifies the automatic growth increment of the Database Engine TempDB log file in MB.
SQLTEMPDBLOGFILEGROWTH="64"
; Provision current user as a Database Engine system administrator for
 %SQL_PRODUCT_SHORT_NAME% Express.
ADDCURRENTUSERASSQLADMIN="True"
; Specify 0 to disable or 1 to enable the TCP/IP protocol.
TCPENABLED="1"
; Specify 0 to disable or 1 to enable the Named Pipes protocol.
NPENABLED="0"
; Startup type for Browser Service.

BROWSERSVCSTARTUPTYPE="Disabled"
```

> **MORE INFO** **USING CONFIGURATION FILES FOR SQL SERVER INSTALLATIONS**
>
> Using configuration files is good way to automate your SQL Server installs, you can learn more about the options around using them here: *https://docs.microsoft.com/en-us/sql/database-engine/install-windows/install-sql-server-2016-using-a-configuration-file.*

Provision an Azure Virtual Machine to host a SQL Server instance

There are several ways to provision a virtual machine for deploying SQL Server. In this section, you learn how to do it both in the Azure Portal and via PowerShell.

Build a Virtual Machine using the portal

1. To deploy a new VM from the portal first login to the portal as a user who has permissions to create a VM. You will need to be a contributor in the resource group where you are creating this VM.

2. From the portal click the + New in the top left (as highlighted in Figure 1-41).

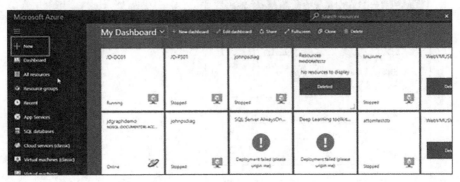

FIGURE 1-41 Azure Portal Open Screen

3. On the next screen, type **Windows Server 2016** in the New box. It will start to auto-populate.

4. Select Windows Server 2016 Datacenter, and click it (see Figure 1-42).

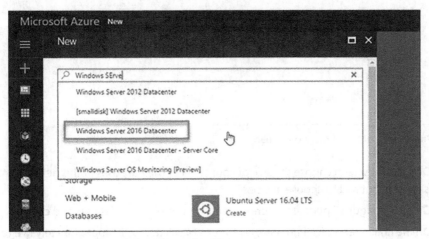

FIGURE 1-42 Selecting Windows Server 2016 Datacenter

5. Accept the default of resource manager and click Create.

6. On the next screen (Figure 1-43), you need to enter a few values for your VM including server name, admin user, admin password, subscription, resource group, and location. Your password is at least 12 characters. Click Next.

FIGURE 1-43 VM Configuration Screen

7. On the next screen choose the size of your VM. For the purposes of this demo a D4S_v3 is chosen, but feel to choose any size.

8. On the Configure Optional Features screen, accept all of the defaults and click OK.

9. On the final screen click Purchase, and your VM will deploy in approximately five to 10 minutes.

Your VM is now ready for adding disks. You can go back to the configuring Storage Spaces section and add disks for your data files and transaction logs.

Deploying an Azure VM with PowerShell

One of the most powerful parts of cloud computing is the ability to transform building infrastructure, which in the past was a time consuming physical process, into repeatable use parameterized code. This process was part of the shift to Azure Resource Manager, which transforms each infrastructure component into objects, with dependencies on each other. ARM also includes a common framework for scripting and automation. This enables you to rapidly deploy large-scale infrastructures like an AlwaysOn Availability Group with minimal effort. One of the things Microsoft has done to make this easier for you is that you can build components using the Azure Portal and then download the template at the end of the process, like you did earlier.

EXAM TIP

Having an understanding of concepts around Azure Resource Manager helps you better understand PowerShell, automation, and other concepts you may be tested on.

After you install Azure PowerShell execute the following steps to deploy your VM.

1. Launch the PowerShell integrated scripting environment by launching the Windows run diaglog (Win+R) and typing **powershell_ise.**

2. On the Powershell_ise, click View, and check the box next to script pane. You will have an interactive scripting window.

3. Paste the following code into the ISE:

```
Login-AzureRmAccount

New-AzureRmResourceGroup -Name myResourceGroup -Location EastUS

# Create a subnet configuration
$subnetConfig = New-AzureRmVirtualNetworkSubnetConfig -Name mySubnet
-AddressPrefix 192.168.1.0/24

# Create a virtual network
$vnet = New-AzureRmVirtualNetwork -ResourceGroupName myResourceGroup
-Location EastUS `
    -Name MYvNET -AddressPrefix 192.168.0.0/16 -Subnet $subnetConfig

# Create a public IP address and specify a DNS name
$pip = New-AzureRmPublicIpAddress -ResourceGroupName myResourceGroup
-Location EastUS `
    -AllocationMethod Static -IdleTimeoutInMinutes 4 -Name
"mypublicdns$(Get-Random)"
    # Create an inbound network security group rule for port 3389

$nsgRuleRDP = New-AzureRmNetworkSecurityRuleConfig
-Name myNetworkSecurityGroupRuleRDP  -Protocol Tcp `
    -Direction Inbound -Priority 1000 -SourceAddressPrefix * -SourcePortRange
* -DestinationAddressPrefix * `
    -DestinationPortRange 3389 -Access Allow

# Create an inbound network security group rule for port 80
$nsgRuleWeb = New-AzureRmNetworkSecurityRuleConfig
-Name myNetworkSecurityGroupRuleWWW  -Protocol Tcp `
    -Direction Inbound -Priority 1001 -SourceAddressPrefix * -SourcePortRange
* -DestinationAddressPrefix * `
    -DestinationPortRange 80 -Access Allow

# Create a network security group
$nsg = New-AzureRmNetworkSecurityGroup -ResourceGroupName myResourceGroup
```

```
        -Location EastUS `
          -Name myNetworkSecurityGroup -SecurityRules $nsgRuleRDP,$nsgRuleWeb

        # Create a virtual network card and associate with public IP address and
        NSG$nic = New-AzureRmNetworkInterface -Name myNic -ResourceGroupName
        myResourceGroup -Location EastUS `
          -SubnetId $vnet.Subnets[0].Id -PublicIpAddressId $pip.Id
        -NetworkSecurityGroupId $nsg.Id

        # Define a credential object
        $cred = Get-Credential

        # Create a virtual machine configuration
        $vmConfig = New-AzureRmVMConfig -VMName myVM -VMSize Standard_DS2 | `
          Set-AzureRmVMOperatingSystem -Windows -ComputerName myVM -Credential $cred | `
          Set-AzureRmVMSourceImage -PublisherName MicrosoftWindowsServer -Offer
        WindowsServer `
          -Skus 2016-Datacenter -Version latest | Add-AzureRmVMNetworkInterface
        -Id $nic.Id

        #Build the VM
        New-AzureRmVM -ResourceGroupName myResourceGroup -Location EastUS -VM $vmConfig

        Get-AzureRmPublicIpAddress -ResourceGroupName myResourceGroup | Select IpAddress
```

When you execute this, you will be prompted twice, the first time will be to login to your Azure account, and then a second time to enter credentials for the virtual machine in your environment. This script will also give you the public IP address at the end. You can then launch a remote desktop session to connect to that IP address with the credentials you created at the second prompt.

You should note the way the VM is created in the resource manager model—the resource group and the network are created first, then the IP addresses and the network security group, and then finally the virtual machine is created. Each of these resources has built-in dependencies and that is the reason for that order. This gives you a quick introduction of what it's like to use PowerShell in Azure. Microsoft has a lot of additional templates on GitHub that you can explore, and in many cases one-click deploy.

> **MORE INFO** **TEMPLATES FOR AZURE FEATURES**
>
> Azure offers a wide variety of templates to meet your needs. You can review some of the of-ferings from Microsoft at Github: *https://github.com/Azure/azure-quickstart-templates*.

Automate the deployment of SQL Server Databases

One of the most prominent programming methodologies in recent years has been the widespread adoption of the Agile methodology, and continuous deployment and continuous integration. This trend has been enhanced by the automation framework that is built into cloud computing—not only can you generate code for your application, you can generate all its underlying infrastructure, and potentially even build out scale-out logic for your application tiers. However, database developers have been slow to adopt these methods, due to the rigorous requirements of databases to ensure and protect production data. There has traditionally been friction between the development and operations teams because the developers wish to push out more changes, and faster, while operations wants to protect the integrity of the data.

Databases can be the bottleneck

It is relatively easy to deploy new code for the front end of a website, for example. The application is still interfacing with the same libraries and classes, and is just calling some new graphic files or style sheets. Changing the database can be significantly more challenging. The challenge with deploying database is that data cannot be dropped in-place, unlike application code which is easily replaced in a deployment. So any changes to the database backend must incorporate and reflect any schema or application changes, while at the same time not having any downtime.

Introducing DACPAC

There are several database version control tools on the market, including many from third-party vendors. However, Microsoft makes a freely available tool called SQL Server Data Tools, which includes a shell version of Visual Studio, and a feature called Data-Tier Application Package or DACPAC. A DACPAC is a single file that contains all the data definition language (DDL) for the schemas in your database. You may also hear of the term BACPAC, which is similar, but includes all the data in the database. You can download SQL Server Data Tools at *https://docs. microsoft.com/en-us/sql/ssdt/download-sql-server-data-tools-ssdt*.

To take advantage of these features, you need to create a Database Project within SQL Server Data Tools. You can create a new project from an existing database, as you'll see in the following example. For this demo, you need SQL Server installed and the AdventureWorks2014 database restored. You can get the database at *https://github.com/Microsoft/sql-server-samples/releases/download/adventureworks2014/adventure-works-2014-oltp-full-database-backup.zip*. Instructions for restoring the database are at *https://github.com/Microsoft/sql-server-samples/releases/download/adventureworks2014/adventure-works-2014-readme.txt*. If you are using Visual Studio 2017, you also want to make sure you have the latest updates. Visual Studio will update as part of Windows Update, you extensions can be updated by clicking the flag next to the "Quick Launch" box in Visual Studio.

1. Launch SQL Server Data Tools.
2. Select File > New Project > SQL Server Database Project.
3. Right-click the Project Name, and Click Import > Database.
4. You will be presented with the dialog box shown in Figure 1-44.

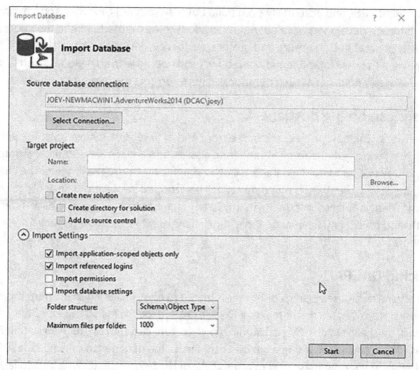

FIGURE 1-44 Import Database Screen from a SQL Server Project

Click the Select Connection Box. You will be directed to a dialog to connect to your SQL Server. Choose the AdventureWorks2014 database and login. Accept the default settings, and click Start. Your database schema (and not your data) will import shortly.

1. In your project in Solution Explorer, click to expand Human Resources > Stored Procedures. Right-click and select Add > New Item (Figure 1-45).

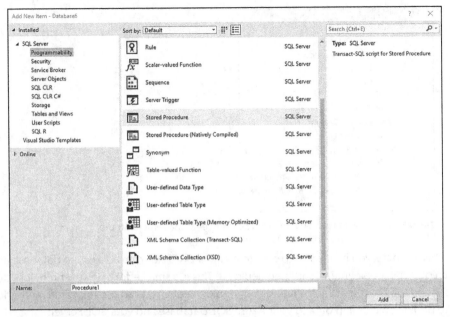

FIGURE 1-45 Add New Item in SQL Server Data Tools

2. Enter the following T-SQL to create a new stored procedure.

```
CREATE PROCEDURE [dbo].[uspGetDate]
AS     SELECT GETDATE()
RETURN 0
```

3. Click the Save icon.

4. Right-click the project Database1 and click publish (Figure 1-46).

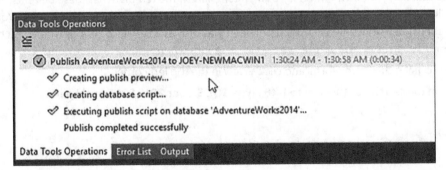

FIGURE 1-46 The Data Tools Operation screen

5. Launch SQL Server Management Studio and connect to your database (Figure 1-47).

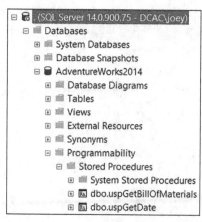

FIGURE 1-47 Object Explorer View from SQL Server Management Studio

In this example, you have learned how to create a DACPAC from an existing database and add an object in deployment, and then deploy it. This is a small effort, however it helps you understand the process for automating your deployments. You can use this same methodology to deploy objects and data to your Azure SQL Database and your SQL Server.

Deploy SQL Server by using templates

Earlier in this chapter you learned about building your own Azure VM for SQL Server, and the process of adding disks, configuring Storage Spaces, and optimizing your settings. In this section you learn about deploying a new SQL Server using the Azure provided templates. Microsoft has added some built-in features to automate some aspects of SQL Server management that you can only take advantage of by using the template. You might ask why would you choose building your own VM versus using a template, if the template has these benefits. Well, much like any other aspect of cloud computing, you are trading control for automation. You make similar decisions when choosing between Platform as a Service offerings where you have less control, versus Infrastructure as a Service offerings where you have more control.

1. Login to the Azure Portal and click +New in the top left corner.

2. In the search box (see Figure 1-48), type **SQL Server 2016 SP1 Developer**.

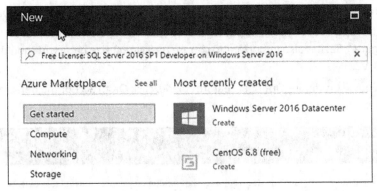

FIGURE 1-48 Search Screen from within Azure Portal

3. You will be taken to the screen to fill in the details of your VM. Enter a name, an admin account and password, a resource group, and a location (Figure 1-49).

FIGURE 1-49 The Server Name screen in the Azure Portal

Note that it is important to create a VM Disk Type of SSD for the purposes of this demo.

1. Next, you choose a size for your VM (see Figure 1-50). Click the View All button, as shown in figure 1-52. It is also important to choose the correct size here; you should choose DS3_V2.

2. On the Settings > Configure Optional Features blade, click OK to accept the defaults and continue.

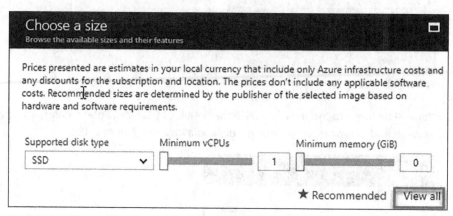

FIGURE 1 50 "Choose a Size Screen" from Azure Portal

3. On the SQL Server Settings Blade, click Enable SQL Authentication. Your username and password from the server should auto populate the field. You should note that logins such as SA and admin are reserved, and cannot be used from this screen.

4. Next, click the Storage Configuration button. This is a cool feature that allows your Storage Spaces volumes to be automatically configured based on the IOPs and Capacity you need (see Figure 1-51). If you have that data from an existing server you can use it here, or just adjust the sliders and watch the number of disks change. You should note that the max IOPs and capacity are correlated to the size of your VM, so if you need more space, you may need a larger VM. You may also choose General, Transaction Processing, or Data Warehousing as the Storage Optimization type. This affects the stripe size of your storage spaces environment.

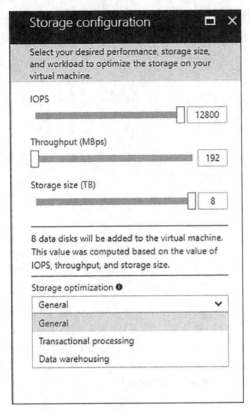

FIGURE 1-51 Storage Configuration Screen for SQL Server VMs

5. Click OK.

6. Click the Automatic Patching button. Click the Enable button and set a time window for when you would like your VM to be patched. Note that if you make this selection, you will incur downtime when the server is patched, so exercise with care in production environments.

7. Click the Automated Backup button. From the blade click Enable. Adjust the retention period slider to meet your requirements (see Figure 1-52). Click Enable on the Encryption button, and supply a password (a minimum of 12 characters is required). You may also wish to configure a custom backup schedule or accept the default value of automated.

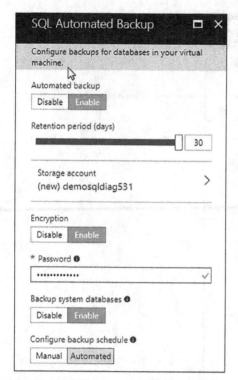

FIGURE 1-52 SQL Automated Backup Blade from the Azure Portal

8. The next button is Key Vault. You can use this to store your keys for encryption if you are using a key vault.

9. Click OK on the SQL Server Settings screen, and click Purchase on the confirmation screen. You VM should deploy in four to five minutes.

Using the Microsoft supplied templates give you more automation and consistent configuration in your Azure deployments. Additionally, you can take advantage of more complex deployment templates like the AlwaysOn Availability Group template to quickly deploy complex environments.

> **MORE INFO AZURE KEY VAULT**
>
> Azure Key Vault is highly secured service to store certificates, keys, and secrets: *https://azure.microsoft.com/en-us/services/key-vault/.*

Skill 1:4: Deploy SQL Server databases to Azure virtual machines

This skill deals with migrating your existing data to Azure, and then supporting your new environment once your workloads are running in the cloud.

> **This skill covers how to:**
> - Migrate an on-premises SQL Server database to an Azure virtual machine
> - Generate benchmark data for performance needs
> - Perform performance tuning on Azure IaaS
> - Support availability sets in Azure

Migrate an on-premises SQL Server Database to an Azure virtual machine

There are several approaches you can take for migrating on-premises workloads into Azure virtual machines. Surprisingly, one of the key components is your network configuration to Azure. Latency and bandwidth and your tolerance for downtime determine your strategy. In this section, you learn about the following approaches:

- Backup and restore to Azure
- Log shipping
- AlwaysOn Availability Groups
- Azure site recovery

Backup and restore to Azure

Of all the options you are going to learn about it, this is the most straightforward. Since SQL Server 2012 SP1 CU2, SQL Server has supported a backup to URL feature that allows you to backup and restore databases directly into an Azure blob storage account. This feature uses HTTPS endpoints, so there is no need for a VPN or any advanced networking configuration like the other options. To get started with this service, you need a storage account in Azure, and a SQL Server instance running either on-premises or in an Azure VM.

1. Login to the Azure Portal and navigate to your storage account. If you do not have a storage account create one. Once your storage account is created, click Blobs in the overview screen, as shown in Figure 1-53.

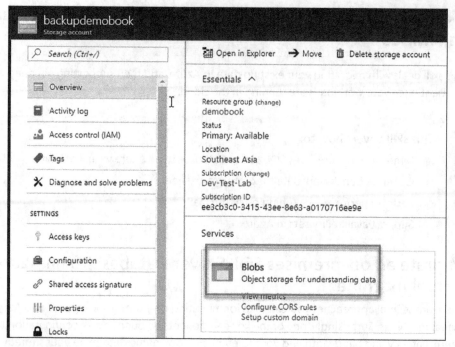

FIGURE 1-53 Azure Storage Account overview screen

2. In the Blob Service screen click the +Container button to create a new container, as shown in Figure 1-54. You should note that both your storage account and your container names must be lower case and not contain spaces or special characters.

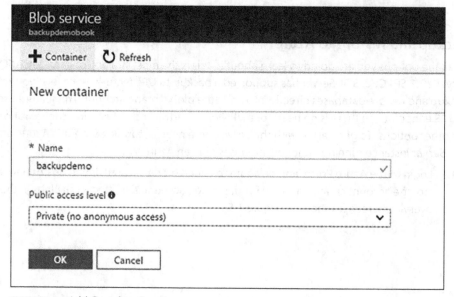

FIGURE 1-54 Add Container Screen

You may notice the access level in this screenshot. It is set to Private, which is what you should use for storing backups.

3. Next, you need to generate a shared access signature for your storage account. Navigate back to the overview of your storage account, and then click the Shared Access Signature button, as highlighted in blue in Figure 1-55.

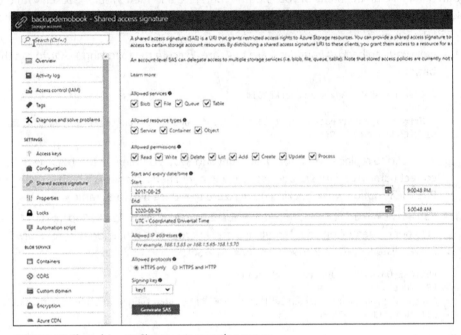

FIGURE 1-55 Shared Access Signature generation screen

A couple of things to note here—you may want to limit the allowed services to blob storage, because that is all SQL Server needs, and the allowed resource types to just containers. You may also want to extend the time on the shared access signature. By default, the expiration is set to eight hours, but for backups it is recommended to set it for much longer. Azure will not remind when your SAS is going to expire, so make note of the date. In this instance, the expiration is set for two years. When you click the blue Generate SAS button, you should copy the SAS token that is first on the screen.

***NOTE:* SAS TOKENS**

When you copy your SAS token from the portal there is a question mark that proceeds the SAS token. You need to remove it before creating your SQL Server credential in T-SQL.

---

4. Launch SQL Server Management Studio and connect to your instance. Launch a new query window. Execute the following T-SQL to create your credential.

```
CREATE CREDENTIAL
[https://$yourstorageaccount.blob.core.windows.net/$yourcontainer] WITH IDENTITY
    = 'shared access signature',
SECRET='$yourSASToken'
```

You need to replace the $yourstorageaccount with the name of your storage account, and $yourcontainer with the name of your storage container, and then $yourSASToken with the value of your SAS token. This credential will be used when you backup your database in the next step.

1. Now you can backup your database to Azure. Execute the following T-SQL to run this backup.

```
BACKUP DATABASE AdventureWorks2014
TO URL =
   'https://$yourstorageaccount.blob.core.windows.net/$yourcontainer/aw2014.bak'
WITH COMPRESSION, STATS=5
```

You need to replace $yourstorageaccount and $yourcontainer in the T-SQL with the correct names for your storage account and containers. It is necessary to use the COMPRESSION option when backing up to Azure to reduce network traffic.

2. You are now ready to restore your database to a new VM in Azure. Repeat step 1 to create your credential on your target instance. In order to do that, login to your new SQL Server instance, and execute the following T-SQL:

```
RESTORE DATABASE AdventureWorks2014
FROM URL =
'https://$yourstorageaccount.blob.core.windows.net/$yourcontainer/aw2014.bak'
WITH REPLACE, STATS=5
```

That is the process of backup and restore to and from Azure. It is a very easy method with the only negative being some amount of downtime for the backup and restore process.

Hybrid network connections

This may seem slightly off-topic, but is a requirement for what you are going to learn about next. Azure supports three types of network connections between your on-premises and cloud environments. For features like AlwaysOn Availability Groups, and Azure Site Recovery having a direct connection to Azure is a necessity.

- **Point to Site VPN**   Point to Site VPNs are a single machine to network VPN using a certificate based VPN. These are best reserved for test and demo systems, and should not be used for a production environment.

- **Site to Site VPN**   This is a dedicated VPN device that connects an on-premises site to Azure. These are best used for smaller migrations with small to medium data footprints.

- **ExpressRoute**   This is an enterprise class, dedicated network connection between your on-premises site and one or more Azure regions. This should be used for large-scale migrations and real-time migrations using Azure Site Recovery.

AlwaysOn Availability Groups

Many organizations choose to take advantage of AlwaysOn Availability Groups for their migrations into the cloud, or even to new hardware. As you read earlier, Availability Groups use Windows Server Failover cluster to orchestrate failover. Many organizations have extended into Azure for Disaster Recovery using Availability Groups. The most important thing in this scenario is to have a very reliable connection to Azure either via a site-to-site VPN or ExpressRoute. In this scenario, you learn about extended an on-premises AG into Azure, with a few mouse clicks. The only prerequisite is that you have an on-premises Availability Group (even if it's one node).

1. From SQL Server Management Studio Connect to your instance, expand AlwaysOn High Availability > Availability Groups, then right-click the name of your Availability Group. Select Add Another Replica.

2. The Add Replica To Availability Group Wizard will then launch. Click Next on the splash screen, then on the next screen click the Connect button to connect to your existing replica(s).

3. On the Add Replica screen, click the button that reads Add Azure Replica as shown in Figure 1-56.

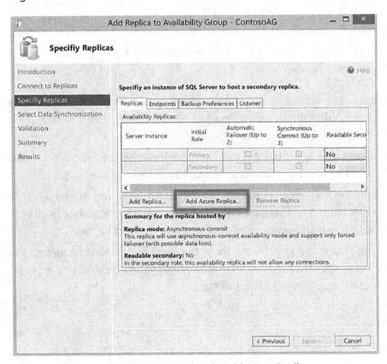

FIGURE 1-56 Add Availability Group Wizard--Add Azure Replica

4. In the next step, you need your subscription ID. You can get your subscription ID by running the PowerShell cmdlet login-azurermaccount and logging in with your credentials. You should paste your subscription ID in the subscription field as shown in Figure 1-57.

FIGURE 1-57 Add Azure Replica Wizard

5. Once you have authenticated to your subscription, you will be able to populate the other fields. The options are standard for a VM, like you have created earlier, but do require the name of your On-Premises domain.

6. When you have completed this, legal terms will be displayed, and you need to click OK. The Add Replica to Availability Group screen will again be displayed. Click OK.

7. The next screen has you select a data synchronization option. You should select Full Synchronization. Note that if you are working with very large databases (> 1 TB) this performs a full backup and restore and may take an extended period.

One other thing you need to do differently for your Availability Group in Azure is to use an Internal Load Balancer in Azure to provide the IP address for your listener. If you are creating a hybrid availability group you still need to do this step.

Azure Site Recovery and SQL Server

Azure Site Recovery (ASR) is a fully featured disaster recovery system. It allows you to do full scale disaster recovery testing with no impact to your production environment. One approach many customers have taken is to use ASR to perform an on-premises to Azure migration. Azure Site Recovery can run with an agent on physical servers and VMWare virtual machines, and natively with Hyper-V virtual machines.

To perform a migration using ASR, you would need to have an Express Route connection, as it replicates block level changes across all of your machines. In terms of SQL Server you can use the following HA/DR options in conjunction with site recovery:

- AlwaysOn Availability Group
- Failover Cluster Instances with Shared Storage
- Database Mirroring
- Standalone instances

Using ASR for migration is good approach for many customers, especially enterprises who still support back versions of SQL Server due to its variety of support. Additionally, ASR offers the ability to migrate all of your infrastructure in one group, versus attempting to do it piecemeal.

Generate benchmark data for performance needs

Trying to size your VMs for SQL Server workloads can be quite challenging. Earlier in this chapter you learned about using Windows Performance Monitor to capture data from existing applications. The other workload capture and replay tool that you will learn about is Distributed Replay in SQL Server.

Distributed Replay

Distributed Replay (see Figure 1-58) is a tool that was introduced in SQL Server 2012 that allows you to capture and replay workloads to test performance of your target environment.

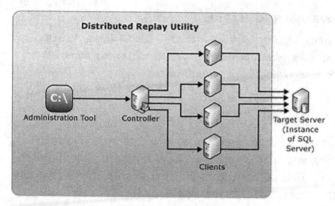

FIGURE 1-58 Distributed Replay architecture

You need to install the distributed replay controller and between 1 and 16 distributed replay clients. You need to add this to your installation of SQL Server, as shown in Figure 1-59.

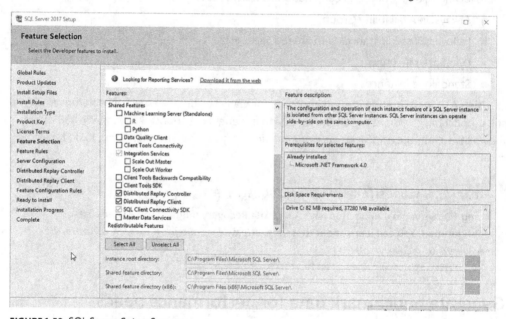

FIGURE 1-59 SQL Server Setup Screen

From there you need to configure both your server and clients. The components install is as follows:

- **Distributed Replay administration tool** A console application, DReplay.exe, used to communicate with the distributed replay controller. Use the administration tool to control the distributed replay.

- **Distributed Replay controller** A computer running the Windows service named SQL Server Distributed Replay controller. The Distributed Replay manages the distributed replay clients. There is only one controller instance in each Distributed Replay environment.

- **Distributed Replay clients** One or more computers (physical or virtual) running the Windows service named SQL Server Distributed Replay client. The Distributed Replay clients work together to simulate workloads against an instance of SQL Server. This client simulates a client application.

- **Target server** An instance of SQL Server that the Distributed Replay clients can use to replay trace data. In this case this would be your Azure environment.

> **MORE INFO SQL SERVER AND DISTRIBUTED REPLAY**
>
> Distributed replay is a fairly complex feature with a large number of configuration options. It does a very good job of simulating the workload against a database server, however it does not measure everything—for example it does not address network throughput: *https://docs.microsoft.com/en-us/sql/tools/distributed-replay/sql-server-distributed-replay*.

Perform performance tuning on Azure IaaS

Azure Virtual Machines are somewhat like on-premises virtual machines, in that you are not locked into a specific hardware platform, and you can enact changes in your hardware with minimal downtime. What this means is that you can balance performance and cost, and if your initial sizing estimate is off the mark, you can quickly change to a new hardware platform. Most of your performances tuning opportunities lie within storage, however you should try to tune SQL Server first.

Tuning SQL Server on Azure IaaS

Fundamentally, there is no difference to tuning SQL Server on Azure IaaS versus any other environment. The one major difference is that I/O performance tends to be more of a focus. The move to premium storage has reduced this, however you should still take advantage of features like data compression to reduce the I/O workload and improve memory utilization on your machine. You should follow other best practices like not using auto shrink and actively managing your data and log file growth. Another I/O issue you may adjust is TempDB—this you can consider moving tempdb to the D: drive to take advantage of its lower latency. You may also wish to take advantage of SQL Server's wait statistics to understand what the database engine is waiting on.

> **MORE INFO SQL SERVER WAIT STATISTICS**
>
> SQL Server tracks everything any operation is waiting on. This can help you tune the system based on what resources are causing the delays: *https://blogs.msdn.microsoft.com/sqlserver-storageengine/2017/07/03/what-are-you-waiting-for-introducing-wait-stats-support-in-query-store/*.

Another pattern you want to follow in Azure VMs (and Azure SQL Database) is to be more aggressive with indexes than you ordinarily might be in an on-premises environment. If you are on SQL Server 2016 or 2017, you can take advantage of the Query Store feature to identify missing indexes for you.

Using the query store

The Query Store is a feature that was introduced in SQL Server 2016, and captures query compilation information and runtime execution statistics. This gives you a powerful history of performance in your environment, and highlights execution plan changes, query regressions (executions that are suddenly slower than past executions), and high resource consuming queries.

You need to enable the Query Store (see Figure 1-60) for your database(s), which you can do by executing the following T-SQL:

```
ALTER DATABASE YourdatabaseName SET QUERY_STORE = ON
```

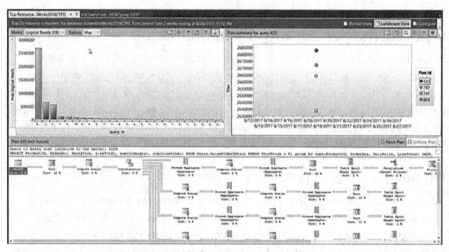

FIGURE 1-60 Top Resource Consumer View from Query Store

You can use the following query to pull missing index requests out of the Query Store data in your database.

```
SELECT  SUM(qrs.count_executions) * AVG(qrs.avg_logical_io_reads) AS
est_logical_reads ,
        SUM(qrs.count_executions) AS sum_executions ,
        AVG(qrs.avg_logical_io_reads) AS avg_avg_logical_io_reads ,
        SUM(qsq.count_compiles) AS sum_compiles ,
        (   SELECT TOP 1 qsqt.query_sql_text
            FROM   sys.query_store_query_text qsqt
            WHERE  qsqt.query_text_id = MAX(qsq.query_text_id)) AS query_text ,
        TRY_CONVERT(XML, (   SELECT   TOP 1 qsp2.query_plan
                             FROM     sys.query_store_plan qsp2
                             WHERE    qsp2.query_id = qsq.query_id
```

```
                              ORDER BY qsp2.plan_id DESC )) AS query_plan ,
        qsq.query_id ,
        qsq.query_hash
FROM    sys.query_store_query qsq
        JOIN sys.query_store_plan qsp ON qsq.query_id = qsp.query_id
        CROSS APPLY ( SELECT TRY_CONVERT(XML, qsp.query_plan) AS query_plan_xml )
 AS qpx
        JOIN sys.query_store_runtime_stats qrs ON qsp.plan_id = qrs.plan_id
        JOIN sys.query_store_runtime_stats_interval qsrsi ON qrs.runtime_stats_
interval_id = qsrsi.runtime_stats_interval_id
WHERE   qsp.query_plan LIKE N'%<MissingIndexes>%'
        AND qsrsi.start_time >= DATEADD(HH, -24, SYSDATETIME())
GROUP BY qsq.query_id ,
        qsq.query_hash
ORDER BY est_logical_reads DESC;
GO
```

The Query Store is a powerful new feature that can supply you with important data about your environment and help you tune the performance of your SQL Server quickly.

Support availability sets in Azure

The Azure cloud has a lot of automation and availability options built into it. However, Microsoft has to perform the same sort of maintenance operations like patching hardware and software that you would do in your on-premises environment. You have learned about building availability into your SQL Server environment, and now you learn about adding availability into your Azure environment. Availability Sets protect your Azure workloads from both unplanned outages due to things like hardware maintenance or physical infrastructure problems, and planned outages to software updates.

You do this in Azure by using the Availability Set construct. For example, you would put all the members of your AlwaysOn Availability Group into an Availablity Set (see Figure 1-61). It is important to note that you must create the availability set at the time you create your VMs. This means you can't add an existing VM to an availability set after the fact.

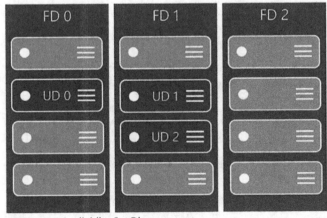

FIGURE 1-61 Availablity Set Diagram

The basic concepts of an availability set are update domains and fault domains. Update domains ensure that your VMs are spread across multiple physical hosts to protect against downtime for planned updates. Fault domains share a common power source and network source. Availability sets spread your virtual machines across three fault domains and up to five update domains. Availability sets also work with managed disks to protect your disks as part of your availability set.

Thought experiment

In this thought experiment, apply what you've learned in this Chapter. You can find answers to this thought experiment in the next section.

You are a consultant to the Contoso Corporation. Contoso is a mid-sized wholesaler, which currently has a customer facing ordering system where each customer has their own set of tables, and a backend business intelligence system that is 10 TB. Business users search the business intelligence system using full text search for product name sales. Contoso has around 100 customers, with each customer averaging about 4 GB of data.

Contoso's CIO is trying to shut down their on-premises data center, due to concerns about PCI compliance and two recent power outages that resulted in days of downtime. Contoso is looking for guidance around a migration path to Azure. Contoso is also looking to provide increased availability for the customer facing systems. With this information in mind answer the following questions.

1. What should be the solution for the business intelligence system?
2. How should Contoso approach building a new customer facing system?
3. How should Contoso address the availability concern?
4. How should Contoso migrate the customer data?

Thought experiment answers

This section contains the solution to the thought experiment. Each answer explains why the answer choice is correct.

1. Contoso should migrate the business intelligence system to SQL Server running in an Azure VM. The size makes it prohibitive to move to SQL DB, and the full text search options limits the use of SQL DW.
2. Contoso should split out each customer into their own database, and migrate the platform to Azure SQL Database using elastic pools to optimize cost and management.
3. Contoso can use active geo-replication in conjunction with the elastic pools in Azure SQL Database
4. Constoso should build BACPACs for each customer's data, and migrate into their new database.

Chapter summary

- You Azure SQL Database Server name must be globally unique.
- Choosing a service tier for your Azure SQL Database is important.
- Azure SQL Database offers automatic tuning via adding and removing indexes automatically.
- Compatibility level 140 offers advanced performance enhancements to both Azure SQL Database and SQL Server 2017.
- Changing service levels for Azure SQL Database may be a time-consuming operation for a large database.
- You can create an Azure SQL Server using the portal, PowerShell, the Azure CLI, or the Rest API.
- You need to open firewall rules for your application to talk to Azure SQL Database.
- Azure SQL Database provides high availability inherently, but you must configure multi-region availability.
- Long term backup retention is available and configured with Azure Backup Vaults.
- Your Azure SQL Database sysadmin account should be an Azure Active Directory Group.
- Elastic pools are a very good fit for many small databases.
- Pools have similar sizing characteristics to individual databases, but simplify management.
- Elastic jobs allow to run scripts across all your databases.
- Elastics jobs can use geo-replication for databases or across multiple databases.
- It is important to understand the SQL Server licensing rules when planning your architecture.
- Migrating existing applications is easier than building for a new application because you can capture performance data from the existing environment.
- Capturing data from performance monitoring is a good way to size your architecture.
- Balancing CPU, memory, and storage performance are the keys to good SQL Server performance.
- Choosing the size for your Azure VM is a balance of cost and performance.
- Azure Compute Units offer a way to compare relative performance of given Azure VM tiers.
- The G series of VMs offer premium performance for your heaviest workloads.
- Use Storage Spaces in Windows Server to add disk storage and IOPs capacity.
- Use Premium Storage exclusively for your production workloads.
- Consider using the temporary D drive for high write TempDB workloads.
- SQL Server on Azure IaaS should use Instant File Initialization.

- Properly size your data files to avoid auto-growth events on your SQL Server on Azure.
- Using DACPACs can help you automate the deployment of schema and DDL to your Azure SQL Databases and SQL Server instances.
- Migration to Azure can take advantage of built-in features like AlwaysOn Availability Groups, or take advantage of Azure Site Recovery.
- Distributed Replay is an excellent way to capture and replay a workload for testing purposes.
- The Query Store is an excellent way to easily capture performance information from either your SQL Server instance or your Azure SQL Database.
- Use Availability Sets to protect your workloads from Azure outages.

## CHAPTER 2

Manage databases and instances

Managing relational databases on the Azure platform requires the understanding of several key concepts and technologies that are crucial to a successful cloud implementation. While several of these concepts apply to both on-premises as well as the cloud, a more comprehensive understanding of effectively configuring security, monitoring database performance, and managing server instances in a PaaS offering is necessary.

Skills in this chapter:

- Skill 2.1: Configure secure access to Microsoft Azure SQL databases
- Skill 2.2: Configure SQL Server performance settings
- Skill 2.3: Manage SQL Server instances

Skill 2.1: Configure secure access to Microsoft Azure SQL databases

Azure SQL Database secures your data at multiple layers to provide enterprise-level security and to meet industry security standards. SQL Database provides encryption for data in motion using Transport Layer Security, for data at rest using TDE (Transparent Data Encryption), and for data in use using Always Encrypted.

This skill focuses on the approach and steps necessary to effectively secure your relational databases and appropriately implement key security features in Azure SQL Database. Some of these steps can be quite different from an on-premises implementation of SQL Server.

This skill covers how to:

- Configure firewall rules
- Configure Always Encrypted for Azure SQL Database
- Configure cell level encryption
- Configure Dynamic Data Masking
- Configure Transparent Data Encryption

Configure firewall rules

As explained in Chapter 1, "Implement SQL in Azure," one of the key concepts and benefits of Azure SQL Database is that it is accessible from nearly anywhere by exposing it over the internet with a TCP endpoint via port 1433., Microsoft provides multiple layers and levels of security to ensure that your database and data is secure and protected. One of those layers is firewall rules. The firewall is the means by which access is granted to a server and or database based on the originating IP address of the incoming request.

By default, all Transact-SQL (T-SQL) access (incoming requests) to your Azure SQL server is blocked by the firewall, and in order to allow incoming requests at least one server-level firewall rule is needed. Firewall rules specify which IP address ranges from the internet are allowed and can be applied at both the server and database levels.

Chapter 1 also provides an overview of how the firewall rules process works. Incoming connection attempts must pass through the firewall in order to access the specified database or server. The firewall first checks that the IP address of the incoming client request falls in the range of any of the specified firewall rules specified at the database-level of the database the client is trying to connect to (as specified in the connection string). If there is a match, the connection is allowed only on the specified database. If there is no match, the firewall makes the same request to the rules specified at the server-level. If there is still no match, the connection fails. If there is a match at the server level (the logical instance level), the client has access to all the databases on the Azure SQL server.

Server-level firewall rules

Server-level firewall rules grant access to all the databases within the same logical server. Server-level firewall rules are stored in the master database and can be created and configured through the following methods:

- Azure Portal
- T-SQL
- Azure PowerShell
- Azure CLI
- REST API

PORTAL

Server-level firewall rules can be created and updated via the Azure portal through the Firewall Settings page, which can be accessed from either the Server Overview page shown in Figure 2-1, or the Database Overview page show in Figure 2-2.

From the Server Overview page, you can access the Firewall Settings page by either clicking Firewall in the left-hand menu under Settings, or by clicking the Show Firewall Settings link in the Server Overview page, as shown in Figure 2-1.

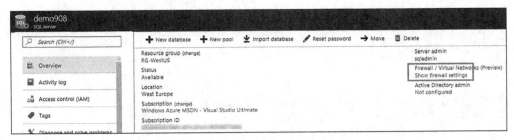

FIGURE 2-1 Accessing the Firewall Settings page via the Server Overview page

From the Database Overview page, you can access the Firewall Settings page by clicking Set Server Firewall on the toolbar, as shown in Figure 2-2.

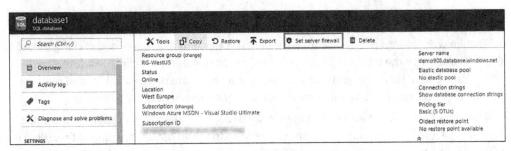

FIGURE 2-2 Accessing the Firewall Settings page via the Database Overview page

Regardless of whether you go through the Server Overview page or the Database Overview page, either option will open the Firewall Settings page, shown in Figure 2-3. The Firewall Settings page is where firewall rules are managed at the server-level. By default, when a server and database are first created, no firewall rules exist and therefore at least one server-level firewall rule must be created, even before adding any database-level firewall rules.

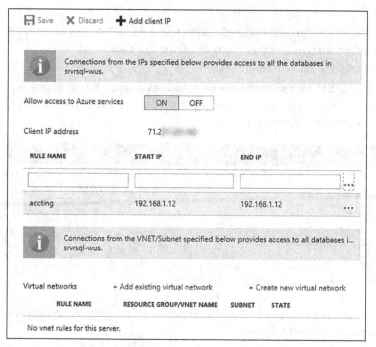

FIGURE 2-3 Configuring Server-level firewall rules

The Firewall Settings page will automatically list your client IP address, and clicking the Add Client IP button on the toolbar will add a single firewall rule using the client IP address as the Start IP and End IP (don't forget to click Save). In order to create server-level firewall rules via the Azure portal, you must be the subscription owner or a subscription contributor.

The Allow Access To Azure Services option, when enabled, allows applications and connections from Azure to connect to the Azure SQL server. Using this option, an internal firewall rule with a starting and ending IP address of 0.0.0.0 is created, indicating that connections from within Azure are allowed, such as from Azure App Services. It is important to understand that enabling this option allows connections from Azure, including connections from other subscriptions. Thus, care and best practices should be implemented to make sure login and user permissions are only allowed to authorized users.

Azure SQL Database supports a maximum of 128 server-level firewall rules, but creating a large number of server-level firewall rules is not recommended. Uses for server-level firewall rules will be discussed shortly.

The Firewall Settings page only allows one operation per save action. For example, adding multiple IP address ranges, or adding an IP address range and deleting another range before saving the changes is not permitted. A single create/delete/edit operation is permitted per save action.

Server-level firewall rule names must be unique. When adding a firewall rule via the portal, and the name of the new firewall rule matches the name of an existing rule, you will be informed that firewall rule names must be unique and you will not be allowed to create the new rule as shown in Figure 2-4. Existing rules can be edited simply by clicking in the appropriate field.

It is a best practice to name the firewall rule so it will help you remember what the server-level firewall setting is for.

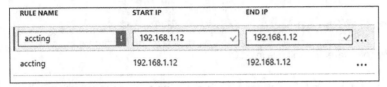

RULE NAME	START IP	END IP	
accting	192.168.1.12	192.168.1.12	...
accting	192.168.1.12	192.168.1.12	...

FIGURE 2-4 Unique firewall rule names

T-SQL

Server-level firewall rules can be managed and maintained using T-SQL through a set of system stored procedures and catalog views, including:

- **sp_set_firewall_rule**   System stored procedure to create a new or update an existing server-level firewall rule.
- **sp_delete_firewall_rule**   System stored procedure to delete server-level firewall rules.
- **sys.firewall_rules**   Catalog view that lists the current server-level firewall rules.

The following code example uses the sp_set_firewall_rule system stored procedure to create a new firewall rule with the name "accting," a starting IP address of 192.168.1.11, and an ending IP address of 192.168.1.30. The sp_set_firewall_rule system stored procedure must be run in the master database.

```
EXECUTE sp_set_firewall_rule @name = N'accting', @start_ip_address = '192.168.1.11',
  @end_ip_address = '192.168.1.30'
```

Figure 2-5 shows the results of the T-SQL execution. First, the sys.firewall_rules catalog view is called to display the existing firewall rules, followed by the execution of sp_set_firewall_rule system stored procedure to create the new firewall rule. The procedure sys.firewall_rules is again called to show the creation of the new firewall rule.

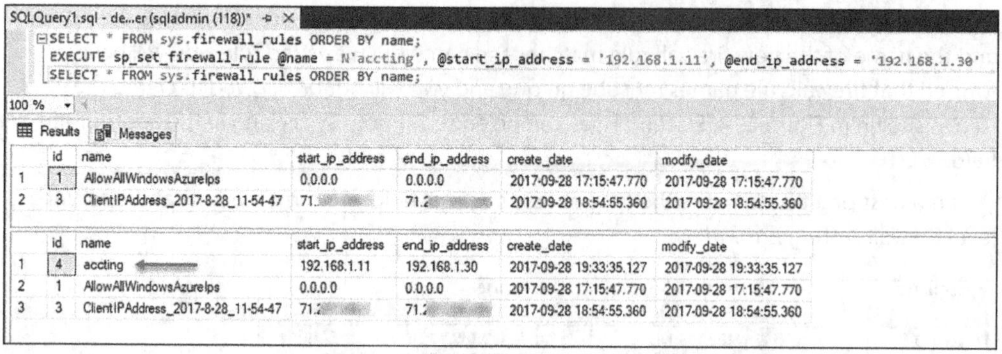

FIGURE 2-5 Creating a new server-level firewall rule in T-SQL

Both system stored procedures and the catalog view is available only in the master database to the server-level principal login or Azure Active Directory principal.

Unlike the Azure portal, when creating a new firewall rule via T-SQL and specifying an existing firewall rule name as a parameter to sp_set_firewall_rule system stored procedure, Azure will update the existing firewall rule and not generate an error. It should also be noted that the very first server-level firewall rule cannot be created using T-SQL, but all subsequent rules can be. Initial server-level firewall rules must be created using the Azure portal, the Azure Power-Shell, the Azure CLI, or the REST API.

When creating server-level firewall rules via T-SQL, you must connect to the SQL Database instance as a server-level principal or an Active Directory Administrator.

AZURE POWERSHELL

Azure PowerShell provides a set of cmdlets in which to manage server-level firewall rules, including:

- **Get-AzureRmSqlServerFirewallRule**   Returns a list of the existing server-level firewall rules.

- **New-AzureRmSqlServerFirewallRule**   Creates a new server-level firewall rule.

- **Set-AzureRmSqlServerFirewallRule**   Updates an existing server-level firewall rule.

- **Remove-AzureRmSqlServerFirewallRule**   Deletes the specified server-level firewall rule.

Microsoft provides two ways to execute these PowerShell cmdlets; through the PowerShell IDE or through the Azure Cloud Shell in the Azure Portal. The Azure Cloud Shell brings the PowerShell experience into the Azure Portal and allows you to easily discover and work with all Azure resources. The above PowerShell cmdlets work seamlessly in both, but the example below uses the Azure Cloud Shell.

The following code example creates a new server-level firewall rule named "engineering" on the server "demo908" in the RG-WestUS resource group with a starting IP address of

192.168.1.31 and an ending IP address of 192.168.1.40. Be sure to replace the resource group name with the appropriate name for your resource group.

```
New-AzureRmSqlServerFirewallRule -ResourceGroupName "RG-WestUS" -ServerName "demo908"
-FirewallRuleName "engineering" -StartIpAddress "192.168.1.31" -EndIpAddress
"192.168.1.40"
```

Figure 2-6 shows the execution of the New-AzureRmSqlServerFirewallRule PowerShell cmdlet to create a new firewall rule. The cmdlet was executed in the Azure Cloud Shell which creates a Cloud Shell and a PowerShell environment. The benefit to this is that because you are authenticated in the portal already, you can execute cmdlets such as New-AzureRmSqlServer-FirewallRule without the necessity of executing additional cmdlets to authenticate and obtain other Azure environment and subscription information. In addition, the Azure Cloud Shell maintains the latest version of the Azure PowerShell cmdlets, thus you can be confident that you are working with the latest version in every Cloud Shell session.

Figure 2-6 also shows the Firewall Settings page with the newly created server-level firewall rule. The takeaway here is that PowerShell makes it easy to manage server-level firewall rules through a small set of cmdlets.

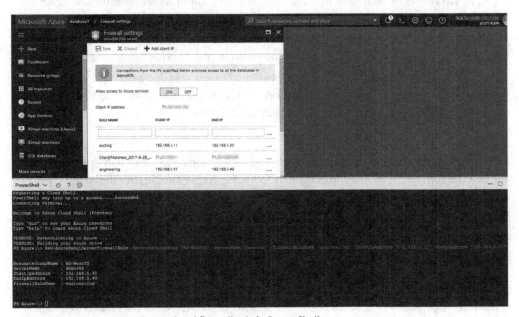

FIGURE 2-6 Creating a new Server-level firewall rule in PowerShell

You'll notice that there are differences in creating and managing firewall rules when using T-SQL versus PowerShell. For example, PowerShell provides individual cmdlets to create, update, and delete firewall rules, whereas T-SQL uses a single system stored procedure to create and update a firewall rule. Items such as these are good to keep in mind when navigating between the technologies.

AZURE CLI

The Azure CLI 2.0 is Azure's new command-line interface for working with and managing Azure resources. It is optimized to work with Azure resources via the command line that work against the Azure Resource Manager. The following commands are used with the Azure CLI to manage server-level firewall rules:

- **az sql server firewall create**   Creates a server-level firewall rule.
- **az sql server firewall delete**   Deletes a server-level firewall rule.
- **az sql server firewall list**   Lists current server-level firewall rules.
- **az sql server firewall rule show**   Shows the details of a server-level firewall rule.
- **az sql server firewall rule update**   Updates an existing server-level firewall rule.

Similar to PowerShell, there are two ways in which to work with the Azure CLI. The first is to download and install the Azure CLI installer, which provides the command-line experience through a command window. This client can be installed on Windows, Linux, and the macOS.

You can either run the Azure CLI through the Bash Shell or through a normal Windows command window. If using a command window, open a command prompt as an administrator and execute the following to log in with your default subscription:

```
az login
```

You will be prompted to log in and enter an authentication code. Once authenticated, you can execute commands simply and easily. The following code example uses the Azure CLI to create a new server-level firewall rule directly within the command prompt window. Be sure to replace the resource group name with the appropriate name for your resource group.

```
az sql server firewall-rule create --resource-group RG-WestUS --server demo908 -n mrking
  --start-ip-address 192.168.1.41
--end-ip-address 192.168.1.50
```

Figure 2-7 shows the execution of the Azure CLI command and the new firewall rule in the Firewall Settings page in the Azure portal as the result of the Azure CLI command execution.

FIGURE 2-7 Creating a new Server-level firewall rule with the Azure CLI 2.0

Similar to PowerShell, the Azure CLI can be accessed through the Azure portal via the Azure Cloud Shell. Launch the Cloud shell from the top navigation bar in the Azure portal, then select the Bash option from the shell drop-down list, as shown in Figure 2-8.

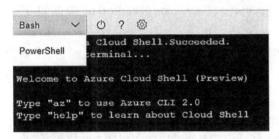

FIGURE 2-8 Using the Azure CLI in the Azure Cloud Shell

The Azure CLI via the Azure Cloud Shell provides a streamlined experience similar to the PowerShell experience. The Azure CLI is best used for building automation scripts to work with the Azure Resource Manager.

Here are some closing thoughts on server-level firewall rules. As firewall rules are temporarily cached, it is recommended that you execute DBCC FLUSHAUTHCACHE on occasion, which will remove any cached entries and clean up the firewall rule list, thus improving connection performance.

Server-level firewall rules should be used sparingly. Consider the following for using server-level firewall rules:

- For administrative functions
- Multiple databases have the same access requirements

- Amount of time spent configuring each database individually

It is highly recommended that no firewall rules be created with a starting IP address of 0.0.0.0 and an ending IP address of 255.255.255.255.

Database-level firewall rules

Database-level firewall rules provide a more granular level of security by allowing access only to a specified database. Unlike server-level firewall rules, database-level firewall rules can only be created using T-SQL.

The following T-SQL system stored procedures and catalog views are used to manage database-level firewall rules:

- **sys.database_firewall_rules**   Catalog view which lists the current database-level firewall rules.

- **sp_set_database_firewall_rule**   System stored procedure to create a new or update an existing database-level firewall rule.

- **sp_delete_database_firewall_rule**   System stored procedure to delete database-level firewall rules.

The following code example uses the sp_set_database_firewall_rule system stored procedure to create a new firewall rule with the name "accting," a starting IP address of 192.168.1.11, and an ending IP address of 192.168.1.30.

```
EXECUTE sp_set_database_firewall_rule @name = N'accting', @start_ip_address =
'192.168.1.1',
@end_ip_address = '192.168.1.10'
```

Figure 2-9 shows the results of the T-SQL execution. First, the sys.database_firewall_rules catalog view is called to display the existing firewall rules for the selected database, followed by the execution of sp_set_database_firewall_rule system stored to create the new firewall rule. The catalog view sys.database_firewall_rules is again called to show the creation of the new firewall rule.

FIGURE 2-9 Creating a database-level firewall rule with T-SQL

Similar to server-level firewall rules, you can have a maximum of 128 database-level firewall rules. It is also recommended that database-level firewall rules be used whenever possible to help ensure the portability of your database.

As a reminder, the order in which the incoming connection checks the firewall rules is important. The firewall first checks the incoming IP against the ranges specified at the database-level. If the incoming IP address is within one of the ranges, the connection is allowed to the SQL Database. If the incoming IP does not match one of the specified ranges at the database-level, the server-level firewall rules are then checked. If there is still no match, the connection request fails. If there is a match at the server-level, the connection is granted and the connection is granted to all databases on the logical server.

Troubleshooting the database firewall

Even though you may have your firewall rules configured correctly, there may still be times when you cannot connect, and the connections experience does not behave as you would expect. As such, the following points can help you pinpoint the connection issue.

- **Local firewall configuration**   Azure SQL Database operates over TCP endpoint 1433. If this port is not opened and enabled on your computer or company firewall, you will not be able to connect.

- **Login and Password issues**   Many times the connections issues are login and password related. For example, perhaps the user name and password are not typed correctly, or the login does not have permissions on the Azure SQL Database or server.

- **NAT (Network address translation)**   There will be times when the IP address displayed on the Firewall Settings page is different from the IP address being used to connect to Azure. You can see an example of this in Figure 2-10. This typically happens when your computer is behind a company firewall due to NAT. An example of this can be seen in Figure 2-10. The IP address that should be used is the external (NAT) IP address, shown in Figure 2-10, is the one specified from the SQL Server login dialog.

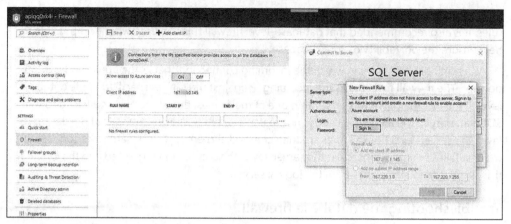

FIGURE 2-10 Different IP address due to NAT

Microsoft states that it may take up to five minutes for the new firewall rules to take effect. Additionally, if your IP address is a dynamic IP (for example, your network provider changes your IP address every few days), this could also be a symptom.

A key takeaway from these points is that the firewall rules only provide clients with an opportunity to attempt to connect to the server and database. Appropriate and necessary credentials must still be provided to connect.

Configure Always Encrypted for Azure SQL Database

SQL Database provides encryption for data in use using Always Encrypted, a featured designed specifically to protect and safe-guard sensitive data such as social security numbers, national identification numbers, credit card numbers, and phone numbers, just to name a few.

One of the main benefits of Always Encrypted is that it provides client applications to safely and securely encrypt and decrypt data without ever revealing the encryption keys to the database engine. Thus, by providing a necessary separation between those who can view the data and those who manage the data, Always Encrypted ensures that no unauthorized users have access to the encrypted data.

Always Encrypted is achieved by installing an Always Encrypted enabled driver on the client machine (for example, .NET Framework 4.6 or later, JDBC, or Windows ODBC), making encryption completely transparent to the application. The driver has the responsibility of automatically encrypting and decrypting sensitive data at the client within the application. When data is generated at the client, the driver encrypts the data before sending it to the database engine. Likewise, the driver transparently decrypts incoming data from query results retrieved from encrypted database columns.

As mentioned earlier, Always Encrypted uses keys to encrypt and decrypt data. Two types of keys are used; a column encryption key (CEK) and a column master key (CMK). Column encryption keys are used to encrypt data in an encrypted column. Column master keys are key-protecting "keys," in that they encrypt one or more column encryption keys. It is up to you to specify the information about the encryption algorithm and cryptographic keys to be used when configuring column encryption.

The database engine never stores or uses the keys of either type, but it does store information about the location of the column master keys. Always Encrypted can use external trusted key stores such as Azure Key Value, Windows Certificate Store on a client machine, or a third-party hardware security module. Since this skill focuses on Azure SQL Database, the example will use Azure Key Vault.

Whenever the client driver needs to encrypt and decrypt data, the driver will contact the specified key store, which contains the column master key. It then uses the plaintext column encryption key to encrypt the parameters. The retrieved key is cached to reduce the number of trips to the key store and improve performance. The driver substitutes the plaintext values of the parameters for the encrypted columns with their encrypted values, which it then sends to the entire query for processing.

To enable Always Encrypted within the application, you must first set up the required authentication for the Azure Key Vault (for this example), or whatever key store you are using. When the application requests the key from the key store, it needs authentication to do so. Thus, the first step is to set up a user that will be used to authenticate the application.

In the Azure portal, select the Azure Active Directory option from the left navigation pane. In the App registrations pane, click the New application registration button on the toolbar, which will open the Create pane, shown in Figure 2-11. In the Create pane, provide a Name and Sign-on URL. The Sign-on URL can be anything as long as it is a valid URL. For example, in Figure 2-11 the Name is myClientApp and the Sign-On URL is *http://myClientApp*. Leave the Application type as Web App / API. Click Create.

FIGURE 2-11 Registering a new Azure active directory application

Back in the App registrations pane, click on your newly created app, which will open the Settings pane. In the Settings pane, click on the Required Permissions option, which will open the Required Permissions pane, shown in Figure 2-12.

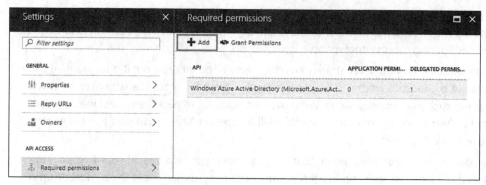

FIGURE 2-12 Adding application permissions

In the Required Permissions pane, click on the Add button on the toolbar, which will open the Add API access pane. In the API access pane, select the Select API option, which will open the Select an API pane shown in Figure 2-13.

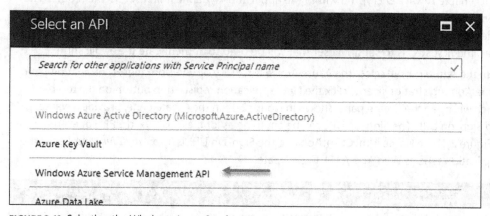

FIGURE 2-13 Selecting the Windows Azure Service Management API

In the Select an API pane, select Windows Azure Service Management API option, then click Select to close the Select an API pane. The Enable Access pane will automatically open, shown in Figure 2-14. Check the box in the Delegated Permission section for Access Azure Service Management as organization users (preview), then click Select.

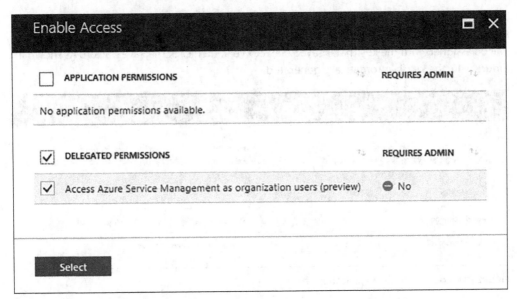

FIGURE 2-14 Enabling delegated permissions to the API

Back on the Add API access pane, ensure that there are green checkmarks for items 1 and 2, then click Done. The Required Permission pane should now list two APIs: the Windows Azure Service Management API which you just added, and the Windows Azure Active Directory API. Close the Required Permissions pane.

Back on the App registrations settings pane for the client application, click the Keys option which will open the Keys pane, shown in Figure 2-15.

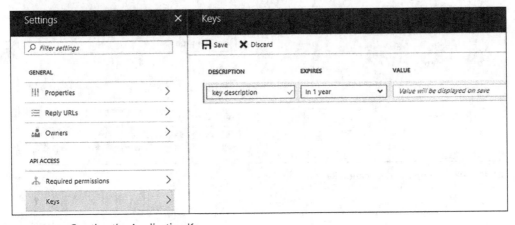

FIGURE 2-15 Creating the Application Key

In the Keys pane you need to create a new key. Enter a description and set the expiration date. Your options for the expiration date are 1 year, 2 years, or Never Expires. The key value will be assigned with the key that is saved. Select 1 year, then click the Save button. As shown in Figure 2-16, the key is automatically generated.

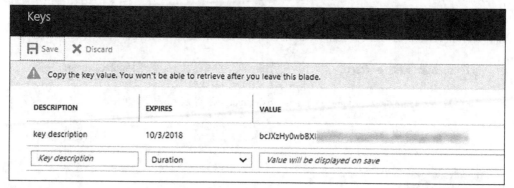

FIGURE 2-16 Copying the new Application key

You will need this key in your application, so copy this key and save it somewhere, then close the Keys blade. You also need the Application ID for this application, so back on the Settings blade, click the Properties option and copy the Application ID from the Properties pane, shown in Figure 2-17. Save this value somewhere as you will use it shortly as well.

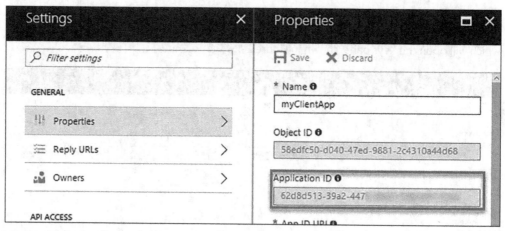

FIGURE 2-17 Getting the Application ID

The next step is to create the Azure Key Value in which to store the Always Encrypted keys. In the Azure portal, click New, then select Security + Identity, then select the Key Vault option shown in Figure 2-18.

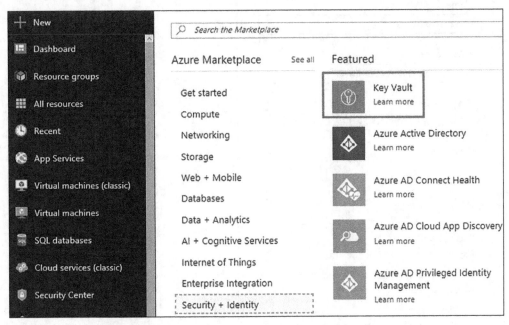

FIGURE 2-18 Creating a new Azure Key Vault

The Create key vault pane will open, shown in Figure 2-19. In this pane, provide a Name, select the appropriate Resource Group (or leave the Create new option selected if a Resource Group does not exists), accept the default values for the Pricing Tier Access Policies, and Advanced Access Policies, ensure the Pin to dashboard option is checked, then click Create.

FIGURE 2-19 Configuring the Azure Key Vault

When the Key Vault is created, open the Key Vault by clicking on the tile on the dashboard. In the Key Vault Properties pane, click the Access Policies tile, which will open the Access Policies pane. One user should be listed, which should be you, becauseyou are the creator and owner of the Key Vault.

However, the client application needs to authenticate to the Key Vault via a user that has permissions to the Key Vault. That could be you and your user listed, but that is not best practice. This is the reason you went through the steps of creating a new Active Directory application for authenticating to the Key Vault.

Click Add New in the Access Policies pane, then in the Add Access Policy pane, expand the Select principal option that opens the Principal pane, shown in figure 2-20.

FIGURE 2-20 Adding a new user access policy

In the Principal pane, start typing the name of the application you created in Azure Active Directory. In this example, the application was named myClientApp, so as I started to type "myc,, the myClientApp was displayed. Click on the appropriate principal and click Select.

In the Add access policy pane, click on the dropdown arrow for the Key permissions. Select the following Key permissions as shown in Figure 2-21:

- Get
- List
- Create
- Unwrap Key
- Wrap Key
- Verify
- Sign

The above list are the minimal permissions needed for the principal to access and use the keys for Always Encrypted. You may choose more, but the list above is the minimum needed.

The Wrap Key permission uses the associated key to protect a symmetric key, while the Unwrap Key permission uses the associated key to unprotect the wrapped symmetric keys.

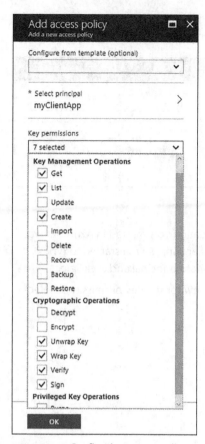

FIGURE 2-21 Configuring access policy permissions

Click OK on the Add access policy pane. The Access policies pane should now look like Figure 2-22.

FIGGURE 2-22 Newly added User Access Policy

So far you have used the portal to configure the Azure Key Vault, but this configuration can also be done via PowerShell. PowerShell contains two cmdlets that allow you to create the Azure Key Vault and set the access policy. Again, in your code be sure to replace the name of the Resource Group with the name of your Resource Group. If you already have an Azure Key Vault with the name specified below, be sure to supply a different name in the code.

```
New-AzureRmKeyVault -VaultName 'aekeyvault' -ResourceGroupName 'RG-WestUS' -Location
 'West US'

Set-AzureRmKeyVaultAccessPolicy -VaultName 'aekeyvault' -ResourceGroupName 'RG-WestUS'
-ServicePricipleName 'myClientApp' -PermissionsTokeys
 get,wrapkey,unwrapkey,sign,verify,list,get,create
```

At this point you are ready to implement and configure Always Encrypted. First, create a database in which you can work with. You can do that via the Azure portal or via T-SQL.

```
CREATE DATABASE [database1]  (EDITION = 'Basic', SERVICE_OBJECTIVE = 'Basic', MAXSIZE =
2 GB);
GO
```

With the database created, use the following T-SQL to create a table.

```
CREATE TABLE [dbo].[Customer](
  [CustomerId] [int] IDENTITY(1,1),
  [FirstName] [nvarchar](50) NULL,
  [LastName] [nvarchar](50) NULL,
  [MiddleName] [nvarchar](50) NULL,
  [StreetAddress] [nvarchar](50) NULL,
  [City] [nvarchar](50) NULL,
  [ZipCode] [char](5) NULL,
  [State] [char](2) NULL,
  [Phone] [char](10) NULL,
  [CCN] [nvarchar](16) NOT NULL,
  [BirthDate] [date] NOT NULL
  PRIMARY KEY CLUSTERED ([CustomerId] ASC) ON [PRIMARY] );
 GO
```

The created table has several columns in which sensitive data is gathered, such as credit card number (CCN) and birth date. This example will use those columns to implement and configure Always Encrypted.

Once the table is created, right-mouse click on the table in the Object Explorer window in SQL Server Management Studio and select Encrypt Columns, as shown in Figure 2-23.

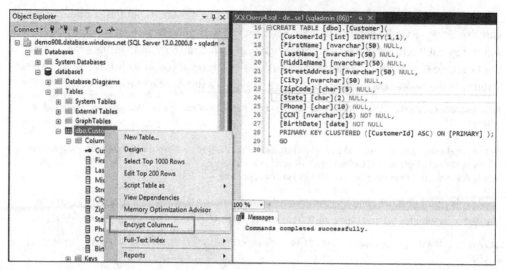

FIGURE 2-23 Starting the Always Encrypted wizard

The Always Encrypted Wizard opens with the Introduction page. Click Next to move to the Column Selection page, shown in Figure 2-24. The Column Selection page is where you select the columns you want to encrypt, the type of encryption, and what column encryption key to use. Select the CCN and Birthdate columns as shown in Figure 2-24.

Once those columns are selected, you now need to select the encryption type. Click the encryption type dropdown arrow for each column. Notice that you have two options for the encryption type: Deterministic and Randomized.

Deterministic encryption uses a method that always generates the same encrypted value for any given plain text value. Deterministic also allows you to group, filter, join tables, and do equity searches on encrypted values.

Randomized encryption uses a method that encrypts data in a less predictable manner. This encryption is more secure, but does not allow grouping, indexing, joining, or equity searches.

Notice that the Encryption Key value defaults to CEK_Auto1 (New), meaning that since you have yet to create any keys, the wizard will create a new column encryption key for you.

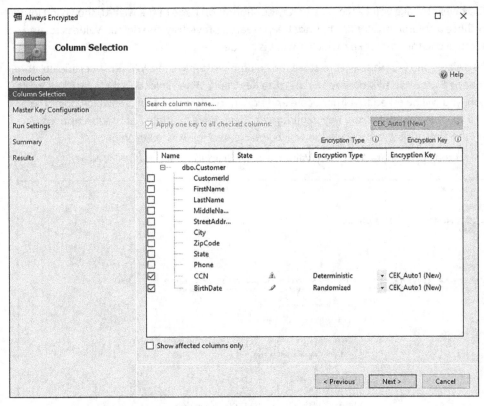

FIGUIRE 2-24 Selecting the columns to be encrypted

Also notice in Figure 2-24 that there is a warning on the CCN column. This is just for informational purposes, alerting how it will change collation of the column to binary collation. Always Encrypted only supports binary collations, so the wizard will be changing the collation for that column so that it can encrypt the column. You should take note of what the current collation of the column is in case you need to roll it back. The wizard has no knowledge of the columns prior state.

Also note that indexed columns encrypted using randomized encryption is not supported. Additionally, the following column characteristics are not supported:

- Columns that are keys for nonclustered indices using a randomized encrypted column as a key column.

- Columns that are keys for clustered indices using a randomized encrypted column as a key column.

- Primary key columns when using randomized encryption.

Click Next to take you to the Master Key Configuration page of the wizard, shown in Figure 2-25. Since a column master key has not been created previously, the default value is to auto generate a column master key, which is what is needed.

By default, the wizard selects to store the column master key in a Windows certificate store, so change the option to store the key in Azure Key Vault. When selecting the Azure Key Vault option, you will be asked to authenticate and sign in to Microsoft Azure, at which point the wizard will retrieve your Azure Key Vault names. If you have multiple Azure subscriptions, select the appropriate subscription in which you created the Azure Key Vault.

Select the appropriate Azure Key Vault from the dropdown and then click Next.

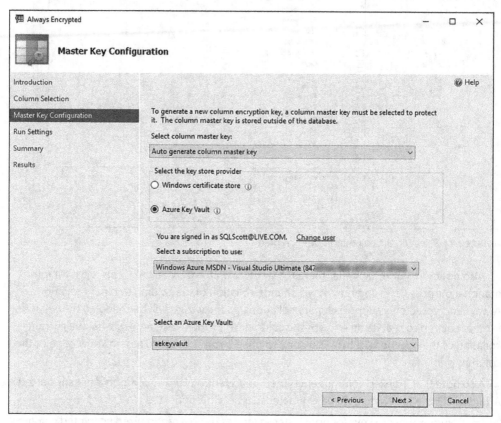

FIGURE 2-25 Master Key configuration

The Run Settings page of the wizard simply gives you a couple of options of proceeding. One of the options will generate a PowerShell script that you can then run later to set up and configure Always Encrypted, and the other option is to proceed and finish now.

Also on this page is several warnings. The first warning states that while the encryption/decryption is taking place, no write operations should be performed on the table. Any write operations that are performed during the encryption/decryption process may cause a loss of data.

The other warning simply states that depending on the SQL Database performance SKU (Basic, Standard, Premium), the performance may vary. In this case, it's a small table with no data so it does not take too long. Click Next on the Run Settings wizard to kick off the process and take you to the Results page, shown in Figure 2-26.

There are three steps in the process. The first step creates the column master key, the next step creates the column encryption key, and the last step performs the actual encryption. Again, since there is no data to encrypt, the process is quite fast. Depending on how much data exists in the table and the type of data, the last step in the process could take some time.

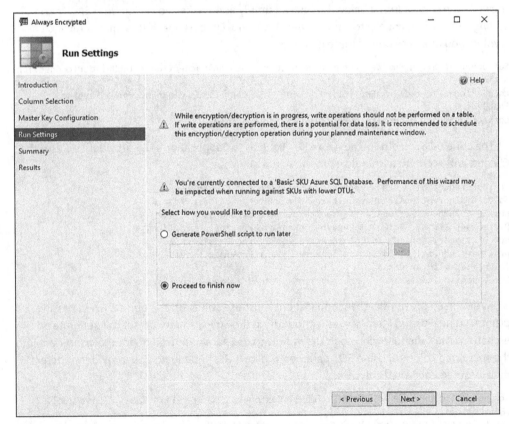

FIGURE 2-26 Always Encrypted process completion

When the encryption process is complete, click Close. At this point, Always Encrypted for Azure SQL Database has been configured. The following code snippets show how to implement Always Encrypted in your application. The full code can be downloaded from this book's homepage.

First, you will need the database connection string, which you can get from the Azure portal. You will then need the ClientId and Secret key. The ClientId is the ApplicationId you copied in Figure 2-17. The Secret is the key value you copied in Figure 2-17.

```
static string connectionString = @"<connection string from portal>";
static string clientId = @"";
static string clientSecret = "";
```

The following code snippet is the critical piece of code that enables Always Encrypted in your database connection string. You can either use the SqlConnectionStringBuilder class as shown in the code snipped below, or you can simply add the keywords "Column Encryption Setting=Enabled" manually to your connection string. Either is fine, but to enable Always Encrypted, you must use one of these methods.

```
SqlConnectionStringBuilder connStringBuilder = new SqlConnectionStringBuilder(connection
String);
connStringBuilder.ColumnEncryptionSetting = SqlConnectionColumnEncryptionSetting.
Enabled;
connectionString = connStringBuilder.ConnectionString;
```

The code below registers the Azure Key Vault as the application's key provider and uses the ClientId and Secret to authenticate to the Azure Key Vault.

```
_clientCredential = new ClientCredential(clientId, clientSecret);
SqlColumnEncryptionAzureKeyVaultProvider azureKeyVaultProvider =
new SqlColumnEncryptionAzureKeyVaultProvider(GetToken);
Dictionary<string, SqlColumnEncryptionKeyStoreProvider> providers =
new Dictionary<string, SqlColumnEncryptionKeyStoreProvider>();
providers.Add(SqlColumnEncryptionAzureKeyVaultProvider.ProviderName,
 azureKeyVaultProvider);
SqlConnection.RegisterColumnEncryptionKeyStoreProviders(providers);
```

As discussed previously, client applications must use SqlParameter objects when passing plaintext data. Passing literal values without using the SqlParameter object will generate an exception. Thus, the following code shows how to use parameterized queries to insert data into the encrypted columns. Using SQL parameters allows the underlying data provider to detect data targeted encrypted columns.

```
string sqlCmdText = @"INSERT INTO [dbo].[Customer] ([CCN], [FirstName], [LastName],
[BirthDate])
VALUES (@CCN, @FirstName, @LastName, @BirthDate);";
SqlCommand sqlCmd = new SqlCommand(sqlCmdText);
SqlParameter paramCCN = new SqlParameter(@"@CCN", newCustomer.CCN);
paramCCN.DbType = DbType.String;
paramCCN.Direction = ParameterDirection.Input;
paramCCN.Size = 19;
sqlCmd.ExecuteNonQuery();
```

When running the full application code, the encrypted data is decrypted at the client and displayed in clear text as seen in Figure 2-27.

FIGURE 2-27 Viewing decrypted data via an application

However, as seen in Figure 2-28, querying the data directly from within SQL Server Management Studio shows the data encrypted, as it should be.

FIGURE 2-28 Viewing encrypted data in the database

To test this further, right mouse click in the query window in SQL Server Management Studio and select Connection > Change Connection from the context menu, opening up the SQL Server connection dialog, shown in Figure 2-29. In the connection dialog, click the Options button to display the connection properties. Click the Additional Connection Parameters tab and add the following (as shown in Figure 2-29):

```
Column Encryption Settings=Enabled
```

Click the Login tab and type in your authentication password, then click Connect. Once authenticated, re-execute the SELECT statement to query the table, and you will see that the encrypted data now comes back as clear text, as shown in Figure 2-30.

Connect to Server
SQL Server
Login
Connection Properties
Additional Connection Parameters
Enter additional connection string parameters (will be sent in clear text):
Column Encryption Setting = True
(Note: Connection string parameters override graphical selections on other panels)
Connect
Cancel
Help
Options <<

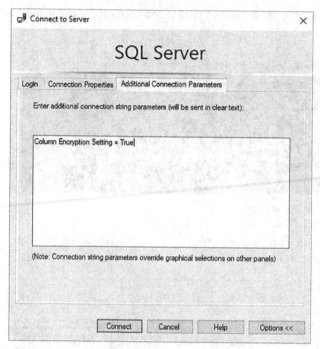

FIGURE 2-29 Setting the Always Encrypted additional connection string parameter in SSMS

The data comes back as clear text because the same client driver used in the client application was also called and used when the query was executed in the query window. When the SELECT statement was issued, the Column Encryption Setting=Enabled connection string parameter was added to the query connection string, at which point the data was encrypted.

SELECT * from Customer;
100 %
Results
Messages

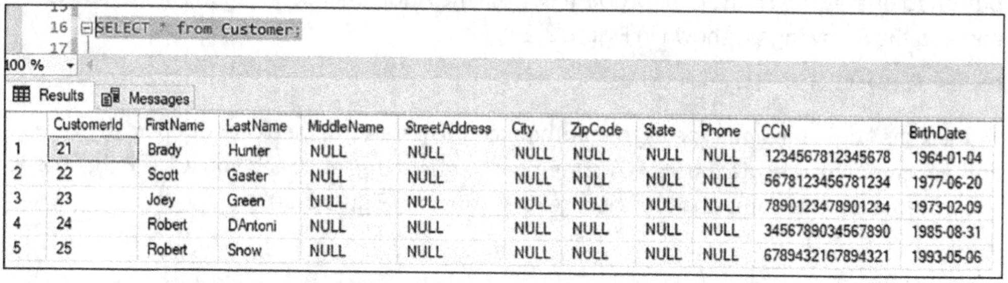

	CustomerId	FirstName	LastName	MiddleName	StreetAddress	City	ZipCode	State	Phone	CCN	BirthDate
1	21	Brady	Hunter	NULL	NULL	NULL	NULL	NULL	NULL	1234567812345678	1964-01-04
2	22	Scott	Gaster	NULL	NULL	NULL	NULL	NULL	NULL	5678123456781234	1977-06-20
3	23	Joey	Green	NULL	NULL	NULL	NULL	NULL	NULL	7890123478901234	1973-02-09
4	24	Robert	DAntoni	NULL	NULL	NULL	NULL	NULL	NULL	3456789034567890	1985-08-31
5	25	Robert	Snow	NULL	NULL	NULL	NULL	NULL	NULL	6789432167894321	1993-05-06

FIGURE 2-30 Viewing decrypted data in the database

The principal objective of Always Encrypted is to ensure that sensitive data is safe and secure, regardless of where your data resides (on-premises or in the cloud). A key value-proposition of Always Encrypted is that it assures users that sensitive data can be stored in the cloud safely and securely.

To further ensure proper security, there are a few key management considerations to keep in mind.

- Never generate column master keys or column encryption keys on a computer that is hosting your database. Use a separate computer to generate the keys which should be dedicated for key management.

- Implement a key management process. Identify roles of who should and should not have access to keys. A DBA, for example, may not generate keys, but may manage the key metadata in the database since the metadata does not contain plaintext keys.

- Periodically replace existing keys with new keys, either due to compliance regulations or if your keys have been compromised.

Always Encrypted can be configured either using SQL Server Management Studio, Power-Shell, or T-SQL. T-SQL has a limitation in that you cannot provision column master or column encryption keys, nor can you encrypt existing data in selected database columns. The following table details what tasks can be accomplished with SSMS, PowerShell, and T-SQL.

TABLE 2-1 Always Encrypted functionality with the different tools

Task	SSMS	PowerShell	T-SQL
Provision CMK and CEK	Yes	Yes	No
Create key metadata in the database	Yes	Yes	Yes
Create new tables with encrypted columns	Yes	Yes	Yes
Encrypt existing data in selected database columns	Yes	Yes	No

Configure cell level encryption

Another method for encrypting your data is via cell-level encryption (CLE) to help protect and secure your data at the data tier. Similar to Always Encrypted, in which specific columns are en-crypted, cell-level encryption is used to encrypt specific columns or cells. Cell-level encryption uses a symmetric encryption and is often referred to or called column-level encryption. A key benefit of cell-level encryption, like Always Encrypted, is that you can encrypt individual cells/columns with different keys. Cell-level encryption is also quite fast and is a great option when working with large amounts of data.

With Cell-level Encryption, encryption and decryption is done by explicitly calling the EN-CRYPTBYKEY or DECRYPTBYKEY functions. These functions require the use of a symmetric key, which must be opened to be used. Both ENCRYPTBYKEY or DECRYPTBYKEY return a varbinary type, thus when storing CLE-encrypted data, the column type must be varbinary with a maxi-mum size of 8000 bytes.

Cell-level encryption uses a database master key for its encryption, which is a symmetric key used to protect private keys and asymmetric keys within the database. When created, the database master key is encrypted using the AES_256 algorithm along with a user-supplied password. A database master key is created by issuing the following T-SQL statement:

```
CREATE DATABASE [database2]  (EDITION = 'Basic', SERVICE_OBJECTIVE = 'Basic', MAXSIZE =
2 GB);
GO
USE database2
GO
CREATE MASTER KEY ENCRYPTION BY PASSWORD = 'AwesomeP@ssw0rd'
GO
```

In order to create the database master key and any certificates, you need the following permisions:

- CONTROL permission on the database
- CREATE CERTIFICATE permission on the database
- ALTER permission on the table

With the master key created, you need to create a certificate and symmetric key, which can be done via the following T-SQL:

```
CREATE CERTIFICATE CreditCardCert01
    WITH SUBJECT = 'Customer Credit Card Numbers';
GO

CREATE SYMMETRIC KEY CreditCards_Key01
    WITH ALGORITHM = AES_256
    ENCRYPTION BY CERTIFICATE CreditCardCert01;

GO
```

The Create Certificate statement creates a database-level securable that follows the X.509 standards. Because the certificate was created with the database master key, the ENCRYPTION BY PASSWORD option is not required.

The certificate can be time-based, meaning, by supplying a START_DATE and EXPIRY_DATE parameter you can specify when the certificate becomes valid and when it expires. By default, if the START_DATE parameter is not specified it becomes valid when the certificate is created. Likewise, if the EXPIRY_DATE parameter is not specified, the certificate expires one year from when after the START_DATE.

The Create Symmetric statement creates a symmetric key in the database and is encrypted using the certificate created above. A symmetric key must be encrypted using either a certificate, password, another symmetric key, or asymmetric key. A single symmetric key actually be encrypted using multiple encryption types.

In this example, the key was encrypted with the AES_256 algorithm. Starting with SQL Server 2016, all algorithms other than AES_128, AES_192, and AES_256 are no longer supported.

To be cell-level encryption to work, execute the following T-SQL to create a table and insert records into the table.

```
CREATE TABLE [dbo].[Customer](
  [CustomerId] [int] IDENTITY(1,1),
  [FirstName] [nvarchar](50) NULL,
  [LastName] [nvarchar](50) NULL,
  [MiddleName] [nvarchar](50) NULL,
  [StreetAddress] [nvarchar](50) NULL,
  [City] [nvarchar](50) NULL,
  [ZipCode] [char](5) NULL,
  [State] [char](2) NULL,
  [Phone] [char](10) NULL,
  [CCN] [nvarchar](19) NOT NULL,
  [BirthDate] [date] NOT NULL
  PRIMARY KEY CLUSTERED ([CustomerId] ASC) ON [PRIMARY] );
  GO
INSERT INTO Customer (FirstName, LastName, CCN, BirthDate)
VALUES ('Brady', 'Hunter', '1234-5678-1234-5678', '01/04/1964')
INSERT INTO Customer (FirstName, LastName, CCN, BirthDate)
VALUES ('Scott', 'Gaster', '5678-1234-5678-1234', '06/20/1976')
INSERT INTO Customer (FirstName, LastName, CCN, BirthDate)
VALUES ('Phillip', 'Green', '7890-1234-7890-1234', '09/02/1973')
INSERT INTO Customer (FirstName, LastName, CCN, BirthDate)
VALUES ('Joey', 'Klein', '3456-7890-3456-7890', '08/31/1985')
INSERT INTO Customer (FirstName, LastName, CCN, BirthDate)
VALUES ('Robert', 'DAntoni', '6789-4321-6789-4321', '05/06/1991')
GO
```

Next, execute the following T-SQL, which will modify the table and add a column in which to store the encrypted credit card numbers. As mentioned earlier, the EncryptByKey and Decrypt-ByKey functions return a varbinary type and since the encrypted data will be stored in this new column, the data type will be varbinary.

```
ALTER TABLE Customer
    ADD CCN_Encrypted varbinary(128);
GO
```

In order to use the EncryptByKey function, the symmetric key must first be opened to encrypted data. The next statement encrypts the values in the CCN column using the Encrypt-ByKey function (which uses the symmetric key) and saves the results in the CCN_Encrypted column.

```
OPEN SYMMETRIC KEY CreditCards_Key01
    DECRYPTION BY CERTIFICATE CreditCardCert01;
UPDATE Customer
SET CCN_Encrypted = EncryptByKey(Key_GUID('CreditCards_Key01')
    , CCN, 1, HashBytes('SHA1', CONVERT( varbinary
    , CustomerId)));
GO
```

You can view the results of the encryption by executing a simple SELECT statement. The encrypted data is shown in Figure 2-31.

```
SELECT FirstName, LastName, CCN, BirthDate, CCN_Encrypted FROM Customer
GO
```

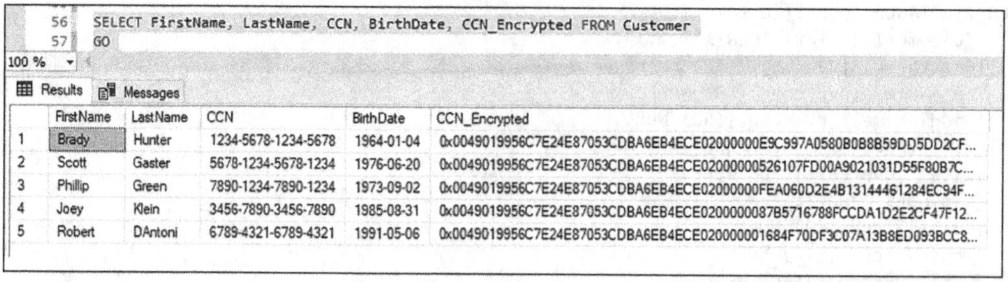

FIGURE 2-31 Viewing encrypted data with Cell-level Encryption

To verify that the encryption, reopen the symmetric key and then issue the following T-SQL which uses the DecryptByKey function to decrypt the values in the CCN_Encrypted column. If the decryption was successful, the original number will match the decrypted number, as shown in Figure 2-32.

```
SELECT CCN, CCN_Encrypted
    AS 'Encrypted card number', CONVERT(nvarchar,
    DecryptByKey(CCN_Encrypted, 1 ,
    HashBytes('SHA1', CONVERT(varbinary, CustomerID))))
    AS 'Decrypted card number' FROM Customer;
GO
```

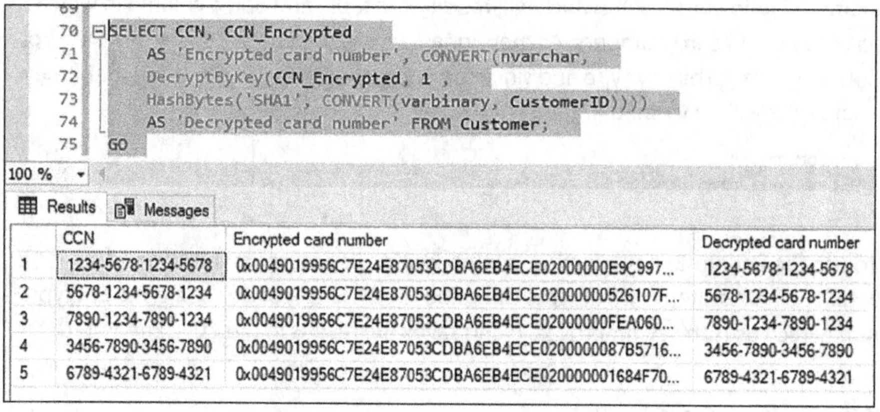

FIGURE 2-32 Using symmetric keys to decrypt data

In this example, the HashBytes function was used to hash the input. When using the Hash-Bytes function, algorithms of MD2, MD4, MD5, SHA, SHA1, and SHA2 can be used. Also, in this example an authenticator was used. Authenticators are additional data that gets encrypted along with the data to be stored encrypted. When the data is decrypted, the authenticator is also specified. If the incorrect authenticator is not specified, the data is not decrypted and a NULL is returned. In this example, the column CreditCardID is used as the authenticator.

You likewise could encrypt data using simple symmetric encryption. For example:

```
UPDATE Customer
SET CCN_Encrypted = EncryptByKey(Key_GUID('CreditCards_Key01'), CCN);
GO
```

While a case for using TDE and CLE together could be made, they are typically used for different purposes. CLE has advantages over TDE when encrypting small amounts of data, but when performance is not too much of a concern, then CLE should be considered. With CLE, the data is still encrypted when it is loaded into memory and allows for a higher degree of customization.

On the other hand, TDE can be very simple to deploy with no changes to the application or database and the performance is better over CLE.

Configure Dynamic Data Masking

Dynamic Data Masking (DDM) is a security feature that limits data exposure by masking it to non-privileged users. It provides the ability to designate how much of the sensitive data should be readable with minimal impact on the application layer. Dynamic data masking simply hides the sensitive data in the result set of a query, while keeping the database unchanged. Masks are applied at query time when the results are returned.

Dynamic data masking can be applied to any data deemed as sensitive data by you, such as credit card numbers, social security or national identification numbers, email address, or phone numbers. Dynamic data masking includes several built-in masking functions, but also provides the ability to create a custom mask.

The following example will walk through implementing Dynamic Data Masking. To begin, create a new Azure SQL Database either via SQL Server Management Studio or the Azure portal. Once created, connect to that database with SQL Server Management studio and execute the following T-SQL which creates a Customer table with several columns that will contain sensitive data (such as email, credit card number, and social security number). The script then inserts five rows of data.

```
CREATE TABLE [dbo].[Customer](
  [CustomerId] [int] IDENTITY(1,1),
```

```
[FirstName] [nvarchar](50) NULL,
[LastName] [nvarchar](50) NULL,
[MiddleName] [nvarchar](50) NULL,
[StreetAddress] [nvarchar](50) NULL,
[City] [nvarchar](50) NULL,
[ZipCode] [char](5) NULL,
[State] [char](2) NULL,
[Phone] [char](10) NULL,
[Email] [nvarchar] (50) NULL,
[SSN] [char] (11) NOT NULL,
[CCN] [nvarchar](19) NOT NULL,
[BirthDate] [date] NOT NULL
PRIMARY KEY CLUSTERED ([CustomerId] ASC) ON [PRIMARY] );
GO

INSERT INTO Customer (FirstName, LastName, Email, SSN, CCN, BirthDate)
VALUES ('Brady', 'Hunter', 'bhunter@live.com', '999-99-0001', '4833-1200-7350-8070',
 '01/04/1964')
INSERT INTO Customer (FirstName, LastName, Email, SSN, CCN, BirthDate)
VALUES ('Scott', 'Gaster', 'sgaster@gmail.com', '999-99-0002', '5145-1800-0184-8667',
 '06/20/1976')
INSERT INTO Customer (FirstName, LastName, Email, SSN, CCN, BirthDate)
VALUES ('Phillip', 'Green', 'pgreen@hotmail.com', '999-99-0003', '3767-6401-5782-0031',
 '09/02/1973')
INSERT INTO Customer (FirstName, LastName, Email, SSN, CCN, BirthDate)
VALUES ('Joey', 'Klein', 'jklein@fastfreddies.com', '999-99-0004',
'3797-0931-5791-0032', '08/31/1985')
INSERT INTO Customer (FirstName, LastName, Email, SSN, CCN, BirthDate)
VALUES ('Robert', 'DAntoni', 'rdantoni@urawesome.com', '999-99-0005',
'4854-1299-2820-4506', '05/06/1991')
GO
```

Once the script executes, log in to the Azure Portal and go to the database you created and click on the Dynamic Data Masking option that will open the Masking Rules pane, shown in Figure 2-33.

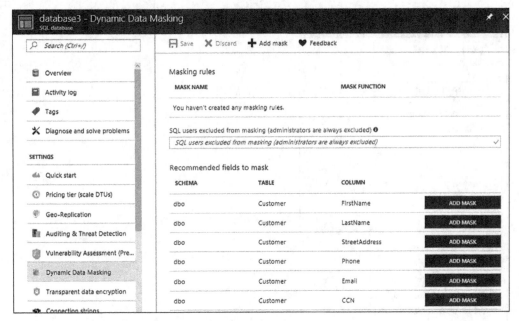

FIGURE 2-33 Selecting the columns to mask

No masking rules have been created, but the pane does show recommended columns to mask. You can click on the Add Mask button for the specific column, or you can click on the Add Mask button on the toolbar.

Clicking the Add Mask button next to the recommended field is a quick way to add the mask. Many times the portal is smart enough to recognize what type of field it is and apply the appropriate mask. However, it is not guaranteed, so the quickest and most efficient way to add the column mask is to click the Add Mask button on the top toolbar that opens the Add masking rule pane, shown in Figure 2-34. This pane will also open if the portal can't appropriately apply the mask when clicking the Add Mask button next to the recommended field.

In the Add masking rule pane, simply select the column you want to mask and then select the appropriate mask. In Figure 2-34, the credit card number column is select and thus the credit card mask is selected.

FIGURE 2-34 Configuring a column mask

Notice the different types of default masks, including:

- **Default** Full masking according to the data types of the designated fields.
- **Credit Card** Exposes the last four digits of the credit card number and adds a constant string as a prefix in the form of a credit card.
- **Email** Exposes the first letter, then replaces the domain with XXX.com.
- **Random Number** Generates a random number based on the supplied upper and lower boundaries.
- **Custom Text** Exposes the first and last characters based on the supplied Prefix and Suffix, then adds a custom padding string in the middle.

The custom text masking function can be used to mask a social security number. Figure 2-35 shows how to use the Prefix and Suffix and padded string to mask all but the last four numbers of a social security number.

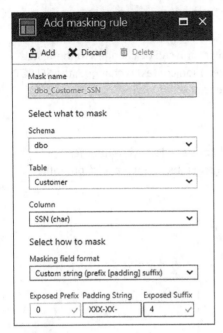

FIGURE 2-35 Creating a custom data mask

Be sure to click the Add button on the Add masking rule pane once the masking rule is configured. After all the masks are applied, click the Save button back on the Masking rules pane. If you don't click Save, the masking rules will not be applied.

Querying the data shows data unmasked, as shown in Figure 2-36. Even though the masking rules have been applied, the data is returned in clear text because the user that is logged in is an administrator.

```
13    SELECT FirstName, LastName, Email, SSN, CCN FROM Customer
```

	FirstName	LastName	Email	SSN	CCN
1	Brady	Hunter	bhunter@live.com	999-99-0001	4833-1200-7350-8070
2	Scott	Gaster	sgaster@gmail.com	999-99-0002	5145-1800-0184-8667
3	Phillip	Green	pgreen@hotmail.com	999-99-0003	3767-6401-5782-0031
4	Joey	Klein	jklein@fastfreddies.com	999-99-0004	3797-0931-5791-0032
5	Robert	DAntoni	rdantoni@urawesome.com	999-99-0005	4854-1299-2820-4506

FIGURE 2-36 Query data with unmasked results

To test the masking, a new user can be created, which simply has SELECT permissions on the table. The following T-SQL creates a new user called TestUser and grants SELECT permission on the Customer table.

```
CREATE USER TestUser WITHOUT LOGIN;
GRANT SELECT ON Customer TO TestUser;
```

To test masking, the execution context of the current session can be changed to the TestUser, as shown in the following T-SQL. Once the session execution context is changed, the SELECT statement can be reissued, which will be executed in the context of the TestUser.

```
Execute AS USER = 'TestUser'
SELECT FirstName, LastName, Email, SSN, CCN FROM Customer
```

As shown in Figure 2-37, the Email, SSN, and CCN columns are displayed with their appropriate masks. It should be noted that the data in the underlying table is not masked, but rather the data is displayed with the corresponding mask.

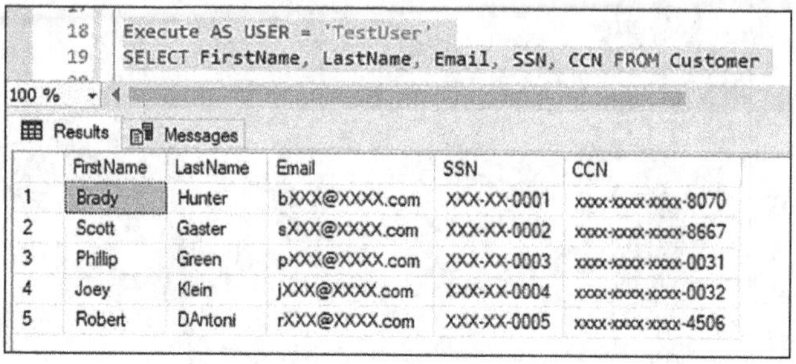

	FirstName	LastName	Email	SSN	CCN
1	Brady	Hunter	bXXX@XXXX.com	XXX-XX-0001	xxxx-xxxx-xxxx-8070
2	Scott	Gaster	sXXX@XXXX.com	XXX-XX-0002	xxxx-xxxx-xxxx-8667
3	Phillip	Green	pXXX@XXXX.com	XXX-XX-0003	xxxx-xxxx-xxxx-0031
4	Joey	Klein	jXXX@XXXX.com	XXX-XX-0004	xxxx-xxxx-xxxx-0032
5	Robert	DAntoni	rXXX@XXXX.com	XXX-XX-0005	xxxx-xxxx-xxxx-4506

FIGURE 2-37 Querying data with masked results

The session execution context can be switched back simply be executing the following T-SQL statement:

```
REVERT;
```

Dynamic Data Masking policies are made up of three components:

- **Users excluded from masking** These are either SQL users or Azure Active Directory identities that get automatically unmasked data.
- **Masking rules** Rules that define the designated fields to be masked and their corresponding masking functions.
- **Masking functions** The methods/functions that control the data exposure.

Figure 2-33 shows these three components on the Masking rules blade. The top portion of that blade lists any defined masking rules. Once a masking rule is defined, such as the ones defined in Figures 2-34 and 2-35, it will be listed in the Masking Rules section.

Directly below that section is a section on the blade titled SQL Users Excluded From Masking. This is where you can specify a semicolon-separated list of users (either SQL users or Azure Active Directory identities) in which data masking will not apply.

Lastly, the masking functions are the built-in functions used to mask the data, which you can see in Figure 2-34. Together, these three components help define the data masking policies.

Managing DDM using T-SQL

Dynamic Data Masking can also be configured using T-SQL. The following T-SQL creates a table called Customer2 and defines built-in masking functions applied during table creation.

```
CREATE TABLE [dbo].[Customer2](
  [CustomerId] [int] IDENTITY(1,1),
  [FirstName] [nvarchar](50) NULL,
  [LastName] [nvarchar](50) NULL,
  [MiddleName] [nvarchar](50) NULL,
  [StreetAddress] [nvarchar](50) NULL,
  [City] [nvarchar](50) NULL,
  [ZipCode] [char](5) NULL,
  [State] [char](2) NULL,
  [Phone] [char](10) NULL,
  [Email] [nvarchar] (50) MASKED WITH (FUNCTION = 'email()') NULL,
  [SSN] [char] (11) MASKED WITH (FUNCTION = 'partial(0, "XXX-XX-", 4)') NOT NULL,
  [CCN] [nvarchar](19) MASKED WITH (FUNCTION = 'partial(0, "xxxx-xxxx-xxxx-", 4)')
NOT NULL,
  [BirthDate] [date] NOT NULL
PRIMARY KEY CLUSTERED ([CustomerId] ASC) ON [PRIMARY] );
```

A mask can be removed from a column by using the DROP MASKED statement. For example:

```
ALTER TABLE Customer
ALTER COLUMN Email DROP MASKED;
```

Managing DDM using PowerShell

Dynamic data masking can be configured using PowerShell cmdlets. Azure PowerShell comes with six cmdlets to create and configure masking rules and policies.

- **Get-AzureRmSqlDatabaseDataMaskingPolicy** Gets the data masking policy for a database.

- **Get-AzureRmSqlDatabaseDaaMaskingRule** Gets the data masking rules from a database.

- **New-AzureRmSqlDatabaseDataMaskingRule** Creates a data masking rule for a database.

- **Remove-AzureRmSqlDatabaseDataMaskingRule** Removes a data masking rule from a database.

- **Set-AzureRmSqlDatabaseDataMaskingRule** Sets the properties of a data masking rule for a database.

- **Set-AzureRmSqlDatabaseDataMaskingPolicy** Sets data masking for a database.

A masking policy is simply the combination of the set of rules that define the columns to be masked, the SQL or AAD users that get unmasked data in the query results, and the masking functions that control the exposure of data for the different scenarios. Thus, by creating a rule that applies the credit card mask to a CCN column, and optionally specifying the SQL or AAD users, a policy has been created. The PowerShell cmdlets allow the creation, modification, and retrieval of the rules and policies.

For example, you can create a new masking rule by executing the following (replacing the appropriate resource group and server names to match your names):

```
New-AzureRmSqlDatabaseDataMaskingRule -ResourceGroupName "RG-WestUS" -ServerName
 "demo908"
-DatabaseName "database3" -SchemaName "dbo" -TableName "Customer2"
-ColumnName "Email" -MaskingFunction "Email"
```

It should be clear that dynamic data masking should be used in conjunction with other security features to better secure sensitive data. Dynamic data masking can be used and is a complimentary security feature along with Always Encrypted, Row Level Security, and other security features. The purpose of dynamic data masking exists to limit the exposure of sensitive data to those who should not have access to it.

Creating a mask on a column does not prevent updates to that column. Meaning, even though a user many see the data as masked, that same user can update the data if they have permissions to do so. This means that a proper access control policy should be implemented to limit update permissions.

When using the SELECT INTO or INSERT INTO statements to copy data, if the source data has a masked column, the destination table will result in masked data in the target table. Also, Dynamic Data Masking is applied when running an import or export. Any database that contains masked columns will result in a backup file with masked data.

The system view sys.masked_columns can be queried to see what columns have a mask applied to them and what masking function is used. This view inherits from the sys.columns view that contains an is_masked column and masking_functions column. The following T-SQL returns a good summary view into the columns that are masked and their corresponding masking functions.

```
SELECT c.name, tbl.name as table_name, c.is_masked, c.masking_function
FROM sys.masked_columns AS c
JOIN sys.tables AS tbl
   ON c.[object_id] = tbl.[object_id]
WHERE is_masked = 1;
```

For some final notes, a masking rule cannot be defined on the following column types:

- A column encrypted with Always Encrypted
- FILESTREAM
- COLUMN_SET or a sparse column that is part of a column set
- A computed column

There are a couple of caveats. If a computed column depends on a column with a MASK, then the computed column will return the masked data. Also, a column with data masking applied cannot be part of a FULLTEXT index.

Configure Transparent Data Encryption

Similar to cell-level encryption, Transparent Data Encryption (TDE) is used to encrypt data at rest. There are several differences between cell-level encryption (CLE) and TDE, one of which is that TDE will automatically encrypt and decrypt the data when it reads and writes the data to/from disk, whereas CLE required the use of the EncryptByKey and DecryptByKey functions. Transparent data encryption also differs from cell-level encryption by encrypting the storage of an entire database, not just a single cell or column. Other differences between CLE and TDE were discussed at the conclusion of the CLE section.

Transparent data encryption helps secure and protect your data by performing database encryption real-time without requiring changes to an application. Encryption is accomplished through a symmetric key called a database encryption key (DEK). The DEK key is protected by the transparent data encryption protector, which is either a service-managed certificate or an asymmetric key stored in Azure Key Vault. The transparent data encryption protector is set at the server level.

When the database starts up, the encrypted DEK is decrypted and then used for the encryption and decryption of the database files. Transparent data encryption performs real-time I/O encryption and decryption of the data at the page level, thus each page is encrypted before it is written to disk, and decrypted when read from disk and into memory.

For Azure SQL Database, TDE is enabled by default at the database level, as shown in Figure 2-38. At this level, TDE can either be turned on or off.

FIGURE 2-38 Configuring TDE

At the server level, the default setting for TDE in Azure SQL Database is for the database encryption key to be protected by a built-in server certificated. This certificate is unique for each server, but if geo-replication is enabled and a database is participating in a geo-replication relationship, the geo-secondary database will be protected by the primary server key. As a best practice, Microsoft rotates these certificates every 90 days. As shown in Figure 2-39, the Use Your Own Key option is disabled by default, thus the database encryption key is protected by a built-in certificate.

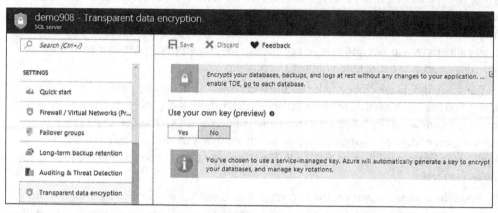

FIGURE 2-39 configuring bring your own key encryption

As mentioned previously, Azure SQL Database also supports Bring Your Own Key (BYOK), which provides the ability to have control over the TDE encryption keys and stores them in Azure Key Vault. To turn on BYOK, simply select Yes for the Use Your Own Key option for TDE at the server level, as shown in Figure 2-40.

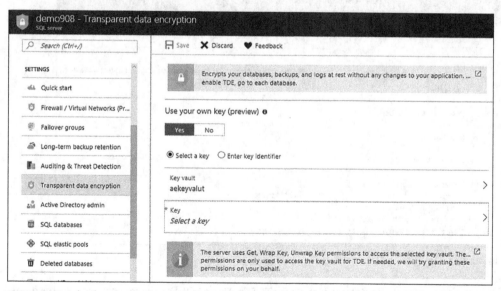

FIGURE 2-40 selecting the key for bring your own encryption key

When selecting the option to Use Your Own Key, you will be prompted to select the Azure Key Vault and the symmetric key from that vault. When selecting the key, an existing key can be selected, or you have the option to create a new key, as shown in Figure 2-41.

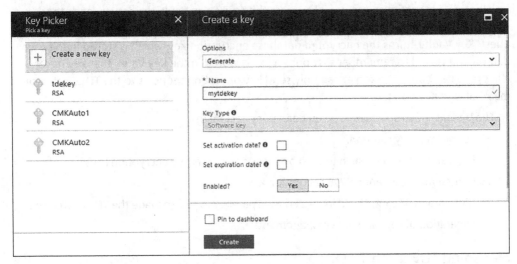

FIGURE 2-41 creating a new encryption key

Once a key is selected or a new key is created, click Save back on the TDE pane.

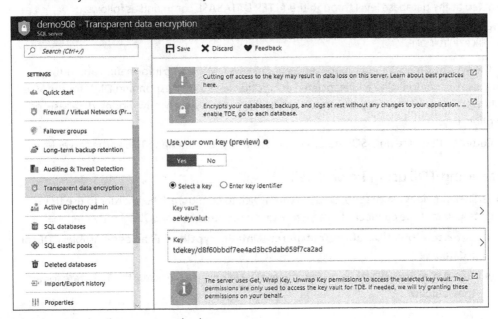

FIGURE 2-42 saving the new encryption key

Clicking save will save the Transparent Data Encryption settings for the server, which is essentially setting the appropriate permissions, ensuring that the database encryption key is protected by the asymmetric key stored in the key vault.

When TDE is configured to use a key from the Azure Key Vault, the server sends the database encryption key of each TDE-enabled database to the Key Vault for a wrapkey request. Key Vault returns the encrypted database encryption key, which is stored in the user database. It is vital to remember that once a key is stored in the Key Vault, that key never leaves the Key Vault. The server can only send key operation requests to the TDE protector material with Key Vault.

The benefits of using Azure Key Vault are many, including:

- Support for key rotation.
- Key Vault is designed such that no one sees or extracts any encryption keys.
- Central management of TDE encryption keys.
- More granular control and increased transparency to self-manage the TDE protector.
- Separation of keys and data management.

Managing TDE using T-SQL

Transparent Data Encryption can be managed with T-SQL at the database level through a small handful of T-SQL statements and DMVs (dynamic management views). TDE can be enabled and disabled at the database level through the ALTER DATABASE command as follows:

```
ALTER DATABASE Database1
SET ENCRYPTION OFF
```

The sys.dm_database_encryption_encryption_keys DMV shows information about the database encryption state and associated encryption keys. A corresponding DMV for the SQL Data Warehouse exists that provides the same information: sysdm_pdw_nodes_database_encryption_keys.

Currently there are no T-SQL statements that allow you to manage TDE at the server level.

Managing TDE using PowerShell

PowerShell provides a nice set of cmdlets with which to configure TDE. In order to use these cmdlets, you must be connected as an Azure owner, contributor, or SQL Security manager.

- **Set-AzureRmSqlDatabaseTransparentDataEncryption**   Enables or disables TDE for a database.
- **Get-AzureRmSqlDatabaseTransparentDataEncryption**   Gets the TDE state for as the database.

- **Get-AzureRmSqlDatabaseTransparentDataEncryptionActivity**   Checks the encryption progress for a database.
- **Add-AzureRmSqlServerKeyVaultKey**   Adds an Azure Key Vault key to a SQL server.
- **Get-AzureRmSqlServerKeyVaultKey**   Gets a SQL server's Azure Key Vault keys.
- **Set-AzureRmSqlServerTransparentDataEncryptionProtector**   Sets the TDE Protector for a SQL server.
- **Get-AzureRmSqlServerTransparentDataEncryptionProtector**   Gets the TDE protector.
- **Remove-AzurermSqlServerKeyVaultKey**   Removes an Azure Key Vault key from a SQL server.

The following code snipped uses the Set-AzureRmSqlDatabaseTransparentDataEncryption cmdlet to enable TDE on database on server demo908 and database database4. When executing, be sure to replace the resources with the appropriate names in your environment.

```
Set-AzureRmSqlDatabaseTransparentDataEncryption -ResourceGroupName "RG-WestUS"
-ServerName "demo908" -DatabaseName "database4" -State Enabled
```

Skill 2.2: Configure SQL Server performance settings

The most recent releases of SQL Server have come with significant built-in performance enhancements to ensure databases perform well. However, simply installing SQL Server is not enough, and there is not a built-in "make it go faster switch." There are several post-installation steps to ensure SQL Server itself, as well as the databases, perform appropriately and effectively.

The knowledge and skill necessary to effectively optimize and improve database performance whether you are on-premises and in the cloud, and the skills in this section focus on the approach and steps necessary to monitor and configure your database for optimum database performance.

> **This skill covers how to:**
> - Configure database performance settings
> - Configure max server memory
> - Configure the database scope
> - Configure operators and alerts

Configure database performance settings

This section will focus primarily on the common configuration steps and tasks necessary to improve overall database performance. While the majority of the configuration settings can be done at the database level, there is one or two which are configured at the server level and should not be overlooked. The server and database level performance configuration settings include:

- Power Plan (Server)
- Trace Flags
- Parallelism
- Query Plan

Many of these performance configuration settings can be done with very little effort but can have a significant performance impact overall, but left unchecked (and improperly configured) can cause your SQL Server to unnecessarily slow down and work harder than it needs to.

Power Plan

Windows Power Plan is a Control Panel configuration setting that was introduced in Windows 2008. A "Power Plan" is a collection of hardware and software settings with the responsibility of managing how your computer manages power. The goal with Power Plan is two-fold; save energy and maximize performance. Thus, the idea behind the "Power Plan" is that Windows may, and does, throttle power to the CPUs to save energy.

The idea and concept behind the Windows Power Plan is good and for the most part, Windows Power Plan does a great job. However, it can wreak havoc on SQL Server. Power Plan throttles CPUs down when they are idle, and throttles them back up when the server is busy, essentially running your server, and SQL Server, at anywhere between 50-70% power.

The reality of this is that CPU-throttling does not respond well to CPU pressure, because in order to get the CPUs back up to 100% utilization, the CPUs need a sustained period of high CPU utilization (of the existing 50-70%) in order to trigger the throttle-up back up to 100% CPU utilization. This does not bode well for SQL Server because overall SQL Server performance will suffer. Queries will take longer to run, transactions will take longer, and on down the line. This applies to both on-premises environments as well as cloud-based IaaS environments.

By default, Windows sets the Power Plan to Balanced, meaning, that Windows will manage the hardware and software and come up with a plan to save energy and maximize performance. Luckily, there are two ways to check the throttling of your CPUs. The first is a third-party tool called CPU-Z (*https://www.cpuid.com*), and the other is through a Windows performance counter.

Figure 2-43 show the output from the CPU pressure on a real SQL Server box. The Specification is the speed that the processor is rated for, and the Core Speed is the actual running speed of the CPU. Here, the rated speed is 4.00 GHz, but the Core Speed is well below that.

In this case there is not a lot of activity on the server so the CPU was fluctuating quite a bit, and would fluctuate as low as 20-25% for the Core Speed.

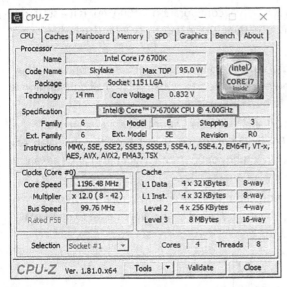

FIGURE 2-43 Comparing rated CPU speed with actual CPU speed

Similar CPU performance information can be obtained through the Windows performance counter Processor Information\% of Maximum Frequency which shows current power level of the CPUs of the maximum frequency. As seen in Figure 2-44, the blue graph bar is tracking the % of Maximum Frequency, and while there are occasional spikes, the average level is around 20%.

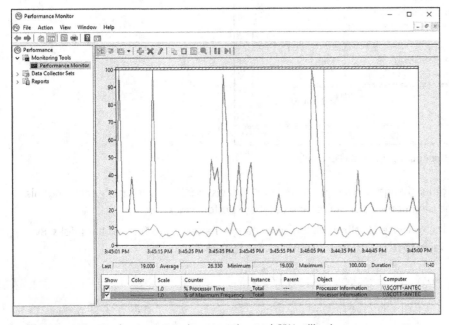

FIGURE 2-44 Using Performance Monitor to track actual CPU utilization

While the Windows Power Plan is not a SQL Server configuration setting, nor is it a setting that is configured at the database level, it is something that needs to be addressed when configuring performance for SQL Server.

This configuration setting can be changed either through the Power Settings option in the Control Panel, or through the BIOS. Depending on the server model, and if the configuration is via the BIOS, power throttling might need to be disable in the BIOS.

To configure the Power Plan in the Control Panel, open the Control Panel and search for Power Options. In the search results, select Power Options, which should show that the Balanced power option is selected. Click the Change plan settings option, then select the Change advanced power settings option, which opens the Power Options dialog.

Figure 2-45 shows the Power Options dialog and the Balanced power plan selected by default. To change the plan, select the drop down, and select High performance to make that power plan the active plan.

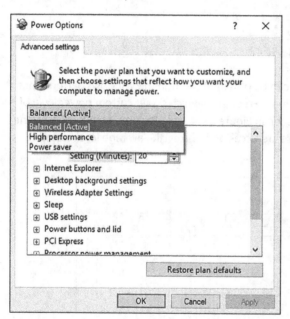

FIGURE 2-45 Configuring Windows Power Plan

With no other changes to the system, either Windows or SQL Server, simply changing this setting alone can improve SQL Server and database performance.

While in the Advanced Settings dialog, also change the setting to Turn off hard disks. By default, the value for this setting is 20 minutes. Set this value to 0.

For Microsoft Azure virtual machines that are created from the Azure portal, both of these settings (Power Plan and Disk sleep setting) are configured appropriately and do not need to be changed. This applies to Windows VMs and SQL Server VMs.

Parallelism

Parallelism is both a server-level and database-level configuration setting that affects the database performance and applies to scenarios where SQL Server runs on a server that has more than one CPU.

Parallelism is the number of processors used to run a single T-SQL statement for each parallel plan execution. When SQL Server is installed on a multi-CPU system, SQL Server does its best to detect the best degree of parallelism.

Parallelism is configured by setting the Maximum Degree of Parallelism, or MaxDOP, value. There is both a server-level configuration value and a database configuration value for MaxDOP. Setting the server-level configuration value sets MaxDOP for all databases on the server. Setting MaxDOP at the database level configures MaxDOP and overrides the server-level configuration value for that database. This section will discuss configuring the setting at the server level.

By default, SQL Server sets the value to 0, which tells SQL Server to determine the degree of parallelism that essentially tells SQL Server to use all the available processors up to 64 processors.

Most PCs today that SQL Server is installed on are NUMA (Non-Uniform Memory Access), meaning that the CPUs are clustered in a way in which they can share memory locally, thus improving performance. Typically, a cluster will consist of four CPUs that are interconnected on a local bus to shared memory.

The easiest way to tell how many NUMA nodes you have is to open Task Manager and select the Performance tab. On the Performance tab, click on the CPU graph that displays a graph on the right. Right-click the graph on the right and select Change Graph To from the context menu. You should see a NUMA node option. If the NUMA node option is grayed out, you have one NUMA node. If it isn't grayed out, then select that option. The number of graphs you see on the right hand side is how many NUMA nodes the computer has.

Knowing the number of NUMA nodes is important to appropriately configuring the MaxDOP setting. Best practice states that for NUMA computers, MaxDOP should be set at the number of CPUs per NUMA node, or eight, whichever is less. Put simply, the proper setting comes down to whether or not you have eight logical cores inside a NUMA node. For a single NUMA node with less than eight logical processors, keep the MaxDOP at or below the number of logical processors. If more than eight, set it to eight. The same thing applies to Multiple NUMA nodes.

Configuring MaxDOP appropriately can have a significant performance implication. Setting the value too high can decrease concurrency, causing queries to back up on worker threads, thus awaiting time to be executed on a CPU. When the number of parallel threads is high, SQL Server will take the path of keeping parallelized tasks within a single NUMA node. Often times this will cause threads of the same query to share CPU time with other threads of the same query. This can cause an imbalance if some CPU threads are handling parallel threads and other threads are handling single threads, resulting in some threads finishing much more quickly than others.

It is recommended that Maximum Degree of Parallelism, or MaxDOP, not be set to a value of one, because this will suppress parallel plan generation.

Another parallelism setting that should be looked at is Cost Threshold for Parallelism, which is an estimate of how much work SQL Server will do to complete a particular query plan task. The default value is five, which may or may not be good because at this value, queries do not need to be particularly large to be a considered for parallelism.

Cost Threshold for Parallelism is a server-level configuration setting. There is no database-level configuration setting for Cost Threshold for Parallelism.

Best practice states that this value be larger, which will prevent smaller queries being parallelized, thus freeing up threads on the CPU to concentrate on larger queries. Smaller queries might take a bit more time to complete, but it will increase concurrency without reducing MaxDOP for larger queries.

While the default value for this configuration setting is five, this is known to be low in most environments. Best practice states that this value be configured with a higher value depending on your workload, with suggested starting values ranging from 25 to 50 and adjusting appropriately.

Cost Threshold for Parallelism does not apply if your computer has only one logical processor, or if your MaxDOP is configured with a value of one.

Both of these settings can be configured through the Advanced page in the Server Properties page in SQL Server Management Studio, as shown in Figure 2-46. In this example, Maximum Degree of Parallelism has been set to a value of four and the Cost Threshold for Parallelism has been configured with a value of 30 for all the databases on the server.

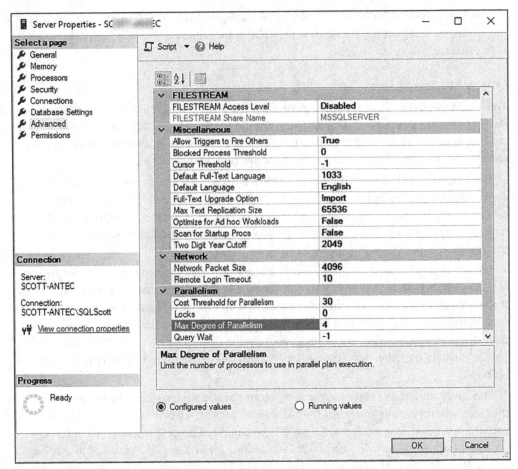

FIGURE 2-46 Configuring Max Degree of Parallelism

Cost Threshold for Parallelism can also be configured in SQL Server using T-SQL as follows:

```
USE master
GO
EXEC sp_configure 'show advanced options', 1 ;
GO
RECONFIGURE
GO
EXEC sp_configure 'cost threshold for parallelism', 30 ;
EXEC sp_configure 'max degree of parallelism', 4;
GO
RECONFIGURE
GO
```

The Cost Threshold for Parallelism cannot be configured in Azure SQL Database, because this is a server-level setting. Configuring MaxDOP at the database level will be discussed later in this chapter.

Query Store

The SQL Server Query Store is a feature introduced in SQL Server 2016 that provides real-time insights into query performance proactively. The idea and goal with Query Store is that it aims to simplify performance troubleshooting of queries by providing detailed look at query plan changes quickly and efficiently to identify poor performing queries.

Query store does this by capturing a history of all executed queries, their plans, and associated runtime statistics. This information is then available for you to examine through a nice user interface. The data is viewable via time slices so that you can see over a given period of time what changed and when and obtain detailed information about the usage patterns of each query.

It is commonly known that query execution plans can change over time for a variety of reasons. The most common reason is due to the change in statistics, but other reasons can include the modification of indexes or schema changes. Regardless of the reason, the problem has been that the cache where the cache plans are stored only stores the most recent execution plan. Additionally, plans can also be removed from the cache for a number of reasons as well, such as memory pressure. Add these all up and it makes troubleshooting query performance a problem.

The query store solves these problems by capturing and storing vital information about the query and their plans and keeps the history so you can track over time what happened and why that caused the performance issues. The benefit of keeping multiple plan information is that allows you to enforce a particular plan for a given query. This is similar to use the USE PLAN query hint, but because it is done through the query store, no application or code changes are needed.

The query store actually is a combination of three separate stores:

- **Plan store**   Contains the execution plan information
- **Runtime stats store**   Contains the execution statistics information
- **Wait stats store**   Contains the wait statistics information

To improve query store performance, plan execution information is written to all three stores asynchronously, and you can view the information in these stores via the query store catalog views.

By default, Query Store is not enabled and must be enabled either via SQL Server Management Studio or via T-SQL. The reasoning behind this is due to the fact that the capture of the query data requires storage space within the database, and while the amount of data is minimal, the option to take up disk space for this purpose is up to the administrator.

The query store can be enabled either via SQL Server Management Studio, or through T-SQL. To enable query store via SSMS, right mouse click on the database for which you want to enable the query store, and select Properties from the context menu. Select the Query Store page, and change the Operation Mode (Request) value from Off to Read Write, as shown in Figure 2-47.

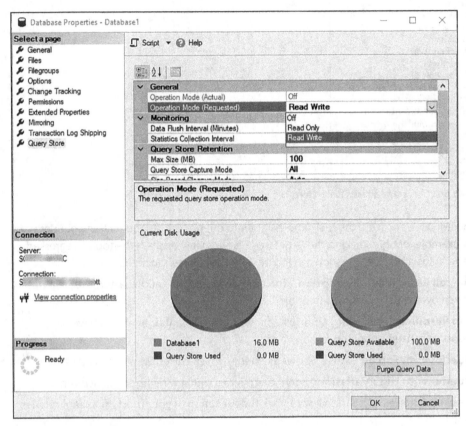

FIGURE 2-47 Enabling Query Store

To enable query store via T-SQL, simply execute the following T-SQL statement in a query window on the database for which you want to enable query store. This statement works for both on-premises SQL Server, SQL Server in an Azure VM, and Azure SQL Database. Replace the database name with the name of your database.

```
ALTER DATABASE database1 SET QUERY_STORE = ON;
```

Once query store is enabled, a new Query Store folder will appear in the Object Explorer windows for the database you have enabled query store. As shown in Figure 2-48, this folder contains a number of built-in views in which to troubleshoot query performance.

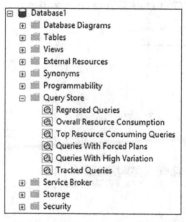

FIGURE 2-48 SQL Server Database Query Store

The built-in views provide the real-time insight into query performance within your database. For example, double-clicking the Regressed Queries view displays the top 25 regressed queries and associated plans, as shown in Figure 2-49. Other views include:

- **Overall Resource Consumption** Identifies resource utilization patterns to help optimized overall database consumption.

- **Top Resource Consuming Queries** shows most relevant queries that have biggest resource consumption impact.

- **Queries with Forced Plans** Shows all queries which currently have forced plans.

- **Queries with High Variation** Identifies queries with a wide performance variant.

- **Tracked Queries** Use this view to track the execution of your most important queries real-time.

The Tracked Queries view is a great resource to use when you have queries for forced plans and you want to make sure the query performance of each query is where it should be.

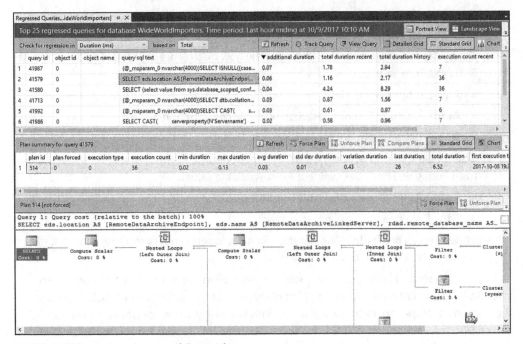

FIGURE 2-49 Query Store Regressed Query View

Given all of this information, simply turning on query store provides a lot of benefit and information. However, to get the most out of query store, ensure that it is properly configured. The Query Store page in the Database Properties dialog allows you to configure the following query store options:

- **Data Flush Interval** The frequency, in minutes, in which the query store data is flushed and persisted to disk. The default value is 15 minutes.

- **Statistics Collection Interval** The granularity in which runtime statistics are aggregated. Available values:

  - 1 Minute
  - 5 Minutes
  - 10 Minutes
  - 15 Minutes
  - 30 Minutes
  - 1 Hour
  - 1 Day

- **Max Size**   The maximum size in MB to allocate to the query store within the host database. The default size is 100 MB.

- **Query Store Capture Mode**   Indicates the how queries are captures. The default value is All. Available values:

  - **All**   Captures all queries

  - **Auto**   Captures queries based on resource consumption

  - **None**   Stops the query capture process

- **Size Based Cleanup Mode**   Data Cleanup mode when the amount of data reaches maximum size. The default value is Auto. Available values:

  - **Auto**   Automatically performs the cleanup.

  - **Off**   Data cleanup does not take place

- **Stale Query Threshold**   The duration, in days, to retain query store runtime statistics. The default value is 30 days.

However, these and additional query store configuration options that can be configured through T-SQL, including the following Max plans per query. The following T-SQL statement sets the max plans per query to a value of five. This statement works for both on-premises SQL Server, SQL Server in an Azure VM, and Azure SQL Database. Be sure to replace the database name with the name of your database.

```
ALTER DATABASE database1 SET QUERY_STORE (MAX_PLANS_PER_QUERY = 5)
```

By default, the Max plans per query option value is 200. Once that value is reached, query store stops capturing new plans. Setting the value to zero removes the limitation with regards to the number of plans captured.

Query store also contains a number of catalog views which represent information about the query store. These catalog views are what the user-interface pull their information from. These catalog views include:

- **sys.database_query_store_options**   Displays the configuration options of the query store.

- **sys.query_store_plan**   Displays query plan execution information.

- **sys.query_store_query_text**   Shows the actual T-SQL and the SQL handle of the query.

- **sys.query_store_wait_stats**   Shows wait stat information for the query.

- **sys.query_context_settings**   Shows information about the semantics affecting context settings associated with a query.

- **sys.query_store_query**   Shows query information and associated aggregated runtime execution statistics.

- **sys.query_store_stats**   Shows query runtime execution statistics.

The key takeaway from the query store is that simply enabling query store provides a wealth of information to help troubleshoot and diagnose query performance problems. However, properly configuring the query store to ensure the right amount of information is also critical.

As eluded to a few times, Query Store is supported in Azure SQL Database as a fully managed feature that continuously collects and displays historical information about all queries. Query Store has been available in Azure SQL Database since late 2015 in nearly half a million databases in Azure, collecting query performance related data without interruption.

There are minimal differences between the Query Store in Azure SQL Database and on-premises SQL Server. Most, if not all, of the best-practice configuration settings are the same including MAX_STORAGE_SIZE (100MB), QUERY_CAPTURE, MODE (AUTO), STALE_QUERY_THRESHOLD_DAYS (30), AND INTERVAL_LENGTH_MINUTES (60). As such, migrating from on-premises to Azure becomes a lot easier.

Missing Index DMVs

One could technical think of identifying missing table indexes as "configuring database performance settings." While working with indexes isn't a configuration setting in and of itself, indexes do play a vital role in database and query performance.

When a query is submitted for execution, it is routed to the query optimizer. The query optimizer has the responsibility of finding or creating a query plan. As part of this process, it analyzes what are the best indexes for the query based on several factors, including particular filter conditions. If the optimal index does not exist, SQL Server does its best to generate a good query plan, but the plan generated will be a suboptimal plan.

To help troubleshoot query performance problems, Microsoft introduced a number of dynamic management views (DMVs) which assist in identifying possible index candidates based on query history. The DMVs that are specific to missing indexes are the following:

- **sys.dm_db_missing_index_details**   Shows detailed information about missing indexes.

- **sys.dm_db_missing_index_columns**   Shows information about table columns that are missing an index.

- **sys.dm_db_missing_index_groups**   Shows information about what missing indexes that are contained in a specific missing index group.

- **sys.dm_db_missing_index_group_stats**   Shows information about groups of missing indexes.

Lets' see these in action. In the WideWorldImports database, the following query selects a few columns from the Sales.Order table filtering on the CustomerID column.

```
USE WideWorldImporters
GO
SELECT OrderDate, CustomerPurchaseOrderNumber, ExpectedDeliveryDate
FROM sales.orders
WHERE CustomerID = 556
```

As shown in Figure 2-50, the sys.dm_db_missing_index_details and sys.dm_db_missing_index_group_stats DMVs are queried. The first query only returns 99 rows (filtering on CustomerID 556), but the important point is the two results that follow. The sys.dm_db_missing_index_details DMV results show that CustomerID was used in the WHERE clause with an equals operator, so the CustomerID is listed in the equity_columns column. Thus, SQL Server is suggesting that CustomerID would be a good index. The inequality_columns column would have data if other operators had been used, such as not equal. Since our filter was an equal operator, no value is listed in this column. The included_columns field is suggesting other columns that could be used when creating the index.

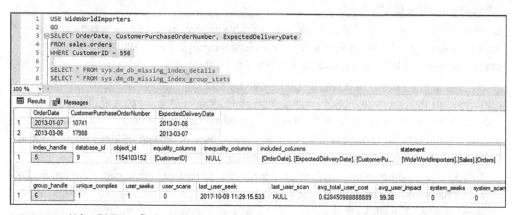

FIGURE 2-50 Using DMVs to find missing indexes

The sys.dm_db_missing_index_group_stats DMV provides additional insight and important information that is useful, including the unique_compiles, user_seeks, and user_scans columns. With this information it is possible to determine how many times the query has been called, and whether a seek or scan performed when the query was executed. The more times this query is run, these numbers should increase.

This information can be nicely laid out by combining the sys.dm_db_missing_index_details and sys.dm_db_missing_index_columns DMVs, as shown in Figure 2-51.

```
25  ⊟SELECT statement AS table_name,
26    column_id, column_name, column_usage
27    FROM sys.dm_db_missing_index_details AS mid
28    CROSS APPLY sys.dm_db_missing_index_columns (mid.index_handle)
29    ORDER BY column_id;
```

100 %

⊞ Results 📄 Messages

	table_name	column_id	column_name	column_usage
1	[WideWorldImporters].[Sales].[Orders]	2	CustomerID	EQUALITY
2	[WideWorldImporters].[Sales].[Orders]	7	OrderDate	INCLUDE
3	[WideWorldImporters].[Sales].[Orders]	8	ExpectedDeliveryDate	INCLUDE
4	[WideWorldImporters].[Sales].[Orders]	9	CustomerPurchaseOrderNumber	INCLUDE

FIGURE 2-51 Joining missing index DMVs

The missing nonclustered index can be applied using the following T-SQL.

```
CREATE NONCLUSTERED INDEX [FK_Sales_Orders_CustomerID]
ON [Sales].[Orders](
[CustomerID] ASC
)
GO
```

With the index applied, the same query can be executed followed by querying the sys.dm_db_missing_index_details DMV, and as shown in Figure 2-52, the query optimizer has found or generated an optimal query plan and therefore does not recommend any indexes.

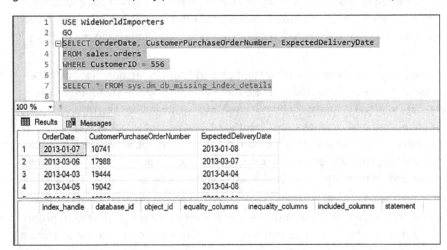

FIGURE 2-52 Missing index query results

The following DMVs are not specific to missing indexes, but are useful in helping identify how indexes are used and if they are providing any value.

- **sys.dm_db_index_usage_stats**   Shows different types of index operations and the time each type was last performed.
- **sys.dm_db_index_operation_stats**   Shows low-level I/O, locking, latching, and access activity for each partition of a table in index.
- **sys.dm_db_index_physical_stats**   Shows data and index size and fragmentation.
- **sys.dm_db_column_store_row_group_physical_stats**   Shows clustered columnstore index rowgroup-level information.

Information stored in the sys.dm_db_missing_index_* DMVs are stored until SQL Server is restarted and not persisted to disk.

Configure max server memory

Probably one of the most misunderstood configuration options in SQL Server is the memory configuration option max server memory. The Maximum server memory option specifies the maximum amount of memory SQL Server can allocate to itself during operation. During operation, SQL Server will continue to use memory as needed, up until the point where it has reached the maximum server memory setting.

As SQL Server runs it will intermittently reach out to the operating system to determine how much free memory is left. The problem with this setting is that if you don't allocate enough memory to the operating system, the operating system will start paging and not enough memory is available to the OS and other applications. SQL Server is designed to release memory back to the operating system if needed, but SQL Server tends to hang on to the memory it already has.

Something else to consider here is the effect that Locked Pages In Memory has on this setting. Locked Pages In Memory is a Windows policy that determines which accounts can use a process to keep data in physical memory and not page it to virtual memory on disk. This policy is disabled by default, and best practice states that this be enabled for SQL Server service accounts. The reason for this is that setting this option can increase SQL Server performance when running in a virtual environment where disk paging is expected. As such, Windows will ensure that the amount of memory committed by SQL Server will be less than, or equal to, the installed physical memory, plus age file capacity.

Leaving the default value in the Maximum server memory configuration setting potentially allows SQL Server to take too much memory and not leave enough for the operating system and other application and resources. SQL Server will, by default, change its memory requirements dynamically as needed, and the documentation recommends that SQL Server be allowed to do that by keeping the Maximum server memory default configuration value.

Depending on the server environment this may not be the best setting. If you need to change the max server memory value, best practice states that you first determine the amount of memory needed by the operating system and other resources, then subtract that number from the total physical memory. The remaining number is the value with which to set the max server memory configuration setting.

If you are unsure of what the best value is for max server memory, a general rule of thumb has been to set it much lower than you think it needs to be and monitor system performance. From there you can increase or lower the value based on analysis. A good way to analyze the available free memory is to monitor the Memory\Available Mbytes performance counter. This counter will tell you how much memory is available to processes running on the machine. After monitoring this information for a period of time, you should know how much memory to dedicate to SQL Server, and this value becomes the value for the max server memory setting.

If you are unsure of the workloads and not sure what value to specify for max server memory, a general practice is to configure as follows based on the amount of physical memory and number of CPUs:

- **4 GB memory with up to 2 CPUs**   At least 1 GB RAM
- **8 GB memory with up to 4 CPUs**   At least 2 GB RAM
- **16 GB memory with up to 8 CPUs**   At least 4 GB RAM
- **32 GB memory with up to 16 CPUs**   At least 6 GB RAM
- **64 GB memory with up to 32 CPUs**   At least 10 GB RAM

SQL Server uses the memory specified in the max server memory setting to control SQL Server memory allocation for resources, including the buffer pool, clr memory, all caches, and compile memory. Memory for memory heaps, thread stacks, and linked server providers are not allocated or controlled from max server memory. When planning maximum memory though, you should account for these settings. Essentially, take the totally physical memory, subtract memory for the OS itself (rule of thumb is 1GB for every 8GB of RM), then subtract memory needed for the additional settings, such as thread stack size (number of worker threads multiplied by thread size). What remains is what you can allocate for SQL Server.

Max server memory can be configured through the Server Properties page in SQL Server Management Studio, or through T-SQL. To configure through SSMS, right mouse click the server in Object Explorer and select Properties from the context menu. In the Server Properties dialog, select the Memory page on the left. Enter the appropriate memory amount in the Maximum server memory field.

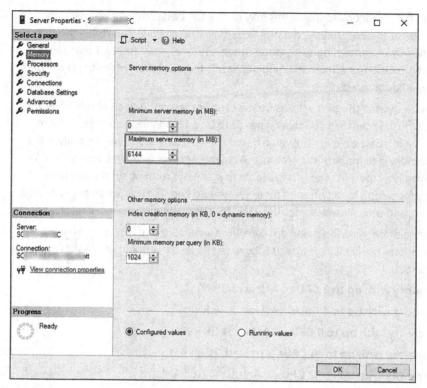

FIGURE 2-53 Configuring Maximum Server Memory

Likewise, max server memory can be configured with T-SQL using the advanced configuration options, as shown in the following code.

```
sp_configure 'show advanced options', 1;
GO
RECONFIGURE;
GO
sp_configure 'max server memory', 6144;
GO
RECONFIGURE;
GO
```

For multiple SQL Server instances running on a single server, configure max server memory for each instance, ensuring that the total memory allowance across the instances is not more than the total physical memory of the machine based upon the memory criteria discussed earlier.

Keep in mind that setting the maximum server memory only applies to on-premises SQL Server or to SQL Server running in an Azure virtual machine. You cannot set the maximum server memory in Azure SQL Database, because this is a server-level configuration setting.

Configure the database scope

Earlier in this chapter, several performance configuration settings were discussed to help improve the performance of SQL Server and databases. There are similar settings at the database level, which also pertain to performance, but also help define the overall behavior of a database. The database-scoped configuration settings that will be discussed are the following:

- Max Dop
- Query Optimizer Fixes
- Parameter Sniffing
- Legacy Cardinality Estimation

Max DOP

The Max DOP configuration setting is the similar to the server-level Max Degree of Parallelism configuration setting, but Max DOP is a database-level configuration setting. As a refresher, Parallelism is the number of processors used to run a single T-SQL statement for each parallel plan execution.

Setting MaxDOP at the database level overrides the server-level configuration value for that database. The same best practices and guidelines that apply at the server-level also apply to the Max DOP setting at the database level. Once configured the setting takes effect immediately without restarting the server.

When using MaxDOP, SQL Server using parallel execution plans when executing queries, index DDL operations, parallel inserts, online alter column statements, and more.

To configure Max DOP, open the Database Properties dialog and select the Options page on the left, then enter the appropriate Max DOP value as shown in Figure 2-54.

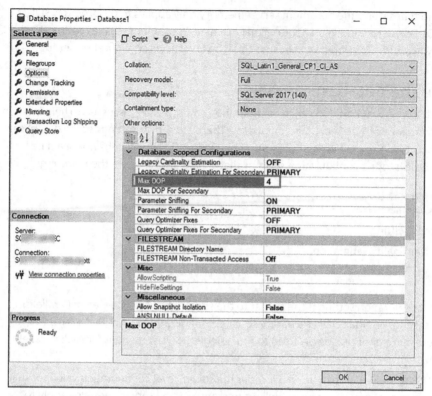

FIGURE 2-54 Configuring Max DOP at the database level

Likewise, Max DOP can be configured at the database level using T-SQL as follows:

```
USE Database1
GO
ALTER DATABASE SCOPED CONFIGURATION SET MAXCOP = 4;
GO
```

Something to keep in mind is that the MaxDOP value can be overridden in queries by specifying the MAXDOP query hint in the query statement.

Query Optimizer Fixes

Prior to SQL Server 2016, whenever a hotfix or CU (Cumulative Update) was released that contained query optimizer improvements, those improvements were not automatically turned on or enabled. This makes sense because of the possibility of the change in query behavior. While you want to assume that optimizer changes were indeed positive, there is always the small chance that the affect could be a negative one. In order to enable the optimizer changes, trace flag 4199 needed to be turned on. This is of course assuming that you installed and tested the hotfix or CU on a test box.

Beginning with SQL Server 2016, query optimizer improvements are now based on the database compatibility level. What this means is that any and all improvements to the query optimizer will be released and turned on by default under consecutive database compatibility levels.

The Query Optimizer Fixes configuration setting, added in SQL Server 2016, enables or disables query optimization hotfixes regardless of the compatibility level of the database, which is equivalent to trace flag 4199. What this means is that with SQL Server 2016 and later, you can safely ignore this setting, which is why by default it is OFF. However, if you are using SQL Server 2016, but have databases that have a previous version compatibility setting, you can consider turning this setting on.

Figure 2-55 shows the Query Optimizer Fixes configuration setting for a database with compatibility level 130 (SQL Server 2016) disabling query optimization hotfixes for the database Database1.

Likewise, this configuration setting can be configured via T-SQL as follows:

```
ALTER DATABASE SCOPED CONFIGURATION SET QUERY_OPTIMIZER_HOTFIXES=ON ;
```

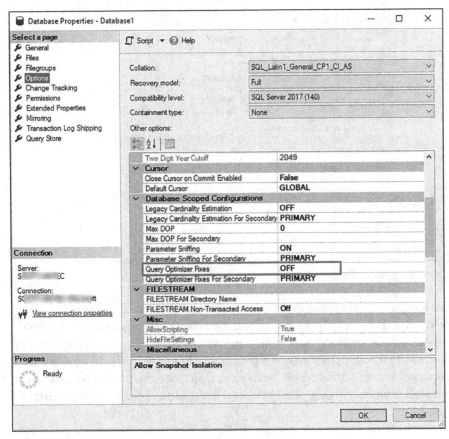

FIGURE 2-55 Configuring Query Optimizer fixes

Parameter sniffing

Parameter sniffing takes place when SQL Server interrogates, or, "sniffs," query parameter values during query compilation and passes the parameters to the query optimizer for the purpose of generating a more efficient query execution plan. Parameter sniffing is used during the compilation, or recompilation, of stored procedures, queries submitted via sp_executesql, and prepare queries.

By default, this configuration is enabled, as shown in Figure 2-56. In earlier versions of SQL Server parameter sniffing was disabled by turning on trace flag 4136.

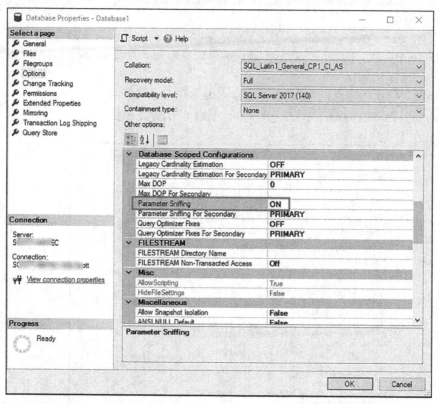

FIGURE 2-56 Configuring Parameter Sniffing

To illustrate how parameter sniffing works and the effect it has on the query plan, the following query as shown in figure 2-57 was run against the AdventureWorks database. The two queries are similar but use different values listed in the WHERE clause. As you can see, different execution plans were generated. The first query performs a clustered index scan while the second query uses a key lookup with a non-clustered index scan. The AdventureWorks database can be downloaded from here: *https://github.com/Microsoft/sql-server-samples/releases/tag/adventureworks2014*.

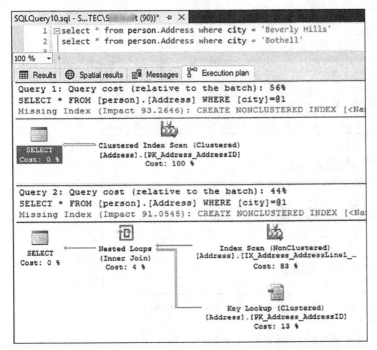

FIGURE 2-57 Different query parameters with different execution plans

As stated earlier, parameter sniffing works when executing stored procedures, so the following code creates a stored procedure which passes in the city name as a parameter.

```
CREATE PROCEDURE sp_GetAddressByCity (@city nvarchar(50))
AS
SELECT AddressLine1, AddressLine2
FROM Person.Address
WHERE City = @city
GO
```

Once the stored procedure is created it can then be called twice passing in the two cities from the queries earlier as parameters. The execution plans of both queries are now the same.

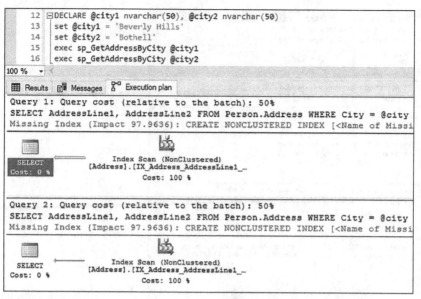

```
 12 □DECLARE @city1 nvarchar(50), @city2 nvarchar(50)
 13  set @city1 = 'Beverly Hills'
 14  set @city2 = 'Bothell'
 15  exec sp_GetAddressByCity @city1
 16  exec sp_GetAddressByCity @city2
100 %  ▾ ◂
⊞ Results  ⊞ Messages  ⅜ Execution plan
Query 1: Query cost (relative to the batch): 50%
SELECT AddressLine1, AddressLine2 FROM Person.Address WHERE City = @city
Missing Index (Impact 97.9636): CREATE NONCLUSTERED INDEX [<Name of Missi

                              Index Scan (NonClustered)
SELECT                        [Address].[IX_Address_AddressLine1_
Cost: 0 %                           Cost: 100 %

Query 2: Query cost (relative to the batch): 50%
SELECT AddressLine1, AddressLine2 FROM Person.Address WHERE City = @city
Missing Index (Impact 97.9636): CREATE NONCLUSTERED INDEX [<Name of Missi

                              Index Scan (NonClustered)
SELECT                        [Address].[IX_Address_AddressLine1_
Cost: 0 %                           Cost: 100 %
```

FIGURE 2-58 Using a stored procedure and parameters with similar execution plans

Stored procedures are precompiled on the initial execution along with the execution plan, and therefore the stored procedure will use the same plan for each execution thereafter notwithstanding the parameter being passed in.

Turning parameter sniffing off will tell SQL Server to ignore parameters and generate different execution plans for each execution of the stored procedure. Best practice states that unless you want more control of the execution plans, leave the Parameter Sniffing configuration setting to ON and don't enable the trace flag.

Legacy Cardinality Estimation

Simply put, cardinality estimation is used to predict how many rows your query is most likely to return. This prediction is used by the query optimizer to generate a more optimal query plan. The better the estimation, the better the query plan.

By default, the Legacy Cardinality Estimation configuration setting is set to OFF because starting with SQL 2014, major updates and improvements were made to the cardinality estimator that incorporated better algorithms and assumptions that are more efficient with the larger OLTP workloads and todays modern data warehouses.

Thus, the Legacy Cardinality Estimation configuration setting exists to allow you to set the cardinality estimation model to SQL Server 2012 and earlier independent of the database compatibility level. Leaving the value to OFF sets the cardinality estimation model based on the database compatibility level of the database.

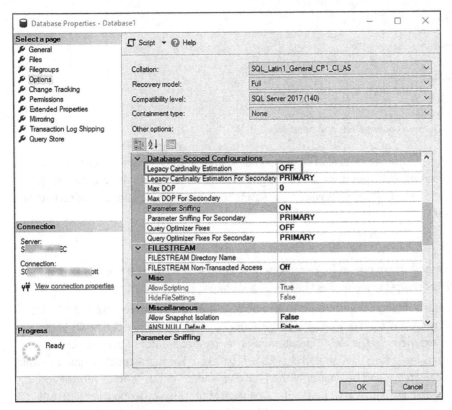

FIGURE 2-59 Configuring Legacy Cardinality Estimation

Unless you are running SQL Server 2012 or earlier, the recommendation is to leave this value to OFF simply due to the fact that the latest cardinality estimator is the most accurate.

The Legacy Cardinality Estimation configuration setting is equivalent to trace flag 9481.

Configure operators and alerts

A lot of the information covered so far in this chapter, and especially here in this skill, has to do with being proactive when it comes to working with and troubleshooting SQL Server. As a database administrator, you will want to know as soon as possible when something goes wrong and what the problem is without too much digging.

SQL Server makes that possible through the SQL Server Agent and the Alerts and Operators, which can be configured to provide proactive insight necessary regarding all aspects of SQL Server, including performance problems. Figure 2-60 shows the Alerts and Operators nodes within the SQL Server Agent in which Operators and Alerts will be created and configured.

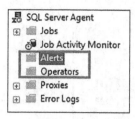

FIGURE 2-60 SQL Server agent alerts and operators

Alerts and Operators are a case of what gets configured first. Alerts are created and assigned to operators. But Operators can be assigned Alerts. So, which do you create first? It doesn't matter really, so Operators will be discussed first because it is easier from a configuration standpoint.

Operators

SQL Server Operators are aliases for people, or groups, which can receive notifications in the form of emails or pages when an alert has been generated.

Creating and defining an operator is quite simple. To create an operator, expand the SQL Server Agent node and right mouse click on the Operators node, and select New Operator from the context menu. In the New Operator dialog, enter an operator name and contact information and make sure the Enabled checkbox is checked. The name must be unique within the SQL Server instance and be no longer than 128 characters. For the contact information, either provide an email address or pager email name, or both. The Pager on duty schedule defines work schedule when the operator can be notified.

In Figure 2-61, the operator has been given a name of Perf_Alerts and an email name of Perf_Alerts@outlook.com. The pager on duty schedule is set for Monday-Saturday from 8am to 6pm. In this example, if an alert is generated on Wednesday after 6pm, the Perf_Alert operator will not be notified via the pager, but will receive an email if an email address is specified.

The Notifications page is where Alerts can be assigned to an Operator. However, since no Alerts have yet been created, we'll come back to this step. Once the Operator has been configured, click OK.

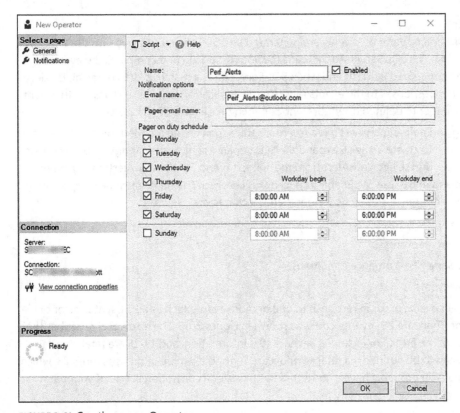

FIGURE 2-61 Creating a new Operator

Best practice for Operators states that pager and net send options not be used as this functionality will be removed in future version of SQL Server.

Operators can also be created with T-SQL as follows (if the Perf_Alerts alert already exists,
change the name of the alert in the code below):

```
USE [msdb]

GO

EXEC msdb.dbo.sp_update_operator @name=N'Perf_Alerts',
@enabled=1,
@weekday_pager_start_time=80000,
@weekday_pager_end_time=180000,
@saturday_pager_start_time=80000,
@saturday_pager_end_time=180000,
@pager_days=126,
@email_address=N'Perf_Alerts@outlook.com',
@pager_address=N''
GO
```

Alerts

During SQL Server operation, events are generated by SQL Server and saved into the Windows application log. The SQL Server Agent reads the application log and compares the events to defined and configured alerts. If and when SQL Server finds a match, it kicks off an alert. Alerts are automated responses to the events found in the application log. These alerts are then sent via email or pager to defined operators who can then take action on the alert.

Creating and defining an alert has a few more steps than create an operator, but it's still not rocket science. To create an alert, expand the SQL Server Agent node and right mouse click on the Alert node, and select New Alert from the context menu. In the New Alert dialog, enter an Alert name and make sure the Enabled checkbox is checked. The name must be unique within the SQL Server instance and be no longer than 128 characters.

There are three types of events from which to generate an alert:

- SQL Server events
- SQL Server Performance conditions
- WMI events

SQL Server events occur in response to one or more events such as a SQL syntax error or syntax error. There are 25 severity codes as shown in Figure 2-62. The error level describes the importance of the error. For example, Severity 10 is information, and 19-25 are fatal. You will definitely want to be notified if a fatal error occurs. A good example of this is severity 23, which suggests that you probably have a corrupted database, or a corruption in one of your databases.

Along with specifying the severity, you also need to select the database name for which this alert is being monitored. You can monitor all database, as shown in Figure 2-62, or a specific database by selecting it from the list.

The Message text allows you to add granularity to the alert by having the alert fire if the event contains certain words or string in the event message.

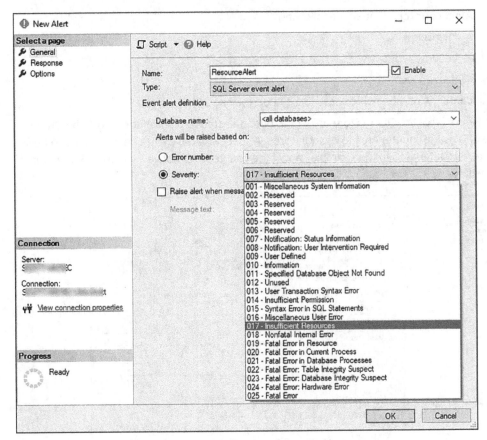

FIGURE 2-62 Selecting the Alert Severity and Alert Type for a new Alert

Instead of raising an alert by severity, you can raise it by Error Number in which case the alert will fire when a specific error occurs. There are too many error messages and their associated numbers to list here, but this link is a good place to start: *https://technet.microsoft.com/en-us/library/cc645603(v=sql.105).aspx*

DBAs are very interested in the performance of their server and databases, and SQL Server Performance Conditions event type allows you to specify alerts which occur in response to a specific performance condition.

For performance conditions, you specify the performance counter to monitor, a threshold for the alert, and the behavior the counter must exhibit for the alert to fire. As shown in Figure 2-63, performance conditions need the following to be configured:

- **Object** The performance counter to be monitored.
- **Counter** The attribute of the object area to be monitored.
- **Instance** The SQL Server instance or database to be monitored.

- **Alert counter**   One of the following:
    - falls below
    - becomes equal to
    - rises above
- **Value**   A number which describes the performance condition.

In Figure 2-63, the Query Store object has been selected to be monitored with the Query Store CPU usage counter area to be monitored. A specific database has been selected to be monitored (Database 1 in this example), and if the counter rises above a value of 75, then the alert will fire.

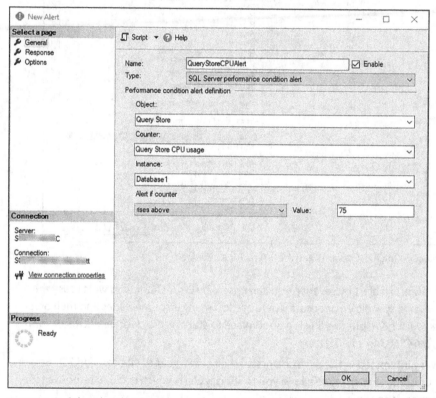

FIGURE 2-63 Select the Alert Type and Performance Conditions for a new Alert

There are over 45 performance condition objects to monitor, each one with their corresponding counters. Another interesting one is the Transactions object and the corresponding Free space in tempdb (KB) counter, which will alert you if the space in TempDB falls below a specific size. These objects are similar to counters you would monitor in Performance Monitor, so if you are planning on working with Alerts, it is recommended that you become familiar with the different objects and their associated counters.

Once the alert type has been defined, the Response page is where the alert is associated to an operator. In Figure 2-64, the alert currently being created is being assigned to the operator Perf_Alert which was created earlier.

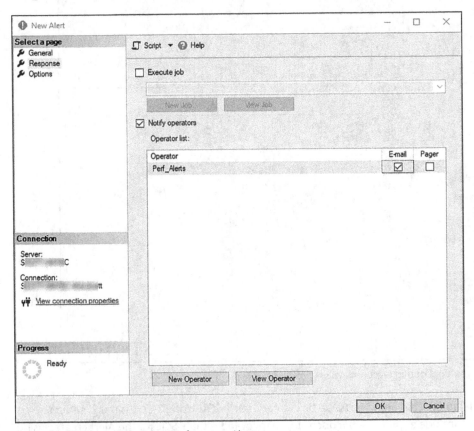

FIGURE 6-64 Selecting the Operator for a new Alert

It is possible to create a new operator or view existing operators.

The Options page of the New Alert dialog is where additional information is configured for the alert. As shown in Figure 2-65, you have the ability to include the alert error text in the message sent either by email or pager, as well as include additional information.

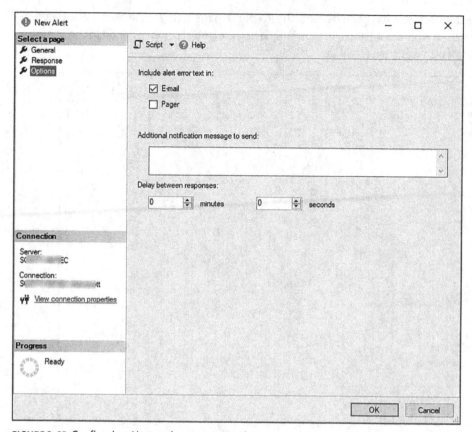

FIGURE 2-65 Configuring Alert options on a new Alert

Similar to the Operator, Alerts can be created with T-SQL. Using T-SQL is much easier to reuse and include as part of a build script. The following is the T-SQL for the Alert created using the UI above.

```
USE [msdb]
GO

EXEC msdb.dbo.sp_add_alert @name=N'QueryStoreCPUAlert',
@enabled=1,
@delay_between_responses=0,
@include_event_description_in=1,
@performance_condition=N'Query Store|Query Store CPU usage|Database1|>|75',
@job_id=N'00000000-0000-0000-0000-000000000000'
GO
EXEC msdb.dbo.sp_add_notification @alert_name=N'QueryStoreCPUAlert',
@operator_name=N'Perf_Alerts', @notification_method = 1
GO
```

As mentioned, Alerts are a great way to proactively know what is going on in your database and SQL Server. However, it is possible to "over alert," and there is a need to find the right balance between being notified when a response is required and not getting notified when a response isn't required.

To help with this you will want to define an alerting strategy, which defines severity categories that alerts fall in to. For example, you might consider categorizing the alerts into three or four buckets of severity such as Critical, High, Medium, and Low, or a subset of these. A critical response is something that requires a response and needs attention immediately. High might be something that is not quite as urgent. For example, the alert can happen overnight, or on the weekend, and can wait until the next day or weekday to address. Medium alerts are good to see on occasion and you might route those to a daily or weekly report. Low alerts are information only and might rarely be looked at.

While the above is an example, the idea is to create a strategy and approach that works best for you and doesn't get into an "over alerting" situation.

Skill 2.3: Manage SQL Server instances

DBAs have the responsibility of configuring and managing each SQL Server instance to meet the needs and the SLA (Service Level Agreement) demands appropriate for the database and workloads planned for the instance.

This skill covers the management of SQL Server instances and the associated databases in order to affectively meet appropriate performance and availability requirements.

> **This skill covers how to:**
> - Manage files and filegroups
> - Create databases
> - Manage system database files
> - Configure TempDB

Manage files and filegroups

SQL Server uses files and filegroups that contain the data and objects necessary to provide the performance and availability of an enterprise database system. This section will discuss both files and filegroups.

Database Files

SQL Server databases have, at a minimum, two file types, but can have up to three types. The database file types are the following:

- **Primary Data** Contains the startup information for the database and contains pointers to other files in the database. Every database has one primary data file. File extension is .mdf. User data and objects are stored in this database.
- **Secondary Data** Optional, user-defined data files. Secondary files can be spread across multiple disks. The recommended file extension is .ndf.
- **Transaction Log** Holds the log information that is used in database recovery. At least one log file is required for each database. The recommended file extension is .ldf.

When creating a database in SQL Server Management Studio using the Create New Database dialog, the General page automatically fills in the Database files with a single data file on the PRIMARY file group and a single log file, as shown in Figure 2-66. Transaction log files are never part of any filegroups.

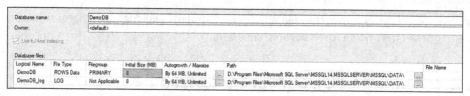

FIGURE 2-66 Data file and transaction log file for a new database

A secondary data file can be added to the database by clicking the Add button on the New Database dialog, as shown in Figure 2-67, and a logical file name is provided.

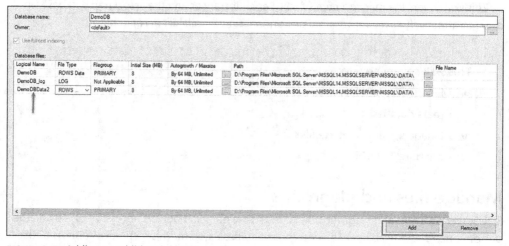

FIGURE 2-67 Adding an additional data file

SQL Server files have two names: a logical file name, and an operating system file name. The logical file name is the name used to refer to the physical file in all of the T-SQL statements, and must be unique among the logical file names in the database. The operating system file name is the name of the physical file in the operating system, including the directory path.

Figure 2-68 shows both the logical file given to the secondary data file as DemoDBData2, and a physical file of Data2.ndf. If a physical file name is not supplied, the physical file name will be derived from the logical file name.

It is recommended that when supplying physical file names that they are given names to make it easy to identify which database the files belong. The same can be said about logical file names as well.

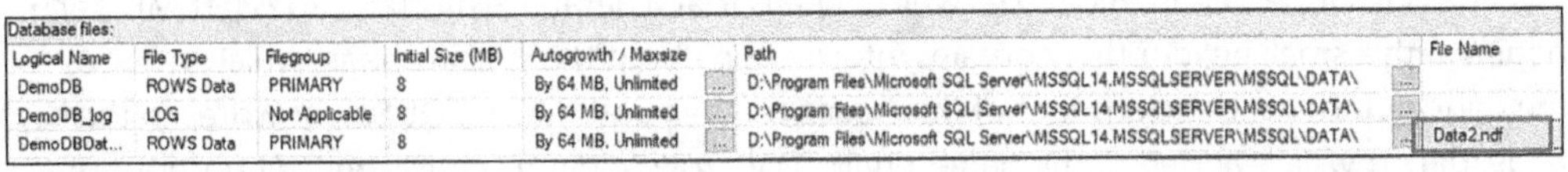

Logical Name	File Type	Filegroup	Initial Size (MB)	Autogrowth / Maxsize	Path	File Name
DemoDB	ROWS Data	PRIMARY	8	By 64 MB, Unlimited	D:\Program Files\Microsoft SQL Server\MSSQL14.MSSQLSERVER\MSSQL\DATA\	
DemoDB_log	LOG	Not Applicable	8	By 64 MB, Unlimited	D:\Program Files\Microsoft SQL Server\MSSQL14.MSSQLSERVER\MSSQL\DATA\	
DemoDBDat...	ROWS Data	PRIMARY	8	By 64 MB, Unlimited	D:\Program Files\Microsoft SQL Server\MSSQL14.MSSQLSERVER\MSSQL\DATA\	Data2.ndf

FIGURE 2-68 Specifying a physical file name

Once the database is created the physical file names can be verified by navigating to the Data directory as shown in Figure 2-69. Notice the Primary data file and transaction log as well as the secondary data file named Data2.

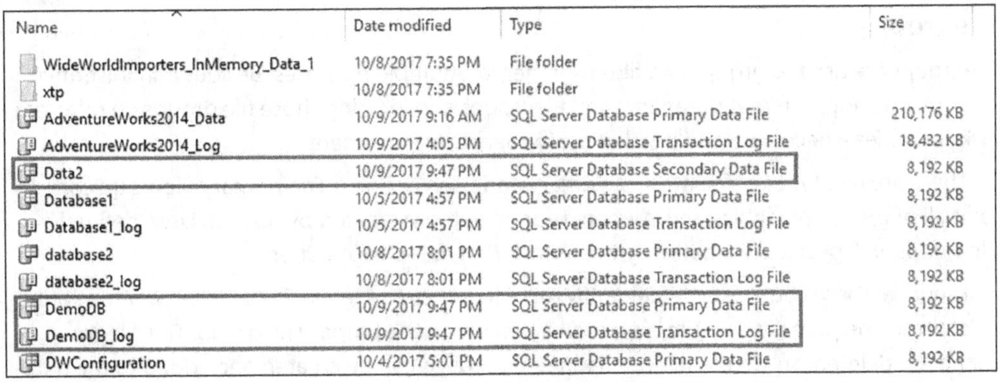

Name	Date modified	Type	Size
WideWorldImporters_InMemory_Data_1	10/8/2017 7:35 PM	File folder	
xtp	10/8/2017 7:35 PM	File folder	
AdventureWorks2014_Data	10/9/2017 9:16 AM	SQL Server Database Primary Data File	210,176 KB
AdventureWorks2014_Log	10/9/2017 4:05 PM	SQL Server Database Transaction Log File	18,432 KB
Data2	10/9/2017 9:47 PM	SQL Server Database Secondary Data File	8,192 KB
Database1	10/5/2017 4:57 PM	SQL Server Database Primary Data File	8,192 KB
Database1_log	10/5/2017 4:57 PM	SQL Server Database Transaction Log File	8,192 KB
database2	10/8/2017 8:01 PM	SQL Server Database Primary Data File	8,192 KB
database2_log	10/8/2017 8:01 PM	SQL Server Database Transaction Log File	8,192 KB
DemoDB	10/9/2017 9:47 PM	SQL Server Database Primary Data File	8,192 KB
DemoDB_log	10/9/2017 9:47 PM	SQL Server Database Transaction Log File	8,192 KB
DWConfiguration	10/4/2017 5:01 PM	SQL Server Database Primary Data File	8,192 KB

FIGURE 2-69 Viewing the physical database files

SQL Server files, both data and transaction log, can and will automatically grow from the original size specified at the time of creation. More about databases and file growth will be discussed later in the "Create Database" section.

Included in every database is a DMV called sys.database_files, which contains a row per file of a database. Querying this view returns information about each database file, including database logical and physical file name (and path), file state (online or not), current size and file growth, and more.

For example, a popular query used to determine current database size and the amount of empty space in database, which uses the sys.database_files view is the following:

```
SELECT name, size/128.0 FileSizeInMB,
size/128.0 - CAST(FILEPROPERTY(name, 'SpaceUsed') AS int)/128.0 AS EmptySpaceInMB
FROM sys.database_files;
```

The basic, yet fundamental, unit of storage in SQL Server is a page. The disk space assigned to a data file in a database, whether it is a .mdf or .ndf, is logically divided into pages numbered contiguously 0 to n. When SQL Server reads and writes data, these operations are done at the page level. In other words, SQL Server reads and writes entire, whole, data pages. Each file in a database has a unique file ID number, and you can see this by querying the sys.database_files view and by looking at the file_guid column.

Pages in SQL Server are 8K in size, which means that a database has 128 pages per MB. Each begins with a small header that contains information about the specific page, which includes the page number and the amount of free space on the page. When SQL Server writes to the page, data rows are added to the page serially. Data rows cannot span pages but portions of a row may be moved off the row's page.

While a deep understanding of data file pages are outside the scope of this skill, it helps to understand the makeup of database files and how SQL Server uses them to store data.

With the foundation of database files, we now turn our attention to database filegroups.

Filegroups

Filegroups are used to group data files together for multiple purposes. Besides administrative reasons, creating different databases and filegroups and locating those file groups on different disks provides a necessary and needed performance improvement.

There are two types of file groups: Primary and User-defined. The primary filegroup contains all of the system tables and is where user objects are created by default. User-defined filegroups are specifically created by the user during database creation.

Every database contains a default PRIMARY filegroup. As seen in Figure 2-66, when creating a database, the primary data file is placed by default on the primary filegroup. This filegroup cannot be deleted. Subsequent, user-defined filegroups can be created and added to the database to help distribute the database files for the reasons previously explained.

When objects are created in the database, they are added to the primary file group by default unless a different filegroup is specified. The PRIMARY filegroup is the default filegroup unless it is changed by the ALTER DATABASE statement.

Filegroups can be created and added during initial database creation, and can be added to the database post-database creation. To add filegroups during database creation, click on the Filegroups page in the New Database dialog and click the Add Filegroup button as seen in Figure 2-70. Provide a name for the new filegroup and make sure the Read Only checkbox is unchecked.

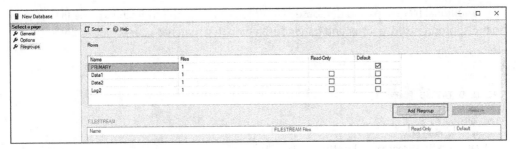

FIGURE 2-70 Creating new Filegroups

Next, click on the General page and as you did with Figure 2-67, add new database files to the database. With additional filegroups created you can now select the new filegroups on which to add the database files, as seen in Figure 2-71.

Database name:		DemoDB							
Owner:		<default>							

Use full text indexing

Database files:

Logical Name	File Type	Filegroup	Initial Size (...	Autogrowth / Maxsize		Path		File Name
DemoDB	ROWS Data	PRIMARY	8	By 64 MB, Unlimited		D:\Program Files\Microsoft SQL Server\MSSQL14.MSSQLSERVER\MSSQL\DATA\		
DemoDB_log	LOG	Not Applicable	8	By 64 MB, Unlimited		D:\Program Files\Microsoft SQL Server\MSSQL14.MSSQLSERVER\MSSQL\DATA\		
DemoDBData1	ROWS Data	Data1	8	By 64 MB, Unlimited		D:\Program Files\Microsoft SQL Server\MSSQL14.MSSQLSERVER\MSSQL\DATA\		DemoDBData1.ndf
DemoDBData2	ROWS Data	Data2	8	By 64 MB, Unlimited		D:\Program Files\Microsoft SQL Server\MSSQL14.MSSQLSERVER\MSSQL\DATA\		DemoDBData2.ndf

FIGURE 2-71 Specifying the Filegroups for new database files

Once the database is created the physical file names can be verified by navigating to the Data directory as shown in Figure 2-72. Notice the Primary data file and transaction log as well as the secondary data files and additional transaction log.

WideWorldImportersTEST_InMemory...	10/18/2017 8:24 PM	File folder	
xtp	10/18/2017 8:25 PM	File folder	
AdventureWorks2014_Data	10/17/2017 1:29 PM	SQL Server Database Primary Data File	210,176 KB
AdventureWorks2014_Log	10/17/2017 1:29 PM	SQL Server Database Transaction Log File	18,432 KB
Database1	10/17/2017 1:29 PM	SQL Server Database Primary Data File	8,192 KB
Database1_log	10/20/2017 1:47 PM	SQL Server Database Transaction Log File	73,728 KB
database2	10/17/2017 1:29 PM	SQL Server Database Primary Data File	8,192 KB
database2_log	10/17/2017 1:29 PM	SQL Server Database Transaction Log File	8,192 KB
DemoDB	10/25/2017 8:35 AM	SQL Server Database Primary Data File	8,192 KB
DemoDB_log	10/25/2017 8:35 AM	SQL Server Database Transaction Log File	8,192 KB
DemoDBData1	10/25/2017 8:35 AM	SQL Server Database Secondary Data File	8,192 KB
DemoDBData2	10/25/2017 8:35 AM	SQL Server Database Secondary Data File	8,192 KB

FIGURE 2-72 Viewing the physical files of a new database using Filegroups

You might think that creating databases with additional files and filegroups is difficult, but it is quite the contrary. The following T-SQL statement shows how to create the above database with additional filegroups and database files. When running this script, change the file location to the appropriate drive letter and folder destination that matches your environment.

```
USE [master]
GO

CREATE DATABASE [DemoDB]
 CONTAINMENT = NONE
 ON  PRIMARY
( NAME = N'DemoDB',
FILENAME = N'D:\Program Files\Microsoft SQL
Server\MSSQL14.MSSQLSERVER\MSSQL\DATA\DemoDB.mdf' ,
SIZE = 8192KB ,
MAXSIZE = UNLIMITED,
FILEGROWTH = 65536KB ),
 FILEGROUP [Data1]
( NAME = N'DemoData1',
FILENAME = N'D:\Program Files\Microsoft SQL Server\MSSQL14.MSSQLSERVER\MSSQL\DATA\
DemoData1.ndf' ,
SIZE = 8192KB ,
MAXSIZE = UNLIMITED,
FILEGROWTH = 65536KB ),
 FILEGROUP [Data2]
( NAME = N'DemoData2',
FILENAME = N'D:\Program Files\Microsoft SQL Server\MSSQL14.MSSQLSERVER\MSSQL\DATA\
DemoData2.ndf' ,
SIZE = 8192KB ,
MAXSIZE = UNLIMITED,
FILEGROWTH = 65536KB )
 LOG ON
( NAME = N'DemoDB_log',
FILENAME = N'D:\Program Files\Microsoft SQL Server\MSSQL14.MSSQLSERVER\MSSQL\DATA\
DemoDB_log.ldf' ,
SIZE = 8192KB ,
MAXSIZE = 2048GB ,
FILEGROWTH = 65536KB )
GO
ALTER DATABASE [DemoDB] SET COMPATIBILITY_LEVEL = 140
GO
```

Using filegroups with database files is a great way to improve performance, because it lets a database be created across multiple disks, disk controllers, or RADI systems. For example, if the machine in which SQL Server is installed has four disks, consider creating a database that is made up of three data files (each on a separate filegroup), one file on each disk, and then the transaction log on the fourth disk. Thus, I/O is spread across the disks and can be accessed in parallel.

Additionally, files and filegroups helps with data and object placement, again increasing performance. For example, an I/O heavy table can be placed in a separate filegroup, which is then placed on a different disk.

Create databases

The last section spent some time on database creation as part of talking about database files, so this section will focus on best practices for creating databases and some of the important database properties to set during database creation.

One of the critical things overlooked when creating a database is the file growth and max size. Beginning with SQL Server 2016, the default autogrowth for both the data file and transaction log file is 64 MB. When creating the database, it is recommended that you make the data files as large as possible, based on the maximum amount of data you initially expect in the database.

It is also recommended to specify a maximum file size so that the database does not take up the entire disk space, especially if the data file is on the OS disk. Best practice states to put the data and transaction log files on separate disks than the OS disk, but sometime this is not possible. Regardless of where the data files reside, put a limit on the growth by specifying a maximum growth file size so that space is left on the hard disk. You should also make certain that the sum total for all databases is less than available disk space.

It is OK to let the data files grown automatically, but this can cause fragmentation. Whenever possible, create the files or filegroups on as many different physical disks. As recommended above, put space and resource intensive objects in different filegroups. While this is a best practice, it still will not solve the issue of fragmentation due to growth events, thus following standard maintenance plans to address fragmentation is needed.

Figure 2-73 shows how to set the autogrowth and maximum file size via SQL Server Management Studio. The UI sets these values in terms of MB, so if the value you need to specify is in GB or larger, you'll need to do that math. For example, in Figure 2-73, the file growth is set to 1GB, or 1,024 MB. The maximum file size is set to 100 GB, or 102,400 MB.

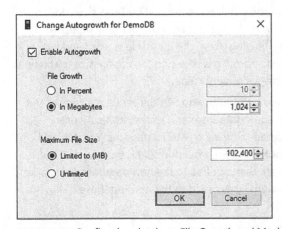

FIGURE 2-73 Configuring database File Growth and Maximum File Size

Setting the file growth size and maximum file size is easier to do in T-SQL when creating databases because you can specify the file growth in terms of MB, GB, TB, and so on, and not have to worry about doing the math for the UI. Again, when running this script, change the file location to the appropriate drive letter and folder destination that matches your environment.

```
CREATE DATABASE [DemoDB]

 CONTAINMENT = NONE

 ON  PRIMARY

( NAME = DemoDB, FILENAME = N'D:\Program Files\Microsoft SQL Server\MSSQL14.MSSQLSERVER\
MSSQL\DATA\DemoDB.mdf' , SIZE = 8192KB , FILEGROWTH = 1GB )

 LOG ON

( NAME = N'DemoDB_log', FILENAME = N'D:\Program Files\Microsoft SQL Server\MSSQL14.
MSSQLSERVER\MSSQL\DATA\DemoDB_log.ldf' , SIZE = 8192KB , FILEGROWTH = 1GB )

GO
```

While on the topic of user databases and transaction logs, a concept worth discussing is that of VLFs, or Virtual Log Files. VLFs split physical database log files into smaller segments, which are required for how log files work in the background. VLFs are created automatically, but you still need to keep an eye on them.

Virtual log files have no fixed size and there is no fixed number of virtual log files for a physical log file. The database engine chooses the size of the virtual log files dynamically when it is creating or extending the log files. The size or number of virtual log files cannot be configured or set by an administrator.

VLFs affect performance based on whether the log files are defined by small size and growth_increment values. If these log files grow to a large size because of many small increments they will have lots of virtual log files, slowing down the database startup and log backup/restore operations. The recommended approach is to assign the log file size to the final size required and have a relatively large growth_increment value.

The model database is a template for all new databases, and SQL Server uses a copy of the model database when creating and initializing new databases and its metadata. All user-defined objects in the model database are copied to newly created databases. You can add any objects to the model database, such as tables, stored procedures, and data types. Thus, when creating a new database, these objects are then applied to the new database. The entire contents of the model database, including options, are copied to the new database.

It is therefore recommended to set the initial database size, filegrowth, and max size in the model database for all new databases created on the server, along with other user-defined objects that are wanted in the new database.

A few more words about the model database. Tempdb is created every time SQL Server is started, and some of the settings of the model database are used when creating tempdb, so the model database must always be present and exist on every SQL Server system. A recommended method is to set the model database to what you want for tempdb and only allow new databases to be created with specified file and filegrowth options.

We'll close this section talking about some of database configuration settings that can be set when creating a database. Some of the configuration settings were discussed in Skill 2.2, including the settings found in the Database Scoped Configurations section of the Database Properties dialog, such as Max DOP, Query Optimizer Fixes, and Parameter Sniffing. These configuration settings have an effect on the database performance, and it is recommended that you review Skill 2.2 to understand how these settings work and affect the performance of your database.

Figure 2-74 shows a few more database configuration settings, from which we will discuss a few. In the Miscellaneous section:

- **Delayed Durability**   Applies to SQL Server transaction commits that can either be fully durable (the default), or delayed durable which is also known as a lazy commit. Fully durable transaction commits are synchronous and are reported as committed only after the log records are written to disk. Delayed durable transactions are asynchronous are report a commit before the transaction log records are written to disk.

- **Is Read Committed Snapshot On**   Controls the locking and row versioning behavior of T-SQL statements via connections to SQL Server.

In the Recovery section:

- **Page Verify**   This setting pertains to data-file integrity. When this value is set to CHECKSUM, the SQL Server engine calculate the checksum over the contents of the whole page and stores the value in the page header when the page is written to disk. When the page is run, the checksum is recomputed and compared to the checksum value stored in the page.

In the State section:

- **Database Read-Only**   Specifies whether the database is read-only. When the value is true, users can only read data, they cannot modify data or database objects.

- **Restrict Access**   Specifies which users may access the database. Values include Multiple, Single, and Restricted. Normal is the default setting, which allows multiple users to connect. Single is for maintenance and allows a single user to connect at any given time. Restricted allows only members of the db_owner, dbcreator, or sysadmin roles to use the database.

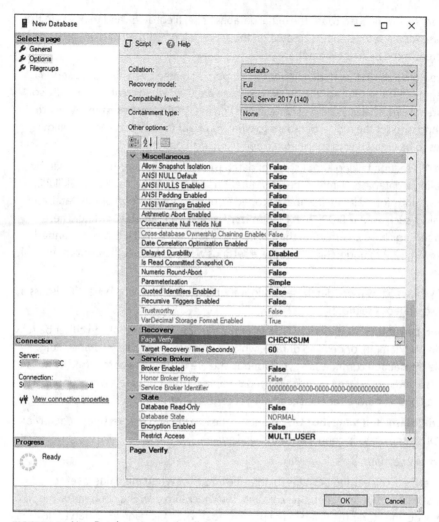

FIGURE 2-74 New Database properties dialog

Turning our attention to the Page Header of the database properties dialog, there are a couple of options to point out there.

- **Recovery Model** Specifies one of the models for recovering the database: Full, Bulk-Logged, or Simple.
- **Compatibility Level** Specifies the version of SQL Server that the database supports.

An example of both Recovery Model and Compatibility Level. In Figure 2-75, the Adventure-Works2014 database has been restored to a computer running SQL Server 2017. The recovery model is Simple and the Combability level is set to SQL Server 2014.

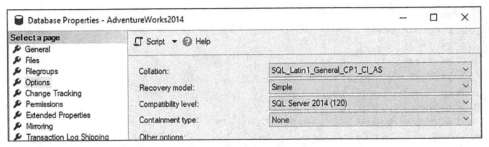

FIGURE 2-75 Compatibility level of a restored SQL Server 2014 database

Similarly, the WideWoldImports sample database was downloaded and restored to the same SQL Server 2017 instance. When restored, the recover model is also Simple and the Compatibility level is set to that for SQL Server 2016.

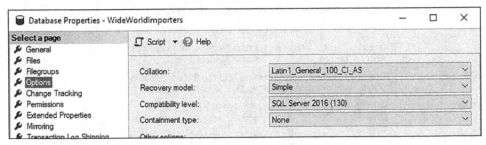

FIGURE 2-76 Compatibility level of a restored SQL Server 2016 database

Database recovery models are designed to control transaction log maintenance. In SQL Server, all transactions are logged, and the Recovery Model database property controls how the transactions are logged and whether the log allows backing up and what kind of restore operations are available. When creating and managing a database, the recovery model can be switched at any time.

With Simple, there are no log backups. With Full, log backups are required and no work is lost due to a lost or damaged data file, Full allows data recovery from an arbitrary point in time.

Manage system database files

When installed, SQL Server includes, and maintains, a set of system-level databases often called system databases. These databases control the overall operation of a single server instance and vigilant care must be taken to ensure they are not compromised.

Depending on your installation options, you will see a list of system databases within the System Databases node in the Object Explorer window in SQL Server Management Studio. A typical installation of a SQL Server instance will show the four common system databases as shown in Figure 2-77.

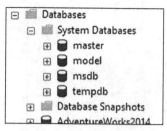

FIGURE 2-77 SQL SERVER SYSTEM DATABASES

A complete list of system databases is summarized in Table 2-2.

TABLE 2-2 Backup best practices of the System Databases

System Database	Description	Backup
master	Contains all system-level information for SQL Server	Yes
model	Template for all databases created on the SQL Server instance	Yes
msdb	Used by the SQL Server Agent for scheduling alerts and jobs. Also contains backup and restore history tables.	Yes
tempdb	Holds temporary or intermediate result sets. Created when SQL Server starts, deleted when SQL Server shuts down.	No
distribution	Exists only if SQL Server is configured as a Replication Distributor. Stores all history and metadata for replication transactions.	Yes
resource	Read-only database that resides in the mssqlsystemresource. mdf file, which contains copies of all system objects.	No

The Backup column in Table 2-2 provides the suggested option for whether the system database should be backed up. The master database should be backed up quite frequently in order to protect the data and instance environment sufficiently. It is recommended that the master database be included in a regularly scheduled backup plan. It should also be backed up after any system update.

The model database should be backed up only as needed for business needs. For example, after adding user customization options to the model database, you should back it up.

The msdb database should be backed up whenever it is updated, such as creating alerts or jobs. A simple recovery model and back up is recommended for the msdb database as well.

Configure TempDB

TempDB is a system database that is a global resource to all user connected to a SQL Server instance.

TempDB is used by SQL Server to do and hold many things among which is the following:

- **Temporary user objects**   Objects that are specifically created by a user, including local or global temporary tables, table variables, cursors, and temporary stored procedures.

- **Internal objects**   Objects that are created by the SQL Server engine such as work tables to store intermediate results for sorting or spooling.

- **Row versions**   Items that are generated by data modification transactions in a database that uses read-committed row versioning isolation or snapshot isolation transactions. Row versions are also generated by data modification transactions for features, including online index operations.

Configuring tempdb is crucial for optimal SQL Server database performance. Prior to SQL Server 2016, the SQL Server installation would create a single tempdb file and associated log. However, starting with SQL Server 2016, the SQL Server installation allows you to configure the number of tempdb files, as shown in Figure 2-78.

The recommended practice for tempdb is to create multiple database files, one per logical CPU processor, but not more than eight. By default, the SQL Server installation does this for you and sets the number of tempdb files the number of logic processors. If the machine has more than eight logical processors, this should still default to eight. If the number of logical processors is greater than eight, set the number to eight to begin.

Having tempdb configured during installation is preferred because it prevents the additional, post-installation steps of configuring multiple tempdb files and setting the size and growth for each file.

The TempDB tab also allows the configuration initial size and growth configuration for all tempdb data and log files, as well as their location. These files should be equal in size with the same autogrowth settings.

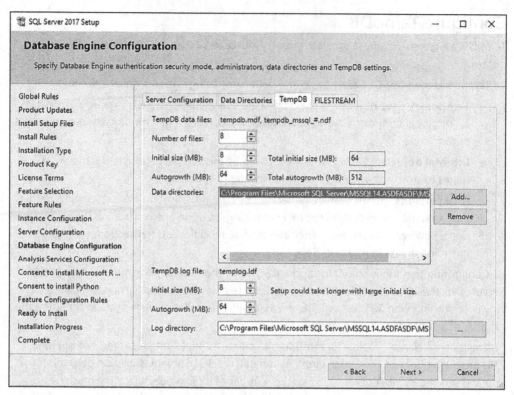

FIGURE 2-78 Configuring TempDB during SQL Server installation

While the SQL Server installation wizard is smart enough to figure out the number of cores and logical processors the machine has, you can find the number of cores and logical processors from Task Manager, as shown in Figure 2-79.

You probably won't need to change anything in the SQL Server setup, but this information is good to know and verify in case you do want to make any configuration changes to tempdb during installation.

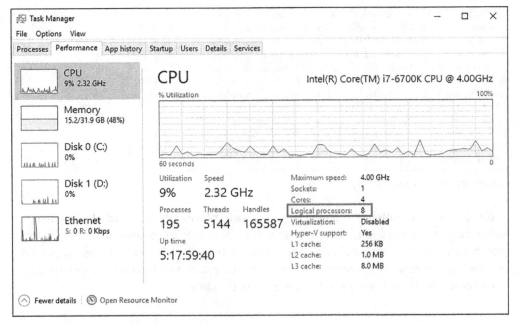

FIGURE 2-79 Determining the logical process count

When the database is created, the physical and logical tempdb configuration is shown in Figure 2-80.

Logical Name	File Type	Filegroup	Initial Size (MB)	Autogrowth / Maxsize	Path	File Name
tempdev	ROWS Data	PRIMARY	8	By 64 MB, Unlimited	D:\Program Files\Microsoft SQL Server\MSSQL14.MSSQLSERVER\MSSQL\DATA	tempdb.mdf
temp2	ROWS Data	PRIMARY	8	By 64 MB, Unlimited	D:\Program Files\Microsoft SQL Server\MSSQL14.MSSQLSERVER\MSSQL\DATA	tempdb_mssql_2.ndf
temp3	ROWS Data	PRIMARY	8	By 64 MB, Unlimited	D:\Program Files\Microsoft SQL Server\MSSQL14.MSSQLSERVER\MSSQL\DATA	tempdb_mssql_3.ndf
temp4	ROWS Data	PRIMARY	8	By 64 MB, Unlimited	D:\Program Files\Microsoft SQL Server\MSSQL14.MSSQLSERVER\MSSQL\DATA	tempdb_mssql_4.ndf
temp5	ROWS Data	PRIMARY	8	By 64 MB, Unlimited	D:\Program Files\Microsoft SQL Server\MSSQL14.MSSQLSERVER\MSSQL\DATA	tempdb_mssql_5.ndf
temp6	ROWS Data	PRIMARY	8	By 64 MB, Unlimited	D:\Program Files\Microsoft SQL Server\MSSQL14.MSSQLSERVER\MSSQL\DATA	tempdb_mssql_6.ndf
temp7	ROWS Data	PRIMARY	8	By 64 MB, Unlimited	D:\Program Files\Microsoft SQL Server\MSSQL14.MSSQLSERVER\MSSQL\DATA	tempdb_mssql_7.ndf
temp8	ROWS Data	PRIMARY	8	By 64 MB, Unlimited	D:\Program Files\Microsoft SQL Server\MSSQL14.MSSQLSERVER\MSSQL\DATA	tempdb_mssql_8.ndf
templog	LOG	Not Applicable	8	By 64 MB, Unlimited	D:\Program Files\Microsoft SQL Server\MSSQL14.MSSQLSERVER\MSSQL\DATA	templog.ldf

FIGURE 2-80 Tempdb database files

For backward compatibility, the primary tempdb data logical name file is called tempdev, but the physical file name is tempdb. Secondary tempdb logical file names follow the temp# naming pattern, and the physical file names follow the tempdb_mssql_# naming pattern. You can see this in both Figure 2-80 and Figure 2-81.

MSDBData	10/4/2017 5:01 PM	SQL Server Database Primary Data File	15,040 KB
MSDBLog	10/8/2017 7:40 PM	SQL Server Database Transaction Log File	1,024 KB
tempdb	10/4/2017 5:02 PM	SQL Server Database Primary Data File	8,192 KB
tempdb_mssql_2	10/4/2017 5:02 PM	SQL Server Database Secondary Data File	8,192 KB
tempdb_mssql_3	10/4/2017 5:02 PM	SQL Server Database Secondary Data File	8,192 KB
tempdb_mssql_4	10/4/2017 5:02 PM	SQL Server Database Secondary Data File	8,192 KB
tempdb_mssql_5	10/4/2017 5:02 PM	SQL Server Database Secondary Data File	8,192 KB
tempdb_mssql_6	10/4/2017 5:02 PM	SQL Server Database Secondary Data File	8,192 KB
tempdb_mssql_7	10/4/2017 5:02 PM	SQL Server Database Secondary Data File	8,192 KB
tempdb_mssql_8	10/4/2017 5:02 PM	SQL Server Database Secondary Data File	8,192 KB
templog	10/4/2017 5:02 PM	SQL Server Database Transaction Log File	8,192 KB
WideWorldImporters	10/8/2017 7:35 PM	SQL Server Database Transaction Log File	102,400 KB

FIGURE 2-81 Tempdb physical files

Best practice recommends to set the recovery model of tempdb to SIMPLE, allowing temp-db to recover and reclaim log space requirements small. It is also recommended to set the file growth increment to a reasonable size. If set too small, tempdb will need to frequently expand which will have a negative impact on performance. Best practice also states to place tempdb on different disks from those where the user database is placed.

Thought experiment

In this thought experiment test your skills covered in this chapter. You will find the answers to this in the next section.

You are a consultant to the Contoso Corporation. Contoso is a mid-sized wholesaler, which currently has an internal customer management and ordering system. Contoso has around 100 customers to track, and different departments within Contoso manage different customer segments and at the rate Contoso is growing, performance is important to keep pace with demand and their expected workload.

Contoso's CIO has made the decision to move their on-premises data center to Azure, but has concerns about PCI compliance, security, and performance. Contoso is looking for guidance around securing their data in Azure to ensure their data and their customers sensitive data is safe-guarded. Contoso is also looking to ensure that their application performance is just as good or better than on-premises. For the most part, the security and performance solutions should work both on-premises and in Azure as they work to migrate.

With this information in mind answer the following questions.

1. What security feature should they consider to ensure data security that works in both environments, requires minimal changes to the application, and secures data in both in motion and at rest?

2. How should Contoso secure their data environment in Azure to ensure only those who are allowed have access to the data?

3. What SQL Server feature should Contoso implement to be able to troubleshoot query performance and query plans to help them with their planned growth?

4. What SQL Server insights can Contoso use to get query improvement information?

Thought experiment answers

This section provides the solution to the thought experiment. Each answer explains why the answer is correct.

1. Contoso should implement Always Encrypted, which provides encryption for data use, is supported in SQL Server and Azure SQL Database, and requires little changes to the application.

2. Once the database and application has been migrated to Azure, Contoso should implement firewall rules at both the server and database levels to ensure that only those who are within the specified environment can access the data. Additionally, with the logins migrated, Contoso should implement Azure Active Directory to centrally manage the identities of the database users.

3. Contoso should use Query Store to provide real-time insight into query performance and provide easier troubleshooting of poor performing queries. Query store is support in both SQL Server and Azure SQL Database, so Contoso can use this feature as they plan for their move to Azure.

4. Contoso should look at using existing missing index DMVs.

Chapter summary

- Azure SQL Server firewall rules can be configured using T-SQL, the Azure Portal, PowerShell, the Azure CLI, and a REST API.
- Azure SQL Database firewall rules can only be configured using T-SQL.
- Azure firewall rules must be unique within the subscription.
- NAT (Network address translation) issues could be a reason your connection to Azure SQL Database is failing.
- Always Encrypted is a must feature either in SQL Server or Azure SQL Database to protect and safe-guard sensitive data.
- If you are using Azure SQL Database, use Azure Key Vault for the Always Encrypted key store provider.
- Consider using Dynamic Data Masking to limit data exposure of sensitive data to non-privileged users for both on-premises and in Azure SQL Database.

- Transparent Data Encryption (TDE) is similar to cell-level encryption, but TDE will automatically encrypt and decrypt the data when it reads and writes data to/from disk. CLE (cell-level encryption) does not.

- TDE requires no changes to your application code.

- TDE supports Bring Your Own Key.

- Instant SQL Server performance can be obtained by changing the Windows Power Option from Balanced to High Performance.

- Use Performance Monitor and the % of Maximum Frequency counter to track the current power level of the CPUs maximum frequency.

- Consider configuring MaxDOP to improve database performance and not leave it at its default configuration setting of 0.

- MaxDOP can be configured at both the server level and the database level. The database-level setting overrides the server-level setting for that database.

- The Query Store is an excellent way to easily capture performance information from your SQL Server instance.

- Consider using the missing index DMVs to identify potential missing indexes to improve performance.

- Change the Maximum server memory configuration option.

- Configure Operators and Alerts to proactively be alerted to SQL Server performance issues.

- Configure tempdb appropriately to improve performance.

## CHAPTER 3

Manage Storage

Managing storage and performing data maintenance on a regular schedule is a critical aspect of ensuring proper performance and availability of SQL Server, both on-premises and in the cloud. A comprehensive understanding of the concepts and technologies is necessary to a successfully running SQL Server environment, and thoughtful and appropriate care must be taken to ensure an appropriate SLA is achieved.

Skills in this chapter:

- Skill 3.1: Manage SQL Storage
- Skill 3.2: Perform database maintenance

Skill 3.1: Manage SQL Storage

Storage is one of the key performance and availability aspects of SQL Server regardless of the size of the instance and environment, and this applies to both on-premises as well as the cloud. At the rate that server processing power is increasing, storage can easily become a bottleneck. These bottlenecks can be avoided with proper understanding of how SQL Server uses storage, and this skill looks at the different storage options for SQL Server and how to properly manage them for performance and availability.

> **This skill covers how to:**
> - Manage SMB file shares
> - Manage stretch databases
> - Configure Azure storage
> - Change service tiers
> - Review wait statistics
> - Manage storage pools
> - Recover from failed storage

Manage SMB file shares

The SMB (Server Message Block) protocol is a network file sharing protocol that provides the ability to access files or resources on a remote server or file share and read/write to files on a network computer. For SQL Server, this means that SQL Server can store use database files on SMB file shares starting with SQL Server 2008 R2. Starting with SQL Server 2008 R2, support for SMB supports SMB for stand-alone SQL Servers, but later releases of SQL Server support SMB for clustered SQL Servers and system databases.

Windows Server 2012 introduced version 3.0 of the SMB protocol, which included significant performance optimizations. One of those optimizations included improvements for small random read/write I/O operations, which is idea for SQL Server. Another optimization is that it turns on MTU (Maximum Transmission Units), which significantly increases performance for large sequential transfers that SQL Server can again take advantage of with SQL Server data warehouse and backup/restore operations.

The addition of the SMB 3.0 protocol in Windows Server 2012 also includes a few performance and availability improvements, such as:

- **SMB Scale Out** Administrators can create file shares that provide concurrent direct access to data files on all nodes in a file server cluster using Cluster Shared Volumes, allowing for improved load balancing and network bandwidth.

- **SMB Transport Failover** Clients can transparently reconnect to another cluster node without interrupting applications writing data to the file shares.

- **SMB Direct** Provides high performance network transport via network adapters that use Remote Direct Memory Access (RDMA). For SQL Server, this enables a remote file server to resemble local storage.

- **SMB Multichannel** Enables server applications to take advantage of all available network bandwidth as well as be resilient to a network failure through the aggregation of network bandwidth and fault tolerance capabilities.

With the improvements to the SMB protocol, this means that SQL Server environments running on Windows Server 2012 or higher (and with SQL Server 2012 or higher) can now place their system database and create user database data files placed on the SMB file shares, knowing it is backed by network performance and integrity.

In order for SQL Server to use the SMB file shares, the SQL Server needs to have the FULL CONTROL permissions and NTFS permissions on the file SMB file share folders. The best practice is that you use a domain account as the SQL Server services account, otherwise you simply need to grant the appropriate permission to the share folder.

To use an SMB file share in SQL Server, simply specify the file path in the form of a UNC path format, such as \\ServerName\ShareName\ or \\ServerName\ShareName. Again, you need to be using SQL Server 2012 or higher, and the SQL Server service and the SQL Agent service accounts need to have FULL CONTROL and NTFS share permissions.

To create a database on an SMB share you can use SQL Server Management Studio or T-SQL. As shown in Figure 3-1, in the New Database dialog box, the primary data file and log file is placed on the default path, and a secondary file is specified with a UNC path to an SMB share.

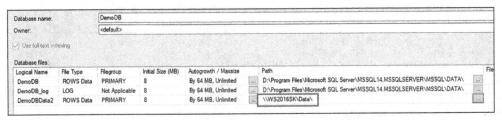

FIGURE 3-1 Creating a database with a secondary data file on an SMB file share

There are a few limitations when using SMB file shares, including the following, which is not supported:

- Mapped network drives
- Incorrect UNC path formats, such as \\...\z$, or \\localhost\...\
- Admin shares, such as \\serername\F$

Likewise, this can be done in Azure using Azure Files, which create SMB 3.0 protocol file shares. The following example uses an Azure Virtual Machine running SQL Server 2016 and an Azure storage account, both of which have already been created. Another section in this chapter discusses Azure storage and walks through creating a storage account.

Once the storage account has been created, open it up in the Azure portal and click the Overview option, which shows the Overview pane, shown in Figure 3-2.

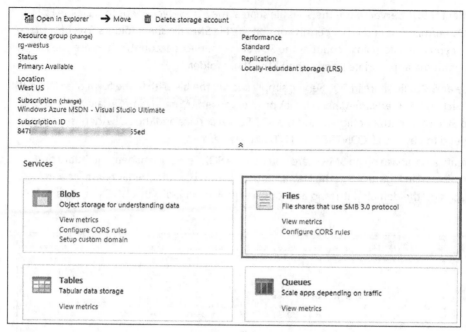

FIGURE 3-2 Azure storage services

The Overview pane shows the available storage services, one of which is the Files service, as shown and highlighted in Figure 3-2. More about this service is discussed later in this chapter. Clicking the File service opens the File service pane, shown in Figure 3-3.

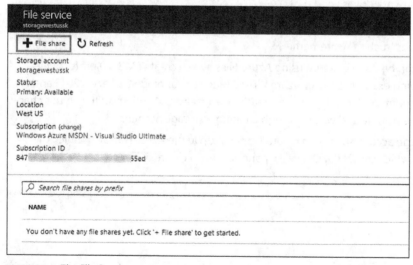

FIGURE 3-3 The File Service pane

The File Service pane shows details about the file service and any file shares that have been created. In this case, no files shares have been created so the list is empty. Therefore, click the + File Share button on the top toolbar to create a new file share, which opens the New File Share pane, shown in Figure 3-4.

Creating a new file share is as simple as providing a file share name and the disk size quota. The quota is specified in GB with a value up to 5120 GB, and in this example a value of 100 GB was specified. Click OK when done, which takes you back to the File Service blade that now displays the newly created file share.

Once the file shares are created they can be mounted in Windows and Windows Server, both in an Azure VM as well as on-premises. They can be mounted using the Windows File Explorer UI, PowerShell, or via the Command Prompt.

When mounting the drive, the operating system must support the SMB 3.0 protocol, and most recent operating systems do. Windows 7 and Windows Server 2008 R2 support SMB 2.1, but both Windows Server 2012 and higher, as well as Windows 8.1 and higher, all include SMB 3.0, although Windows Server 2012 R2 as well as Server Core contain version 3.2, as does Windows Server 2016.

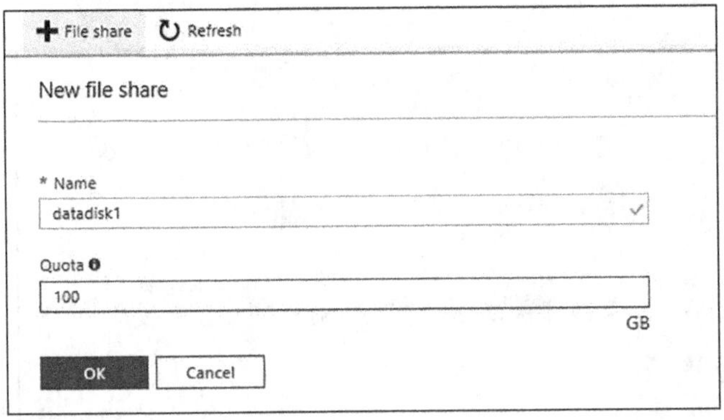

FIGURE 3-4 Configuring a new file share

As previously mentioned, Azure file shares can be mounted in Windows using the Windows File Explorer UI, PowerShell, or via the Command Prompt. Regardless of the option, the Storage Account Name and the Storage Account Key are needed. Additionally, the SMB protocol communicates over TCP port 445, and you need to ensure your firewall is not blocking that port.

The storage account name and key can be obtained from the Access keys option in your Azure storage account. For the storage key, either the primary or secondary key will work.

Probably the easiest way to mount the drive is by using the Windows Command Prompt and the Net Use command and specifying the drive letter, account name, and account key, as shown in the code below. To execute, replace the <account name> with the name of your storage account name, and replace the <storage account key> with the primary key for the storage account.

```
net use Z: \\< account name>.file.core.windows.net\datadisk1 /u:AZURE\<account name>
<storage account key>
```

Figure 3-5 shows the execution of the Net Use command to mount the SMB file share as drive Z, specifying the account name and account key. You will get an error if port 445 is not open on your firewall. Some ISPs block port 445 so you will need to check with your provider.

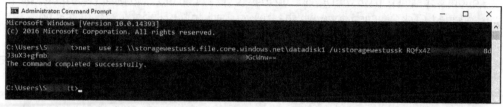

FIGURE 3-5 Mounting the new file share with command prompt

Once the file share is mounted, you can view the new mounted drive in Windows Explorer as a Network location, as shown in Figure 3-6.

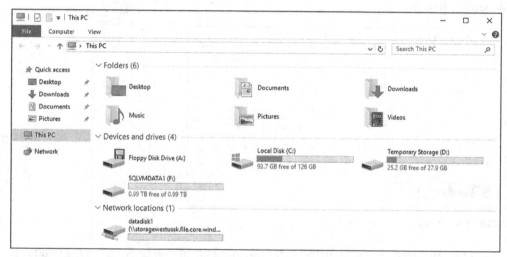

FIGURE 3-6 The new file share in Windows Explorer

With the new SMB file share mounted and ready to use, files and folders can be created on it, including SQL Server data files. For this example, a folder on the file share called Data is created to add SQL Server secondary data files.

Figure 3-7 shows how to create a new database on-premises with a data file on a SMB file share. When creating a new database in SQL Server Management Studio, in the New Database dialog box, the primary data file and log file are placed on the default path, and a secondary file is specified with a UNC path to the Azure file share.

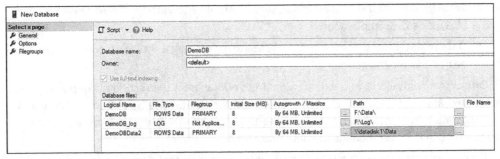

FIGURE 3-7 Creating a database with a secondary data file on an Azure File share with SMB

Similar to on-premises SMB file shares, the same permissions and security requirements apply when using Azure Files. The SQL Server services still needs FULL CONTROL permissions to the share, as well as NTFS. Once this is configured, you are able to create databases using SMB file shares.

It used to be that using file shares as a storage option for data files was unthinkable. The risks were too high; file shares were too slow causing performance issues, data integrity was an issue, and the SMB protocol was not kind to the likes of applications such as SQL Server, which had rigorous I/O workloads.

However, this changed with the release of version 3.0 of the SMB protocol, which addresses these issues by implementing the features and capabilities discussed earlier, allowing SQL Server to be a prime target for using SMB file shares.

Manage stretch databases

Stretch Database is a feature added to SQL Server 2016 with the goal of providing cost efficient storage for your cold data. Hot data refers to data that is frequently accessed on fast storage, warm data is data that is less-frequently accessed data preferably stored on less-performant storage, and cold data refers to rarely accessed data that is hopefully stored on slow storage.

In the SQL Server environment, hot, warm, and cold data is typically stored on the same storage devices for easy access, even though cold data is, as mentioned, rarely accessed. The result of storing cold data causes the database to fill up with unused data, and increases storage costs as the hot/warm data becomes cold data.

Stretch Database aims to address these issues by allowing you to dynamically "stretch" cold transactional data to the cloud where storage is less expensive thus freeing up disk space locally. There are several benefits to using Stretch Database:

- **Low cost** By moving cold data from on-premises to the cloud, storage costs can be up to 40 percent less.
- **No application changes** Even though data is moved to the cloud, there are no application change requirements to access the data.

- **Security** Existing security features such as Always Encrypted and Row-Level Security (RLS) can still be implemented.
- **Data maintenance** On-premises database maintenance, including backups, can now be done faster and easier.

One of the main keys to understand with Stretch Database is the second bullet point; no application changes are required. How does this work? When a table is "stretched" to Azure and the cold data moved into Azure SQL Database, the application still sees the table as a single table, letting SQL Server manage the data processing.

For example, let's say you have an Orders table with orders that date back five years or more. When stretching the Orders table, you specify a filter that specifies what data you want moved to Azure. When querying the Orders table, SQL Server knows which data is on-premises and which has been moved to the cloud, and handles the retrieval of data for you. Even if you execute a SELECT * FROM Orders statement, it retrieves the data from on-premises as well as retrieves the data from Azure, aggregates the results, and returns the data. Thus, there is no need to change the application.

Understand, though, that there is some latency when querying cold data. The latency depends really on how much data you are querying. If you are querying very little, the latency is very small. If you are executing SELECT *, you might need to wait a bit more. Thus, the amount of data you determine as "cold" should be an educated decision.

Another key point is that Stretch Database allows you to store your cold data in Azure SQL Database, which is always online and available, thus providing a much more robust retention period for the cold data. And, with the cold data stored in Azure SQL Database, Azure also manages the storage in a high-performance, reliable, and secure database.

Stretch Database must be enabled at the instance level prior to enabling Stretch at the database or table level. Enabling Stretch Database at the instance level is done by setting the remote data archive advanced SQL Server option via sp_configure.

```
EXEC sp_configure 'remote data archive, '1';
GO
RECONFIGURE
GO
```

At the database level, enabling Stretch Database can be done one of two ways; through T-SQL or through the Stretch Database Wizard, and Stretch must be enabled at the database level before stretching a table. The easiest way to enable stretch at the database level is through the Stretch Database Wizard within SQL Server Management Studio. You can either right mouse click the database for which you want to enable Stretch (Tasks > Stretch > Enable), or right mouse click the specific table you want to stretch (Stretch > Enable), as shown in Figure 3-8.

Either option starts the Stretch Database Wizard and enables stretch, the only difference being that right-clicking on the table will automatically select the table in the Wizard, whereas right-clicking on the database will not select any tables and asks you which tables to stretch.

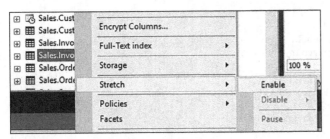

FIGURE 3-8 Launching the Stretch Database Wizard

The first page of the Stretch Wizard is the Introduction page, which provides important information as to what you need in order to complete the wizard. Click Next on this page of the wizard, and then the Select Tables page appears, shown in Figure 3-9.

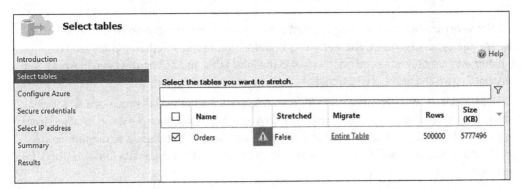

FIGURE 3-9 Selecting the tables to stretch to Azure

In the Select Tables page, select the tables you want to stretch to Azure by checking the check box. Each row in the list of tables specifies whether the tables has been stretched, how much of the table has been stretched, how many rows are currently in the table, and the approximate size of the data.

Figure 3-9 shows that the Orders table has not been stretched, and that the entire table, all 50,000 rows, will be stretched to Azure. A warning is also given, so let's address the warning first. The structure of the Orders table looks like this:

```
CREATE TABLE [dbo].[Orders](
[OrderID] [int] IDENTITY(1,1) NOT NULL,
[CustomerID] [int] NOT NULL,
[SalespersonPersonID] [int] NOT NULL,
[PickedByPersonID] [int] NULL,
[ContactPersonID] [int] NOT NULL,
[BackorderOrderID] [int] NULL,
[OrderDate] [date] NOT NULL,
[ExpectedDeliveryDate] [date] NOT NULL,
[CustomerPurchaseOrderNumber] [nvarchar](20) NULL,
[IsUndersupplyBackordered] [bit] NOT NULL,
[Comments] [nvarchar](max) NULL,
[DeliveryInstructions] [nvarchar](max) NULL,
[InternalComments] [nvarchar](max) NULL,
[PickingCompletedWhen] [datetime2](7) NULL,
[LastEditedBy] [int] NOT NULL,
[LastEditedWhen] [datetime2](7) NOT NULL,
CONSTRAINT [PK_Sales_Orders] PRIMARY KEY CLUSTERED
(
[OrderID] ASC
) ON [PRIMARY]
) ON [PRIMARY] TEXTIMAGE_ON [PRIMARY]
GO
```

Not very exciting, but the thing to point out is that the Orders table does contain a Primary Key on the OrderID column. The warning is therefore informing you that primary keys or unique keys are only enforced on the rows in the local table and not on the table in Azure. Fair enough, so we can move on from that.

The next item of importance is the Migrate column. By default, all the rows of a selected table, the entire table, are set to be migrated to Azure. This is not what we want, recalling from the earlier hot data/cold data discussion. The goal with Stretch Database is to migrate only cold data to Azure; things like closed orders, or orders passed a certain data (order history), for example.

To fix this, click the Entire Table link, which opens the dialog shown in Figure 3-10. This dialog allows you to apply a filter to specify which rows are to be migrated to Azure. To do this, select the Choose Rows option, and then provide a name for the filter function. This function does not need to already exists. Next, define the WHERE clause filter by picking a column from the table on which to filter, specifying the operator, and then providing a value.

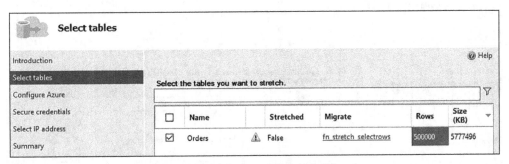

○ Entire Table
◉ Choose Rows

Table name: Orders
Name: fn_stretch_selectrows

Column :   Value :

Where OrderDate   ▾   <   ▾   1/1/2017   Check

```
SELECT TOP 1000 *
FROM [dbo].[Orders]
WHERE [OrderDate] < CONVERT(date, N'1/1/2017)
```

✓ Success

Done   Cancel

FIGURE 3-10 Configuring the rows to migrate to zure

In this example, the OrderDate column is being used as the filter for the WHERE clause, specifying that any order older than January 1, 2017 should be migrated to Azure. To test the query, click the Check button, which checks the function by running a sample query that is displayed in the text box below the filter. This text box is read only and not editable. It is for display purposes only. If the sample query returns rows, the test is reported as successful and you can click Close.

The Migrate column back, the Select tables page of the wizard now shows the name of the function it will use to migrate the data to Azure, as shown in Figure 3-11.

Select tables

Introduction						⊘ Help
Select tables	**Select the tables you want to stretch.**					
Configure Azure						▽
Secure credentials	☐	**Name**	**Stretched**	**Migrate**	**Rows**	**Size (KB)** ▾
Select IP address	☑	Orders	⚠ False	fn_stretch_selectrows	500000	5777496
Summary						

FIGURE 3-11 Configured Select Tables page of the Stretch Database Wizard

Click Next to continue with the wizard, which shows the Configure Azure page, shown in Figure 3-12. The Configure Azure page is where you specify the region in which to either create a new Azure SQL server or select an existing one and in which region, and then supply the credentials for the new or existing server.

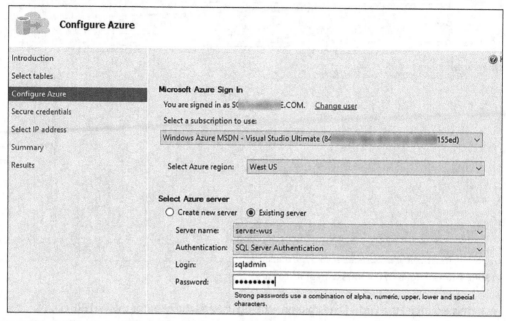

FIGURE 3-12 Selecting and configuring the Azure server

The wizard asks you to sign in to your Azure account in order to access the necessary information, such as existing servers if you have selected that option, such as this example. Once the Configure Azure page is configured, click Next, which displays the Secure credentials page, shown in Figure 3-13.

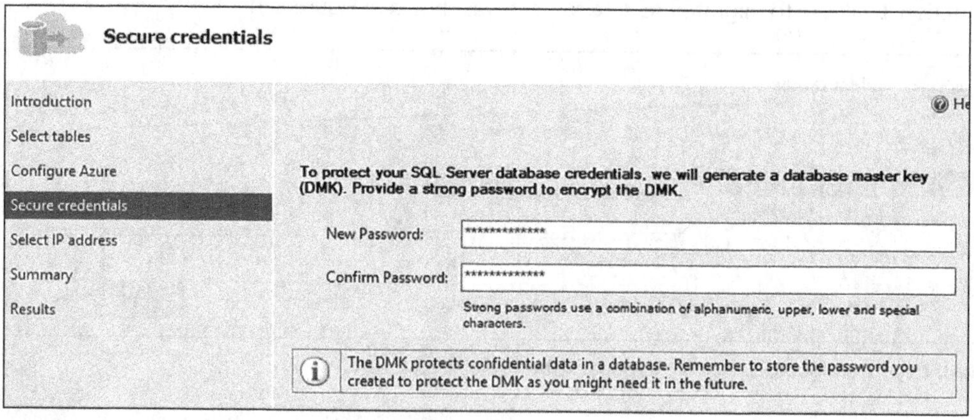

FIGURE 3-13 Providing a database master key password

Enter, and confirm, a password on the Confirm Credentials page. As part of the Stretch migration, the wizard creates a database master key. This key is used to secure the credentials that Stretch Database uses to connect to the remote database in Azure.

If the wizard detects an existing database master key, it only prompts you for the existing password. Otherwise it creates a new key and the wizard prompts you to enter and confirm a password. Click Next to move to the Select IP address page of the wizard, shown in figure 3-14.

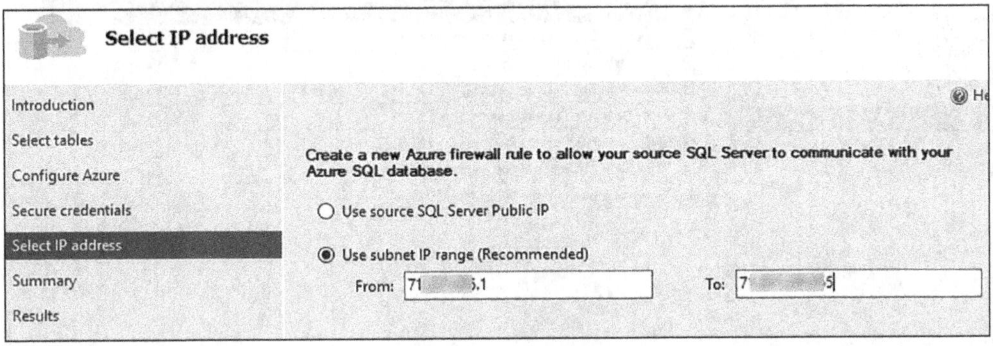

Select IP address

Introduction
Select tables
Configure Azure
Secure credentials
Select IP address
Summary
Results

Create a new Azure firewall rule to allow your source SQL Server to communicate with your Azure SQL database.

○ Use source SQL Server Public IP

◉ Use subnet IP range (Recommended)

From: 71   .1   To: 7   5

FIGURE 3-14 Providing the IP address for the database-level firewall rule

As reviewed in Chapter 2, access to an Azure SQL Database is restricted to a set of known IP addresses through a set of firewall rules. Firewall rules grant access to a database or databases based on the originating IP address of each request. As such, the Select IP Address page of the wizard provides the option to use the public IP address of your SQL Server, or a manually specified IP address range. The recommended option is to manually specify the IP address. The wizard creates the appropriate database-level firewall rule in Azure to allow SQL Server to communicate with the SQL Database in Azure.

Click Next to go to the Summary page, review the details, and then click Next to begin the migration and view the Results page, shown in Figure 3-15.

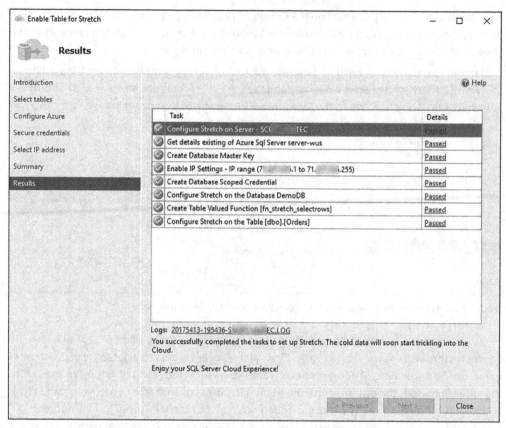

FIGURE 3-15 Completed Stretch Database migration

As you can see in Figure 3-15, there are quite a number of steps. The target database was created on the specified Azure SQL server, the database master key created, the firewall rule created, the function created on the local SQL Server, and then the migration began.

What is interesting to note is that this wizard completed before the migration was 100 percent complete; you'll see that shortly. However, the key point is that Stretch was configured on both ends, on-premises and the cloud, and the migration kicked off. To verify the migration process, connect to the Azure SQL server in SQL Server Management Studio and expand the databases node, wherein you see a Stretch Database-named Orders table, as shown in Figure 3-16.

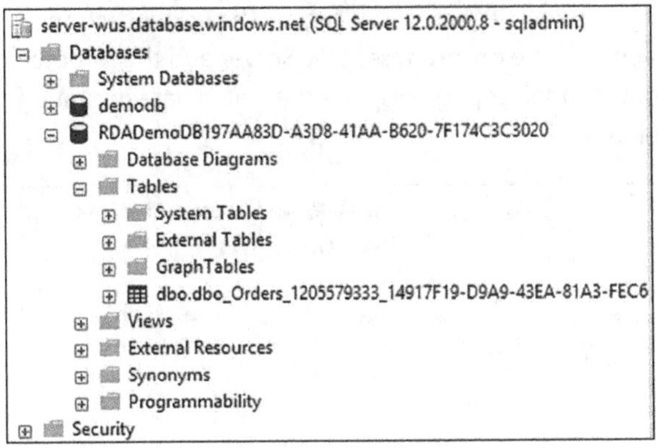

FIGURE 3-16 Stretched table in Azure within SQL Server Management Studio

The stretched Orders table is like any other database. By default, a Standard-tier SQL Database is created, but you can change the service tier to get better performance if you plan on querying the data frequently. However, querying the data frequently sort of defeats the purpose of Stretch Database and cold storage. Thus, you need to decide what the appropriate performance level you need is, and if the default is too much or too little. Service tiers are discussed later in this chapter.

However, because it is a normal database, you can connect to it via SQL Server Management Studio and query the data and see how much data is in there. Because the Stretch Wizard completed prior to 100 percent data migration (which is by design), the data is migrated to Azure over a period of time. Depending on how much data is being migrated, the migration process could be quick, or it could take a while.

There is a better way to see what is going on with the Stretch environment, including the number of rows in each table, the status, and troubleshoot each stretch-enabled database. The Stretch Database Monitor is built into SQL Server Management Studio, and you can get to it by right-clicking the database that has been stretched, and selecting Tasks -> Stretch -> Monitor from the context menu, as shown in Figure 3-17.

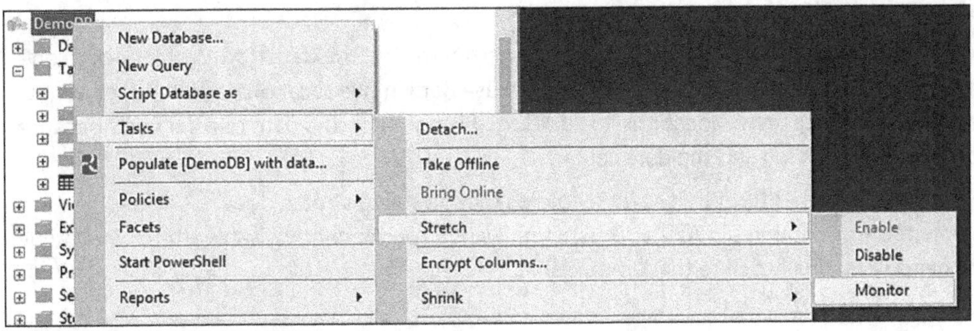

FIGURE 3-17 Opening the Stretch Database monitor

The Stretch Database Monitor, shown in Figure 3-18, has two sections. The upper section of the page displays general information both of the on-premises SQL Server and the remote Azure SQL database. The lower portion of the monitor page displays the status data migration for each stretch-enabled table in the database.

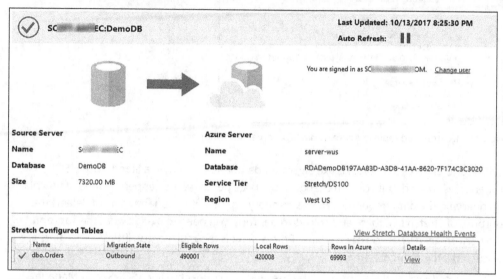

FIGURE 3-18 The Stretch Database Monitor

The monitor page refreshes every 60 seconds, thus if you watch the monitor page long enough you see the Local Rows number decrease and the Rows In Azure number increase, until all the rows that match the filter criteria have been migrated to Azure.

Stretch Database can be disabled either through SQL Server Management Studio or via T-SQL. There are two options when disabling stretch, bringing the data in Azure back to on-premises, or leaving the data in Azure. Leaving the data in Azure abandons the remote data and disables stretch completely. In this scenario, you have data in two locations but not stretched environment. Meaning, you now have to execute a second query to access the cold data.

Bringing the data back to on-premises copies, not moves, the data from Azure back to on-premises and disables stretch. Again, you now have data in two locations, but in this case, you have the same data in two locations. In addition, this option incurs data transfer costs because now you have data leaving the data center.

You should gather from these two scenarios that disabling stretch does not delete the remote table or database in Azure. Thus, if you want to permanently disable stretch for a table, you need to manually delete the remote table.

To disable Stretch, right-click the table you want to stop stretching and select Stretch -> Disable, then select the appropriate option. The Recover Data And Disable Stretch dialog, shown in figure 3-19, shows that Stretch has been disabled successfully.

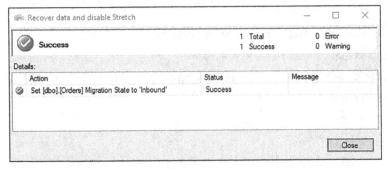

FIGURE 3-19 Disabling Stretch Database

However, if you selected the option to bring data back from Azure, the migration of data back to on-premises is so the actual disabling of Stretch might take a bit depending on how much data is in Azure.

It was mentioned earlier about the difference between hot, warm, and cold data, with cold data typically stored on a slower storage option. One of the great things about Stretch Database is that as a storage option, part of managing Stretch Database is selecting the performance level of the remote storage, which in this case, is an Azure SQL database. The different service tiers and performance levels are discussed later in this chapter.

Identifying databases and tables for Stretch Database

One of the main goals of Stretch Database is to provide cost efficient storage for your cold data. The question then becomes how to identify tables that would make good Stretch Database candidates. While there is no hard, fast rule, the general rule of thumb is any transactional table with large amounts of cold data. For example, the table used in this chapter contains an OrderDate column, and stored orders that date back many years. This example simply says "any order with an order date older than 1/1/2017" is considered cold data. Another approach would have been to include an OrderStatus column, with values of "open," "closed," "Pending," and so on. In this situation we could have defined the filter as any order with an order status of "closed" as cold and migrated to Azure.

Any "history" table is a good candidate for stretch. SQL Server also introduced a feature called Temporal tables, which is a system-versioned temporal table designed to keep a full history of data changes for each point-in-time analysis. These tables are excellent candidates for stretch as you can migrate all or part of the associated history to Azure.

Stretch Database limitations

Stretch Database does have a few limitations that prevents a table from being stretched. They are:

- **Tables**
  - Tables that have more than 1,023 columns or 998 indexes
  - FileTables or tables that contain FILESTREAM data
  - Replicated tables, or tables that use Change Tracking or Change Data Capture
  - Memory-optimized tables
- **Indexes**
  - Full text
  - XML
  - Spatial
  - Indexed Views
- **Data types**
  - sql_variant
  - XML
  - CLR
  - Text, ntext, image
  - timestamp
  - Computed columns
- **Constraints**
  - Default constraints
  - Foreign key constraints that reference the table

Likewise, remote tables have limitations. As reviewed earlier, stretch-enabled tables do not enforce primary keys or unique constraints. You also cannot update or delete rows that have been migrated, or rows that are eligible for migration.

Configure Azure storage

Azure storage is a managed service providing enterprise-ready storage capabilities. Azure storage is comprised of three storage services; Blob, File, and Queue. Until recently, Table storage was also a part of Azure storage, but Azure Table storage is now part of Azure Cosmos DB.

The goal with Azure storage is to provide an array of storage options that are highly available, scalable, secure, and redundant. Azure storage provides this by implementing an architecture that allows for the storage and access of immense amounts of data. Figure 3-20 shows the Azure storage architecture at a high level.

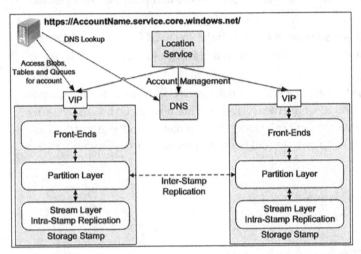

FIGURE 3-20 Windows Azure Storage architecture

As shown in Figure 3-20, Azure storage consists of several components:

- **Storage Stamps** A cluster of N racks of storage nodes, each rack is built out as a separate fault domain. Clusters range from 10 to 20 racks.

- **Stream Layer** Stores the bits on disk and is responsible for distributing and replicating the data across multiple servers for data durability with the stamp.

- **Partition Layer** Provides scalability by partitioning data within the stamp. Also provides transaction ordering and caching data to reduce disk I/O.

- **Front-Ends** Comprised of a number of stateless servers, is responsible for handling incoming requests. Is also responsible for authenticating and authorizing the request.

- **Location Service** Manages all of the storage stamps, and the account namespace across the stamps. This layer also allocates accounts to storage stamps and manages them across the stamp for disaster recovery and load balancing.

The Location Service tracks and manages the resources used by each storage stamp. When a request for a new storage request comes in, that request contains the location (region) in which to create the account. Based on this information, the Location Service selects the storage stamp within that location best equipped to handle the account and selects that stamp as the primary stamp (based on load across stamps and other criteria).

The Location Service stores the account metadata in the selected stamp, informing the stamp that it is ready to receive requests for that account. The Location Service then updates the DNS, allowing incoming requests to be routed from that account name to that storage stamps VIP (Virtual IP). The VIP is an IP address that the storage stamp exposes for external traffic.

Thus, to use any of the storage services of Azure Storage you must first create an Azure Storage account. Azure Storage accounts can be created using the Azure portal, or by using PowerShell or the Azure CLI.

The New-AzureRmStorageAccount PowerShell cmdlet is used to create a general-purpose storage account that can be used across all the services. For example, it can be used as shown in the code snippet below. Be sure to replace <storageaccountname> and <resourcegroupname> with a valid and available storage account name and resource group in your subscription.

```
New-AzureRmStorageAccount
-ResourceGroupName "<resourcegroupname>"
-Name "<storageaccountname>"
-Location "West US"
-SkuName Standard_LRS
-Kind Storage -EnableEncryptionService Blob
```

The Azure CLI is similar (replacing <storageaccountname> and <resourcegroupname> with a valid and available storage account name and resource group in your subscription):

```
az storage account create --name <storageaccountname> --resource-group
<resourcegroupname> --location eastus --sku Standard_LRS --encryption blob
```

Both PowerShell and the Azure CLI can be executed directly from within the Azure Portal. However, this example shows how to create the Storage account in the Azure portal. Within the portal, select New -> Storage, and then select the Storage account option, which opens the Create Storage Account blade, shown in Figure 3-21.

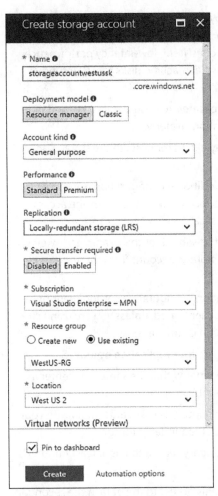

FIGURE 3-21 Creating and configuring an Azure storage account

Configuring Azure storage appropriately is important because there are several options, which can help with performance and availability.

- **Name** The name of the storage account. Must be unique across all existing account names in Azure, and be 3 to 24 characters in length of lowercase letters and numbers.

- **Deployment Model** Use Resource Manager for all new accounts and latest Azure features. Use Classic if you have existing applications in a Classic virtual network.

- **Account Kind** General purpose account provides storage services for blob, files, tables, and queues in a unified account. The other account option, Blob Storage, are specialized for storing blob data.

- **Performance** Standard accounts are backed by magnetic drives and provide the lower cost per GB, and are best used where data is accessed infrequently. Premium storage is backed by SSD (solid state drives) and provide consistent, low-latency performance. Premium storage can only be used with Azure virtual machine disks for I/O intensive applications.

- **Replication** Data in Azure storage is always replicated to ensure durability and high availability. This option selects the type of replication strategy.

- **Secure Transfer Required** When enabled, only allows requests to the storage account via secure connections.

When selecting the Blob Storage Account kind, the additional configuration option of the Access tier is available, with the options of choosing Cool or Hot, which specifies the access pattern for the data, or how frequently the data is accessed.

The Virtual network option is in Preview; thus, it is left disabled for this example. However, this configuration setting grants exclusive access to the storage account from the specified virtual network and subnets.

It should be noted that the Performance and Replication configuration settings cannot be changed once the storage account has been created. As mentioned, unless you are using storage as virtual machine disks, choosing the Standard option is sufficient.

Focusing the Replication configuration option, there are four replication options:

- **Locally Redundant** Replicates your data three times within the same datacenter in the region in which you created the storage account.

- **Zone-Redundant** Replicates your data asynchronously across datacenters with your region in addition to storing three replicas per local redundant storage.

- **Geo-Redundant** Replicates your data to a secondary region that is at least hundreds of miles away from the primary region.

- **Read-Access Geo-Redundant** Provides read-only access to the data in the secondary location in addition to the replication across regions provided by geo-redundant.

In 2014, Azure released the Resource Manager deployment model, which added the concept of a resource group which is essentially a mechanism for grouping resources that share a common lifecycle. The recommended best practice is to use Resource Manager for all new Azure services.

Once the Create storage account page is configured, click Create. It doesn't take long for the account to be created, so the storage account properties and overview panes, shown in Figure 3-22, will open.

The Overview pane contains three sections; the top section is the Essentials section that displays information about the storage account, the middle section shows the services in the storage account (Blobs, Files, Tables, and Queues), and the lower section displays a few graphs to monitor what is happening within the storage account, including total requests, amount of outgoing data, and average latency.

FIGURE 3-22 Azure storage account overview

When the account is created, a set of access keys is generated, a primary and secondary key. Each storage account contains a set of keys, and they can be regenerated if ever compromised. These keys are used to authenticate applications when making requests to the corresponding storage account. These keys should be stored in Azure Key Vault for improved security, and best practice states that the keys be regenerated on a regular basis. Two keys are provided so that you can maintain connections using one key while regenerating the other.

Figure 3-23 shows the Access Keys pane, which shows the two access keys and their corresponding connection strings. When regenerating keys, the corresponding connection strings are also regenerated with the new keys. These keys are used to connect to any of the Azure storage services.

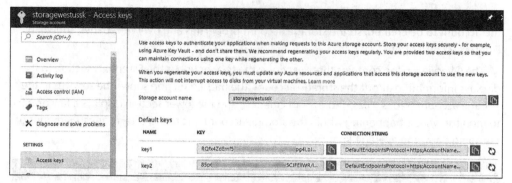

FIGURE 3-23 Retrieving the Azure storage account keys and connection strings

As shown in Figure 3-22, creating an Azure storage account comes with storages services for Blobs, Files, and Queues. Tables is also listed but it is recommended that the new premium Azure table experience be used through Azure Cosmos DB.

Blobs

The Azure Blob service is aimed at storing large amounts of unstructured data and accessed from anywhere. The types of files that can be stored include text files, images, videos, and documents, as well as others. The Blob service is comprised of the following components:

- **Storage Account** The name of the storage account.
- **Container** Groups a set of blobs. All blobs must be in a container.
- **Blob** A file of any time and size.

Thus, a storage account can have one or more containers, and a container can have one or more blobs. An account can contain an unlimited number of containers, and a container can contain an unlimited number of blobs. Think of the structure much like that of Windows Explorer, a folders and files structure with the operating system representing the account.

Because blobs must be in containers, let's look at containers first. Back in the Overview pane for the storage account, shown in Figure 3-22, click the Blobs tile, which opens the Blob service pane, shown in Figure 3-24. The Blob service pane displays information about the storage account and blob service and lists any containers that exist within that storage account. In this example, the storage account has recently been created so no containers have been created yet. To create a container, click the + Container button on the top toolbar in the Blob service pane, shown in Figure 3-24, which opens the New Container dialog shown in Figure 3-25.

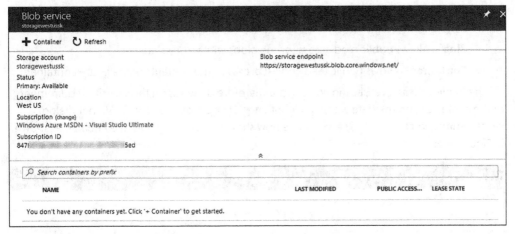

FIGURE 3-24 The Azure blob service pane

Adding and configuring a new container is as simple as providing a container name and specifying a public access level, as you can see in Figure 3-25.

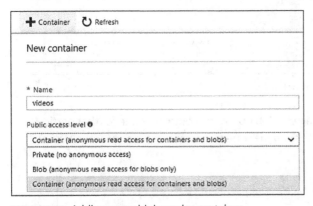

FIGURE 3-25 Adding a new blob service container

Container names must be lower case and begin with a letter or number, and can only contain letters, numbers, and the dash character. Container names must be between three and 63 characters long, and each dash must be immediately preceded by and followed by a letter or number.

As you can see in Figure 3-25, there are three public access level types. The public access level specifies if the data in the container is accessible to the public and how it is accessible.

- **Private**   The default value that specifies that the data within the container is available only to the account owner.
- **Blob**   Allows public read access for the blobs within the container.
- **Container**   Allows public read and list access to the contents of the entire container.

The public access level setting you choose therefore depends on the security requirements of the container and the data within the container. Click OK on the New Container dialog, which returns you to the Blob service pane now showing the newly added container, as shown in Figure 3-26.

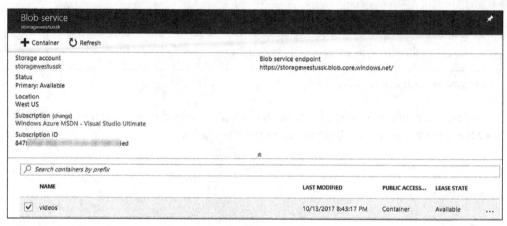

FIGURE 3-26 The blob service pane listing a container

Clicking anywhere on the newly created blob opens the container pane for that particular blob. In Figure 3-27, clicking the Videos container opens the container pane for the Videos container.

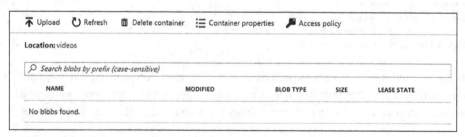

FIGURE 3-27 Listing the contents of the container

The container pane allows you to upload files to the container, delete the container, view the container properties, and more importantly, define access policies. In the container pane, click the Access policy button on the toolbar, which opens the Access policy pane.

The Access policy pane shows defined access policies and if needed, changes the public access level of the container. Leaving the public access level where it is, there should be no policies defined, so click the Add Policy button that opens the Add Policy dialog, shown in Figure 3-28.

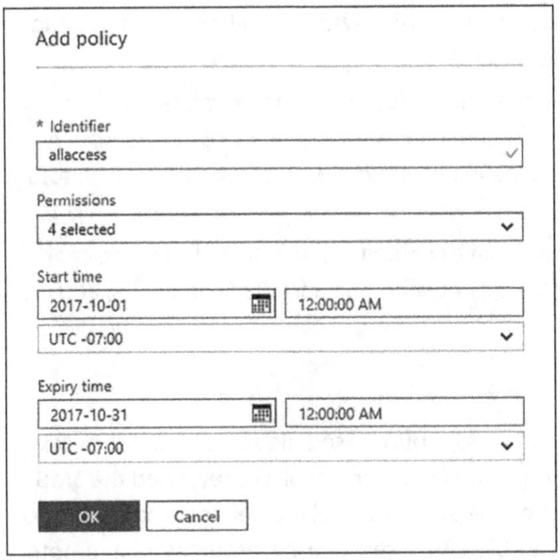

FIGURE 3-28 Defining an access policy on a container

An access policy is defined on a resource, such as in this case, on a container. The policy is used to provide a finer-grained access to the object. When an access policy is applied to a shared access signature (SAS), the shared access signature inherits the constraints of the policy.

For example, in Figure 3-28 the policy is defined with an identifier, with all four permissions selected. The four permissions are Read, Write, Delete, and List. A time limit has also been specified of one month, from 10/1 to 10/31.

A shared access signature provides delegated access to any resource in the storage account without sharing your account keys. This is the point of shared access signatures; it is a secure way to share storage resources without compromising your account keys.

Shared access signatures cannot be created in the Azure portal, but can be created using PowerShell or any of the Azure SDKs including .NET. The idea is that you define the access policy in the portal (as you did in Figure 3-28), and then apply the access policy to a shared access signature to define the level of access.

A few words on blobs before moving on. Azure storage offers three types of blobs:

- **Block**   Ideal for storing text or binary files such as documents, videos, or other media files.

- **Append**   Similar to block blobs but are optimized for append operations, thus useful for logging scenarios.

- **Page**   More efficient for I/O operations, which is why Azure virtual machines use page blogs as operating system and data disks.

Page blobs can be up to 8 TB in size, whereas a single block blob can be made up of up to 50,000 blocks with each block being 100 MB, totaling a bit more than 4.75 TB in total size. A single append block can be made up of up to 50,000 blocks with each block being 4 MB, totaling a little over 195 GB in total size.

Blob naming conventions differ slightly from that of containers, in that a blob name can contain any combination of characters but must be between one and 1024 characters, and are case sensitive.

Files

Azure files provide the ability to create fully managed, cloud-based file shares that are accessible with the industry standard SMB (Server Message Block) protocol. We reviewed the SMB protocol earlier in this chapter, but as a refresher, the SMB protocol is a network sharing protocol implemented in Windows that provides the ability to access files or resources on a remote server or file share and read/write to files on a network computer.

One of the major benefits of Azure files is that the file share can be mounted concurrently both in the cloud as well as on-premises, on Windows, Linux, or macOS. Azure files provide the additional benefit of having additional disk space without the necessity of managing physical servers or other devices and hardware.

Azure File shares are useful when you need to replace, complement, or provide additional storage space to on-premises file servers. Azure file shares can be directly mounted from anywhere in the world, making them highly accessible. Azure Files also enable "lift and shift" scenarios where you want to migrate an on-premises application to the cloud and the application has the requirement of access to a specific folder or file share.

Earlier in this chapter you walked through how to create an Azure File, as seen in Figure 3-4. In the Azure storage overview pane, click the Files tile, which opens the File service pane, shown in Figure 3-29. Earlier you created a file share so that share is listed in the list of file shares.

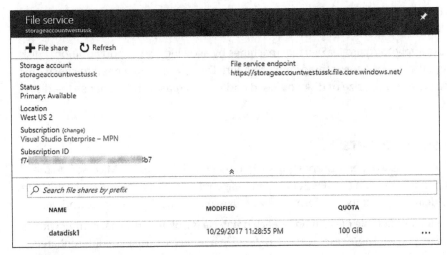

FIGURE 3-29 Azure storage file share

Clicking the file share, open the File Share pane, shown in Figure 3-30. Via the File Share pane you can upload files to the share, add directories, delete the share, update the quota, and obtain the connection information for both Windows and Linux by clicking the Connect button.

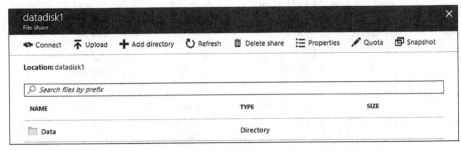

FIGURE 3-30 Adding a folder to the Azure file share

In this example, we added a Data directory that was used earlier to add secondary SQL Server data files. Clicking the directory provides the ability to upload files to that directory, add subdirectories, and delete the directory.

The question then becomes one of when to use what service. When do you decide to use Azure blobs, files, or even disks? Use the following points as a guide.

- **Azure Blobs** Your application needs streaming support or has infrequent access scenarios to unstructured data, which needs to be stored and accessed at scale, plus you need access to your data from anywhere.

- **Azure Files** You have a "lift and shift" scenario and you want minimal to no application changes, or you need to replace or complement existing storage.

Azure Disks apply to Azure IaaS virtual machines by allowing you to add additional disk space through the use of Azure storage. To use Azure Disks, you simply need to specify the performance type and the size of disk you need and Azure creates and manages the disks for you.

Change service tiers

Azure SQL Database is a general-purpose, managed relational database in Microsoft Azure that shares its code base with the SQL Server database engine. As a managed service in Azure, the goal is to deliver predictable performance with dynamic scalability and no downtime.

To achieve the predictable performance, each database is isolated from each other with its defined set of resources. These resources are defined in a service tier that are differentiated by a set of SLA options, including storage size, uptime availability, performance, and price, as detailed in Table 3-1.

TABLE 3-1 Choosing a service tier

	Basic	Standard	Premium	Premium RS
Target workload	Development and Production	Development and Production	Development and Production	*Workloads that can stand data loss
Max. DB Size	2GB	1 TB	4 TB	1 TB
Max DTUs	5	3000	4000	1000
Uptime SLA	99.99%	99.99%	99.99%	**N/A
Backup retention	7 days	35 days	35 days	35 days
CPU	Low	Low, Medium, High	Medium, High	Medium
IO throughput	Low	Medium	Significantly higher than Standard	Same as Premium
IO Latency	Higher than Premium	Higher than Premium	Lower than Basic and Standard	Same as Premium
Columnstore indexing and in-memory OLTP	N/A	N/A	Supported	Supported

*   Data loss is up to 5 minutes due to service failures
**   Not available while Premium RS tier is in preview

Choosing a service tier for our database depends primarily on the storage, uptime, and performance requirements.

DTU

To understand performance in Azure SQL Database is to understand DTUs. DTU, or Database Transaction Unit, is a blended measure of CPU, memory, and I/O. The amount of resources determined per DTU was defined by an OLTP benchmark workload designed and optimized for typical, real-world OLTP workloads. When a performance tier is selected, the DTUs are set aside and dedicated to your database and are not available to any other database, thus the workload of another database does not impact your database or the resources of your database, and likewise your workload does not impact the resources or performance of another database. When your workload exceeds the amount of resources defined by the DTU, your throughput is throttled, resulting in a slower performance and timeouts.

Within each service tier is a set of different performance levels. The following tables (Table 3-2 to Table 3-6) detail the different service tiers and their performance levels.

TABLE 3-2 Basic Service Tier

Performance Level	Basic
Max DTUs	5
Max concurrent logins	30
Max concurrent sessions	300

TABLE 3-3 Standard Service Tier

Performance Level	S0	S1	S2	S3
Max DTUs	10	20	50	100
Max concurrent logins	60	90	120	200
Max concurrent sessions	600	900	1200	2400

TABLE 3-4 Continued Standard Service Tier

Performance Level	S4	S6	S7	S9	S12
Max DTUs	200	400	800	1600	3000
Max concurrent logins	400	800	1600	3200	6000
Max concurrent sessions	4800	9600	19200	30000	30000

TABLE 3-5 Premium Service Tier

Performance Level	P1	P2	P4	P6	P11	P13
Max DTUs	125	250	500	1000	1750	4000
Max concurrent logins	200	400	800	1600	2400	6400
Max concurrent sessions	30000	30000	30000	30000	30000	30000

TABLE 3-6 Premium RS Service Tier

Performance Level	PRS1	PRS2	PRS4	PRS6
Max DTUs	125	250	500	1000
Max concurrent logins	200	400	800	1600
Max concurrent sessions	30000	30000	30000	30000

The Premium RS service Tier was announced and added in early 2017. It is currently in preview and as such the specifics of the tier may change. The Premium RS service tier was specifically designed for I/O intensive workloads that need the premium performance but do not require the highest availability guarantees.

It helps to understand the relative amount of resources between the different performance level and service tiers, and the impact they have on the database performance. The math is quite easy, in that, changing a service tier for a database from a Premium P1 to a Premium P2 doubles the DTUs and increases the performance level of the database by doubling the amount of resources to the database.

As such, as you begin to gain insight into the performance implications a specific service tier has for your database, you should begin to understand the proper service tier your specific database needs and the potential affect that will take place, either positive or negative, as you change between service tiers.

Based on the above information, it should be obvious that you can change service tiers for your database at any time. Setting the initial performance level at database creation time is a good baseline, but workload demand dictates the proper service tier and performance level for your database and thus you can change it as needed.

In fact, a standard practice is to scale the database up during normal business operating hours, and then scale it down during off hours, saving costs dramatically. Changing service tiers has minimal downtime, typically only a few seconds. Thus, scaling a database should be done at proper times when it does not affect users.

Changing a service tier can be done via several methods, including via the Azure portal, T-SQL, and PowerShell. In the Azure portal, select the database for which you want to change the service tier, and in the Overview pane, select the Pricing tier option, as shown in Figure 3-31.

FIGURE 3-31 Configuting the pricing tier for a database

The Configure Performance pane opens, shown in Figure 3-32, which opens showing the current service tier for the database. The top section of the Configure Performance displays the different service tiers via four tabs. The tabs contain a description of the service tier and a start cost for the minimum performance level of that service tier.

In this example, the current service tier is Basic with a maximum storage of 2 GB. Using the slider, we can scale the storage from a maximum of 2 GB to a minimum of 100 MB. For the DTU, the only option is 5 for the Basic service tier so there is no option to change it. Given this configuration, we are then presented with a cost for each item, plus a total monthly cost for the database.

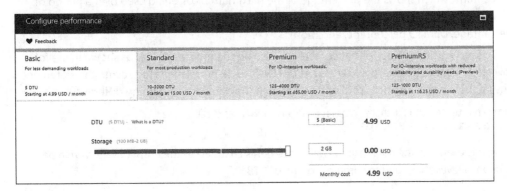

FIGURE 3-32 Configuring performance for a database

To change the service tier and configure a new performance level, simply select the appropriate service tier on the top tabs, and then using the sliders, select the performance tier (DTUs) and storage amount, as shown in Figure 3-33.

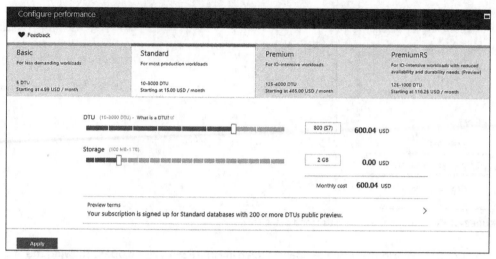

FIGURE 3-33 Changing the performance configuration for a database

Once you have configured your database with the new service tier and performance level, click Apply. Changing the service tier can take anywhere from several minutes to an hour or more depending on the size of the database. Regardless on the length of time, the database will remain online during the change.

A great way to monitor DTU usage for the database is via the DTU usage graph on the Overview pane of the database in the Azure portal. By default, the graph displays the DTU percentage, which shows the percentage of the maximum DTUs being used over a period of time. Clicking on the graph allows you to add additional metrics to the graph, including CPU percentage, Data IO percentage, and more.

The service tier and performance level can also be changed via T-SQL, as shown in the following statement below. You will need ALTER DATABASE permissions to execute the statement. Ensure the database name is correct if you named the database something different.

```
ALTER DATABASE [db1] MODIFY (EDITION = 'Premium', MAXSIZE = 1024 GB,
SERVICE_OBJECTIVE = 'P15');
```

In this example, the database performance tier is changed to the Premium tier with a performance level of P15 and maximum storage of 1 TB.

Review wait statistics

When executing a query, SQL Server requests resources from the system to execute the query. In a heavy workload environment where the database system is extremely busy, these requests might compete for resources and therefore the request might need to wait before proceeding. For example, query B might need to wait for query A to release a lock on a resource it needs.

As reviewed in Chapter 1, "Implement SQL in Azure," SQL Server tracks everything that any operation is waiting on. Thus, SQL Server tracks wait information as wait statistics and summarizes and categorizes this wait information across all connections in order to troubleshoot and monitor performance issues and problems.

SQL Server includes to DMVs (Dynamic Management Views) through which wait statistics are exposed:

- **sys.dm_os_wait_stats**   Aggregated, historical look at the wait statistics for all wait types that have been encountered.
- **sys.dm_os_waiting_tasks**   Wait statistics for currently executing requests that are experiencing resource waits.
- **sys.dm_exec_session_wait_status**   Returns information about all the waits by threads that executed for each session. This view returns the same information that is aggregated in the sys.dm_os_wait_status but for the current session and includes the session_id.

There are more than 900 wait types in SQL Server, all of them important, but some are more important than others. Luckily, this section does not discuss all 900, but review the important and oft-looked at wait stats that can help narrow down performance problems.

Common wait types

The most commonly encountered wait types are listed below. Let's look at what they are and why you might be seeing them listed, and how to address them in some cases.

- **LCK_***   This wait type means that one query is holding locks on an object while another query is waiting to get locks on that same object. For example, one query might be trying to update rows in a table while another query is trying to read them. Blocking is occurring in the system and sessions are waiting to acquire a lock.
- **CXPACKET**   While CXPACKET waits are not necessarily an indication of a problem, they may be a symptom of a different problem. The CXPACKET wait type has to do with parallel query execution and typically is an indication that a SPID is waiting on a parallel query process to start or finish.
- **PAGEIOLATCH_***   These wait types are commonly associated with disk I/O bottlenecks. Typically, this means that SQL Server is waiting to read data pages from storage. If these pages were not cached in memory, SQL Server has to get them from disk. A common root cause of this is a poor performing query or the system not having enough memory.

- **ASYNC_NETWORK_IO** Often incorrectly attributed to network bottlenecks, this wait simply means that SQL Server has the results of a query and is waiting for the application to consume the results. Or in other words, SQL Server is waiting for the client application to consume the results faster because the client app is not processing the results fast enough. The fix for this is usually on the client (application) side.

- **SOS_SCHEDULER_YIELD** This wait signifies that an individual task needs more CPU time. The query could finish faster if it could get more CPU power and the query needs more CPU resources; it does not mean your server needs more CPU. If this wait type appears frequently, look for reasons why the CPU is under pressure. Addressing this issue involves relieving CPU pressure by upgrading the hardware and/or removing existing CPU pressure.

- **OLEDB** Means that the SPID has made a call to an OLEDB provider and is waiting for the data to be returned. Addressing this wait type includes checking Disk secs/Read and Disk secs/Write for bandwidth bottlenecks and adding additional I/O bandwidth if necessary. Also, inspect the T-SQL for RPC and linked server calls which can sometimes cause bottlenecks.

- **WRITELOG** Similar to the PAGEIOLATCH, this is a disk I/O bottleneck for the transaction log. As insert/update/delete operations take place, SQL Server writes those transactions to the transaction log and is waiting for an acknowledgement from the transaction log of the write request. This wait means that the transaction log is having a hard time keeping up for several reasons, including a high VLF count or a high frequency of commits.

- **PAGELATCH_*** This wait pertains to non-IO waits for latches on data pages in the buffer pool. Frequently associated with allocation contention issues, this commonly occurs in tempdb when a large number of objects are being created and destroyed in tempdb and the system experiences contention.

- **THREADPOOL** This thread is specific to the internal thread scheduling mechanism within SQL Server, and means that there are no available threads in the server's thread pool, which can lead to queries not being run.

There are a few more DMVs that can help in understanding these waits and why you might be seeing these wait.

- **sys.dm_exec_requests** Returns information about each request that is currently executing within SQL Server

- **sys.dm_exec_sql_text** Returns the text of the SQL batch that is identified by the specified SQL_handle.

- **sys.dm_exec_text_query_plan** Returns the Showplan in text format for a T-SQL batch or for a specific statement within the batch.

Let's put this to the test. The following query loops 500 times and executes several select statements and executes a couple of stored procedures each loop. It generates random numbers so that different plans are potentially generated each execution. The following block of code is executed against the WideWorldImporters database for SQL Server 2016.

```
DECLARE @counter int, @id int, @id2 int, @date_from DATETIME, @date_to DATETIME;
SET @counter = 1;
WHILE @counter < 501
    BEGIN
        SET @id = (SELECT CAST(RAND() * 1000 AS INT))
        SET @id2 = (SELECT CAST(RAND() * 100 AS INT))
        SET @date_from = '2013-01-01';
        SET @date_to = '2016-05-31';

        SELECT * FROM sales.orders where OrderID = @id
        SELECT * FROM sales.Invoices where OrderID = @id
        SELECT * FROM sales.Invoices where CustomerID = @id2

        SET @date_from = ((@date_from + (ABS(CAST(CAST( NewID() AS BINARY(8)) AS INT)) %
CAST((@date_to - @date_from) AS INT))))
        SET @date_to = DATEADD(m, 1, @date_from)

        EXEC [Integration].[GetOrderUpdates] @date_from, @date_to
        EXEC [Website].[SearchForCustomers] 'GU', 100

        SET @counter = @counter + 1
    END;
GO
```

Before running this code, open a second query window in SQL Server Management Studio and execute the following query. This query is a simple query that shows current session waits and the T-SQL that is causing the wait.

```
SELECT ws.*, t.text
FROM sys.dm_exec_session_wait_stats ws
INNER JOIN sys.dm_exec_requests er ON ws.session_id = er.session_id
CROSS APPLY sys.dm_exec_sql_text(er.sql_handle) t
```

You should only see a small handful of rows that should be of no concern, so now you can execute the big block of code. Once this code is executing, it runs for several minutes. While it is running, go back to the second query window and execute the DMV query again, and this time you should see a few more rows returned showing new waits and that the cause of the wait is the execution of the stored procedure GetOrderUpdates, as shown in Figure 3-34.

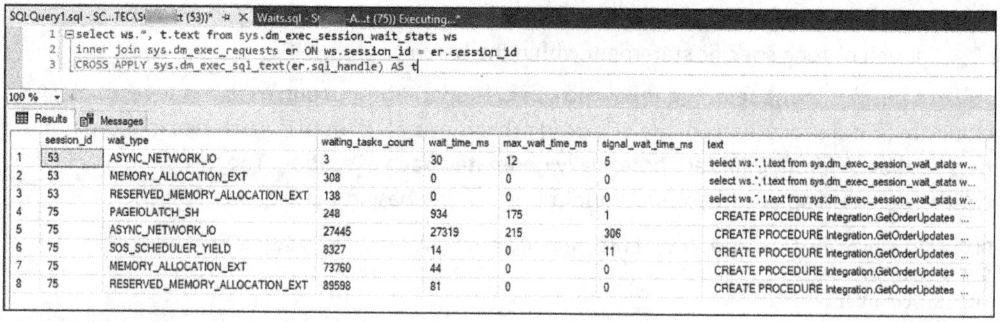

```
SQLQuery1.sql - SC...TEC\S(    t (53))*  + X  Waits.sql - St   -A...t (75)) Executing..."
    1 ⊟select ws.*, t.text from sys.dm_exec_session_wait_stats ws
    2  inner join sys.dm_exec_requests er ON ws.session_id = er.session_id
    3  CROSS APPLY sys.dm_exec_sql_text(er.sql_handle) AS t|
```

	session_id	wait_type	waiting_tasks_count	wait_time_ms	max_wait_time_ms	signal_wait_time_ms	text
1	53	ASYNC_NETWORK_IO	3	30	12	5	select ws.*, t.text from sys.dm_exec_session_wait_stats w...
2	53	MEMORY_ALLOCATION_EXT	308	0	0	0	select ws.*, t.text from sys.dm_exec_session_wait_stats w...
3	53	RESERVED_MEMORY_ALLOCATION_EXT	138	0	0	0	select ws.*, t.text from sys.dm_exec_session_wait_stats w...
4	75	PAGEIOLATCH_SH	248	934	175	1	CREATE PROCEDURE Integration.GetOrderUpdates ...
5	75	ASYNC_NETWORK_IO	27445	27319	215	306	CREATE PROCEDURE Integration.GetOrderUpdates ...
6	75	SOS_SCHEDULER_YIELD	8327	14	0	11	CREATE PROCEDURE Integration.GetOrderUpdates ...
7	75	MEMORY_ALLOCATION_EXT	73760	44	0	0	CREATE PROCEDURE Integration.GetOrderUpdates ...
8	75	RESERVED_MEMORY_ALLOCATION_EXT	89598	81	0	0	CREATE PROCEDURE Integration.GetOrderUpdates ...

FIGURE 3-34 Using Dynamic Management vVew to view wait statistics

Notice that the waits returned are many of the ones listed above, with the biggest culprit being the ASYNC_NETWORK_IO wait, due to the fact that it returns the results of each statement to the SSMS and the UI can't keep up. By letting it run longer and rerunning the DMV query, you'll see that the ASYNC_NETWORK_IO wait is still high, but the SOS_SCHEDULER_YIELD wait is starting to creep up, as shown in Figure 3-35.

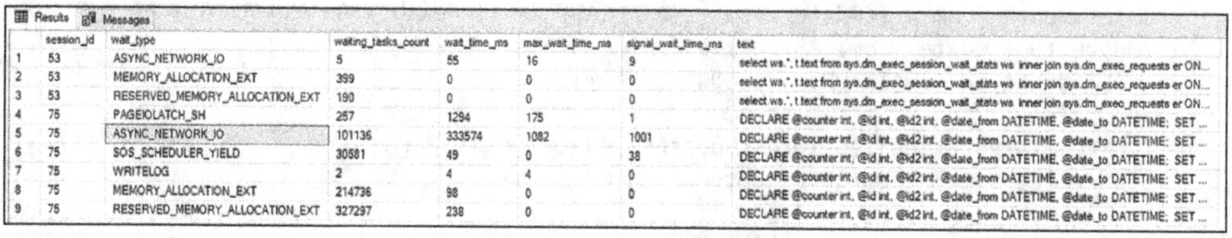

	session_id	wait_type	waiting_tasks_count	wait_time_ms	max_wait_time_ms	signal_wait_time_ms	text
1	53	ASYNC_NETWORK_IO	5	55	16	9	select ws.*, t.text from sys.dm_exec_session_wait_stats ws inner join sys.dm_exec_requests er ON...
2	53	MEMORY_ALLOCATION_EXT	399	0	0	0	select ws.*, t.text from sys.dm_exec_session_wait_stats ws inner join sys.dm_exec_requests er ON...
3	53	RESERVED_MEMORY_ALLOCATION_EXT	190	0	0	0	select ws.*, t.text from sys.dm_exec_session_wait_stats ws inner join sys.dm_exec_requests er ON...
4	75	PAGEIOLATCH_SH	257	1294	175	1	DECLARE @counter int, @id int, @id2 int, @date_from DATETIME, @date_to DATETIME: SET ...
5	75	ASYNC_NETWORK_IO	101136	333574	1082	1001	DECLARE @counter int, @id int, @id2 int, @date_from DATETIME, @date_to DATETIME: SET ...
6	75	SOS_SCHEDULER_YIELD	30581	49	0	38	DECLARE @counter int, @id int, @id2 int, @date_from DATETIME, @date_to DATETIME: SET ...
7	75	WRITELOG	2	4	4	0	DECLARE @counter int, @id int, @id2 int, @date_from DATETIME, @date_to DATETIME: SET ...
8	75	MEMORY_ALLOCATION_EXT	214736	98	0	0	DECLARE @counter int, @id int, @id2 int, @date_from DATETIME, @date_to DATETIME: SET ...
9	75	RESERVED_MEMORY_ALLOCATION_EXT	327297	238	0	0	DECLARE @counter int, @id int, @id2 int, @date_from DATETIME, @date_to DATETIME: SET ...

FIGURE 3-35 Monitoring waits using Dynamic Management View

We also see the WRITELOG wait appear in the second execution of the DMVs, but the numbers are low so it is not a concern. The SOS_SCHEDULER_YIELD wait might be a concern depending on the application and workload, so this one would need to continue to be monitored.

Simply monitoring waits for a few seconds does not yield a true measure of what is going on, but it is a baseline and the idea is to continue to monitor these waits over a period of time, even a week or more depending on the scenario.

These waits apply to both on-premises SQL Server as well as SQL Server in an Azure VM in Azure IaaS. As pointed out in Chapter 1, the one major difference is that I/O performance tends to be more of a focus, thus the I/O waits should be monitored frequently.

Azure SQL Database has a similar DMV called sys.dm_db_wait_stats that returns information about all the waits encountered by threads during execution at the database level. This DMV shows the waits that have completed and does not show current waits. The majority of the same wait types that exist in SQL Server also exist in Azure SQL Database and are grouped by the type of waits.

- **Resource Waits** Occur when a work requests access to a resource that is not available because it is in use by another worker. For example, locks, latches, and disk I/O waits.
- **Queue Waits** Occurs when a worker is idle and waiting to be assigned.
- **External Waits** Occurs when SQL Server is waiting for an external event, such as a linked server query or an extended stored procedure to complete.

Manage storage pools

Windows Server 2012 introduced a concept and functionality called storage pools, which is the ability to group physical disks together to form a pool of resource storage. The idea is that a pool is created and empty disks are added to the pool. Once the pool is created, virtual disks can then be created called storage spaces from the available capacity in the storage pools.

This can be done both on-premises as well as in an Azure IaaS virtual machine, and the following example demonstrates how to create and manage a pool in an Azure virtual machine running Windows Server.

To begin with, we use a Windows Server virtual machine that was previously created. In the Azure portal, in the Overview pane, click the Disks option, which lists the default operating system disk, but no additional data disks have been added, as seen in Figure 3-36.

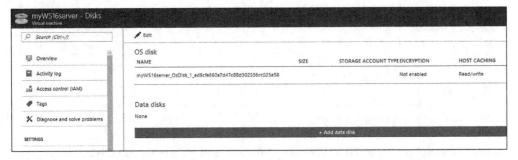

FIGURE 3-36 The managed disks blade in the Azure portal

To add additional data disks, click the Add Data Disk link at the bottom of the Disks pane in the blue bar, which provides the option to create a disk, as shown in Figure 3-37.

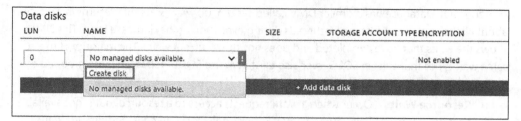

FIGURE 3-37 Creating a new managed disk in the Azure portal

Click the Create Disk link and the Create Managed Disk pane will display, as shown in Figure 3-38. In the Create Managed Disk dialog, enter a disk name, and provide the Resource Group, Account Type, Source Type, and Disk Size.

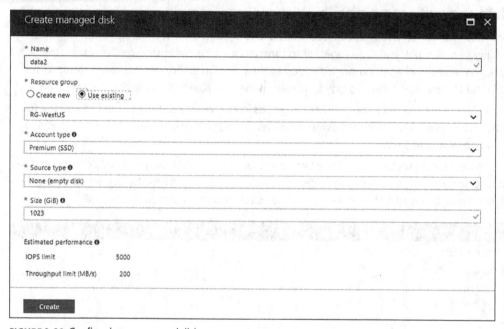

FIGURE 3-38 Configuring a managed disk

The Account Type lets you select between premium SSD disks or standard HDD disks. Because these are used as drives in virtual machines, the best option is to select premium SSD for better performance. The Source Type gives the option to create the disk from an existing source, including a snapshot of another disk, a blob in a storage account, or just to create an empty disk from no source. Select the None option to create an empty disk. Leave the default size set to 1,023 GB, or 1 TB, and then click Create. This adds the disk to the list of Data disks in the Data Disks pane.

Repeat this process to add a few more disks, as shown in Figure 3-39, and then click Save on the Disks blade to save the disks to the virtual machine.

| Data disks | | | | | |
LUN	NAME	SIZE	STORAGE ACCOUNT TYPE	ENCRYPTION	HOST CACHING
0	data2	1023 GiB	Premium_LRS	Not enabled	Read-only
1	data3	1023 GiB	Premium_LRS	Not enabled	Read-only
2	data4	1023 GiB	Premium_LRS	Not enabled	Read-only
3	log2	1023 GiB	Premium_LRS	Not enabled	Read-only
		+ Add data disk			

FIGURE 3-39 Saving managed disks

At this point, the focus is now on creating and managing the storage pool, which is done within the virtual machine. Close the Disks blade in the portal and click the Connect button on the toolbar in the Overview pane, which downloads an RDP file for the VM and prompts you to log into the virtual machine. Be sure that the VM is started, or start it if it has not been started.

Log into the virtual machine and the Server Manager dashboard automatically opens, with the File And Storage Services option in the upper left of the dashboard, as seen in Figure 3-40.

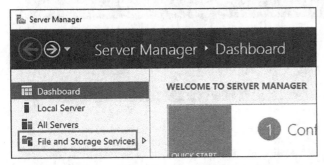

FIGURE 3-40 Windows Server Manager dashboard

The File and Storage Services is one of the many roles within Windows Server and requires nothing but a full and working installation of the operating system. The File and Storage Services within the dashboard lists all disks and volumes currently on the machine. Click File And Storage Services, and the Storage Pools option is presented in the upper left of the dashboard, as shown in Figure 3-41.

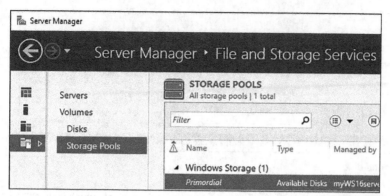

FIGURE 3-41 Working with storage pools in Windows Server Manager

The Storage Pools page of the dashboard shows three windows: the list of available virtual disks, the available physical disks, and the existing storage pools, as shown in Figure 3-42.

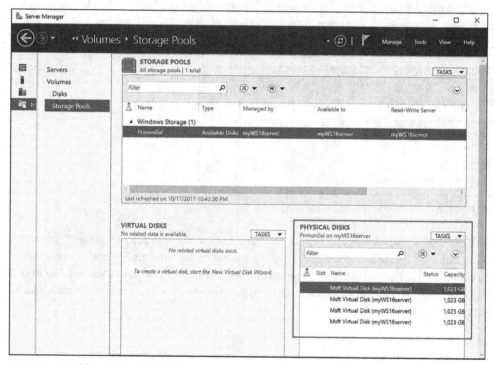

FIGURE 3-42 Adding physical disks to a storage pool

The physical disks section of the Storage Pools page shows the four disks created in the Azure portal, which are deemed "primordial," meaning the physical disks have been added to the server, but not yet added to a storage space. Notice the disks show up as physical disks in the storage dashboard, but they do not show up as disks in Windows Explorer, as seen in Figure 3-43. This is because they have been added to the storage space and a new volume has not been created.

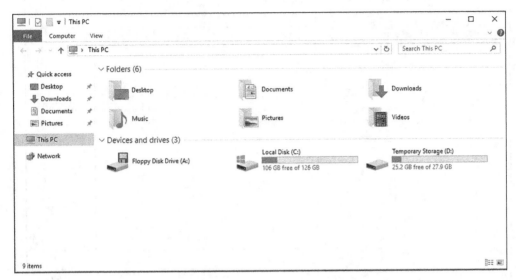

FIGURE 3-43 Local drives in Windows Explorer

The first step is to create a storage pool by clicking Tasks in the upper right of the Storage Pools window, and selecting New Storage Pool, shown in Figure 3-44.

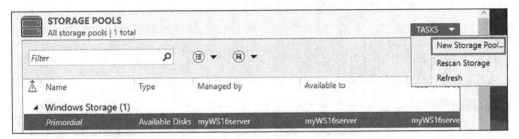

FIGURE 3-44 Adding a new storage pool

In the New Storage Pool Wizard, click Next on the Before You Begin page, and then on the Storage Pool Name page, provide a name for the new storage pool, as shown in Figure 3-45. The page also lists the initial primordial pool from which the storage pools and storage spaces can be created.

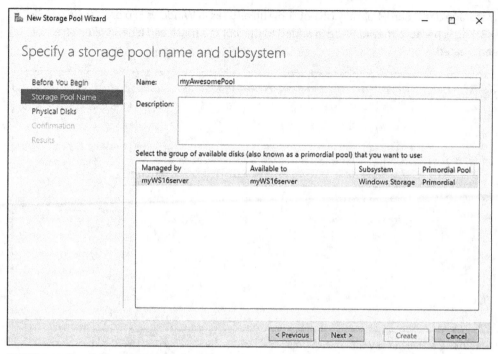

FIGURE 3-45 Specifying a storage pool name

Click next to select the physical disks to add to the storage pool. The four disks created earlier are listed. Select them all, as shown in Figure 3-46.

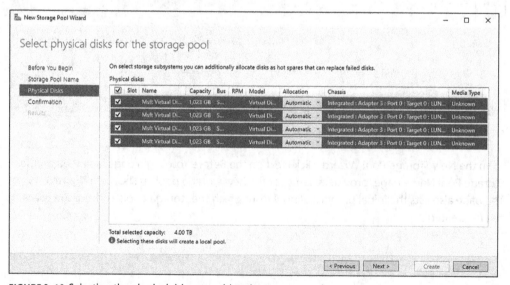

FIGURE 3-46 Selecting the physical drives to add to the storage pool

The Allocation option, when selecting the physical disks, provides three options: Automatic, Hot Spare, and Manual. The allocation options are the default, and the disk space is allocated automatically. If you want to designate a disk as a hot spare, select Hot Spare. A hot spare disk is a disk or group of disks used to automatically or manually replace a failing, or failed, disk.

Click next to go to the Confirmation page of the wizard, and click Create on the Confirmation page. After a minute or so the storage pool is created containing the four physical disks, and the wizard displays the Results page. Click Close on the New Storage Pool Wizard. At this point all that exists is a storage pool containing the four disks, but it is not useful, so the next task is to create a new virtual disk from the storage pool resources.

Thus, right-click the New Storage Pool, and select New Virtual Disk, as shown in Figure 3-47.

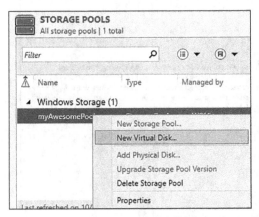

FIGURE 3-47 Creating a new virtual disk from the storage pool

You are first prompted to select the storage pool from which to create the virtual disk. Select the Storage Pool you just created, and click OK. The New Virtual Disk Wizard begins with the Before You Begin page explaining what a virtual disk is and what the wizard does. Click next to take you to the Virtual Disk Name page, and supply a name for the virtual disk and an optional description, and click Next.

The next step of the New Virtual Disk Wizard is the Enclosure Awareness page. Enclosure awareness in storage spaces store copies of your data on separate storage enclosures to ensure resiliency to the entire closure if it fails. The Enclosure Awareness page of the wizard prompts you to enable enclosure awareness, but this option is only enabled if your server has at least three enclosures and the physical disks in each enclosure must have automatic allocation. If this option is disabled in the wizard, click Next.

The Storage Layout page defines the resiliency of the data and this page of the wizard prompts you to select the storage layout by selecting one of three options: Simple, Mirror, or Parity.

- **Simple** Data is striped across physical disks, maximizing capacity and throughput, but has decreased reliability. Requires at least one disk and does not protect from disk failure.

- **Mirror**   Data is striped across physical disks, creating multiple copies of your data which increases reliability. Use at least two disks to protect against single disk failure, and use at least five disks to protect against two disk failures.

- **Parity**   Data and parity information are striped across physical disks, increasing reliability but reducing capacity and performance to a degree. Use at least three disks to protect against single disk failure, and use at least seven disks to protect against two disk failures.

Figure 3-48 shows the Mirror option selected to ensure data reliability. Click Next.

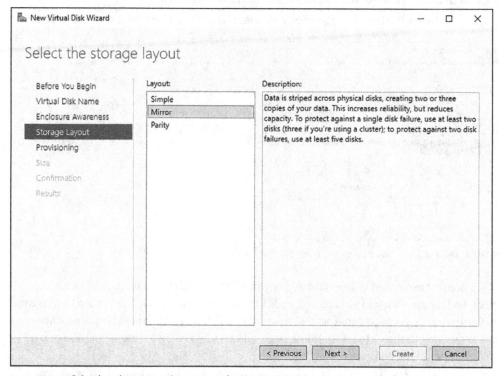

FIGURE 3-48 Selecting the storage layout type for the virtual disk

The Provisioning page of the wizard prompts you to select the provisioning type. The provisioning type has to do with how the disk is provisioned and the space on the disk allocated. The two options are Fixed and Thin.

- **Fixed**   The volume uses all the storage resources from the storage pool equal to the volume size (specified on the next page of the wizard).

- **Thin**   The volume uses storage resources from the storage pool as needed, up to the volume size (specified on the next page of the wizard).

This provisioning optimizes the utilization of available storage by over-subscribing capacity with "just-in-time" allocation, meaning, the pool size used by the virtual disk is the size of the files on the disk. This helps reduce fragmentation tremendously. Fixed, on the other hand, acquires the specified capacity at disk creation time for the best performance, but is more apt to fragmentation.

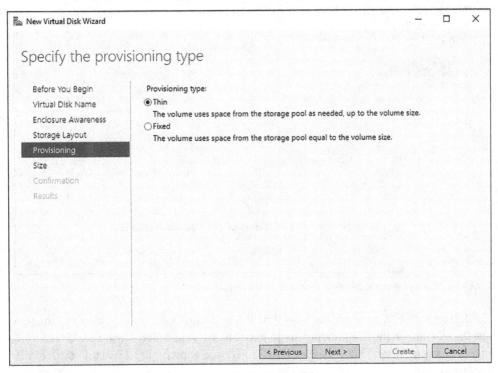

FIGURE 3-49 Configuring the provisioning type for the virtual disk

Depending on the selection made on this page of the wizard determines the options available on the Size page of the wizard. Selecting Thin on the Provisioning page does not allow you to specify the Maximum size on following page of the wizard.

Selecting the Maximum provisioning type allows you to either specify the Maximum size of the disk, or allow you to specify a size up to the available free space. In Figure 3-49 the Thin option is specified, and the Specify size option is selected in the Size page of the wizard, as shown in Figure 3-50. This allows the volume to use the storage pool resources as needed until the 2 TB is used (the value specified in the Specify size option).

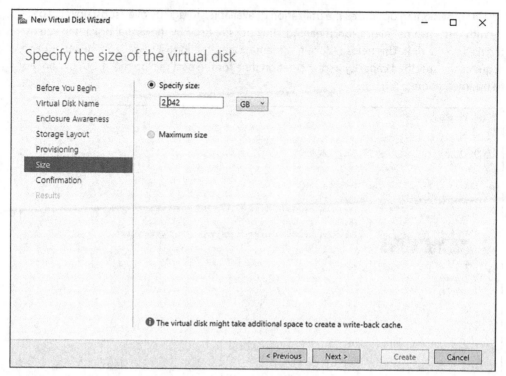

FIGURE 3-50 Specifying the available disk space for the virtual disk

Click Next on the Size page of the New Virtual Disk Wizard, taking you to the Confirmation page. Click Create on the Confirmation page to create the virtual disk, which should take a few seconds. Once the virtual disk is created, the Results page appears displaying the status of the virtual disk creation.

At this point the virtual disk has been created based on the disk resources in the storage pool, but it is not usable yet because a volume needs to be created from the virtual disk.

At the bottom of the Results page, the check box Create A Volume When This Wizard Closes should automatically be checked. Leave it checked and click Close for the New Virtual Disk Wizard. The New Volume Wizard automatically begins, and just like the previous two wizards, begins with a Before You Begin page. Click Next on this page to take you to the Server And Disk selection page, shown in Figure 3-51.

On the Server And Disk selection page, ensure the proper server and disk is selected, and then click Next. The disk should be the virtual disk just created and the server should be the server to which you are adding the volume.

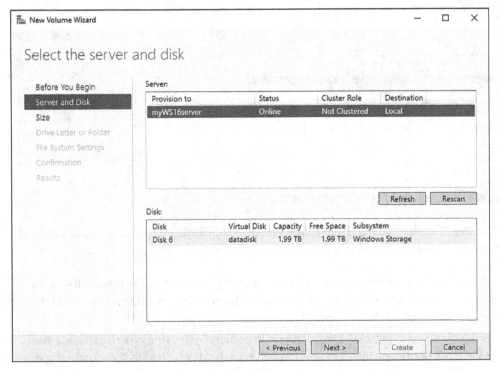

FIGURE 3-51 Creating a new volume from the virtual disk

On the Size page, specify the size of the volume being created. The Volume size defaults to the maximum space available on the virtual disk but you can change the size and the size type (TB, GB, or MB). Click Next.

On the Drive Letter page, specify a drive letter or whether you want to use this volume as a mount point in an empty NTFS folder on another volume. For this example, select Drive Letter and select an available drive letter, and then click next.

On the File System Settings page, select the File System type, which defines the format of the file system. Available options are NTFS and Resilient File System. Select NTFS, and then select the appropriate allocation unit size, and specify the volume label. For SQL Server, the format should be NTFS and supports sizes of 512, 1024, 2048, 4096, 8192, 16K, 32K, and 64K. The allocation unit is the smallest amount of space that a file can consume, and for SQL Server, the best setting for the allocation unit size should be at least 64K for OLTP workloads, and 256K for data warehouse workloads. SQL Server does I/O in extents, which is 8x8 pages, thus, 64K.

Provide a name for the volume (the Volume label), and then click Next.

On the Confirmation page, make sure the configuration settings are correct and click OK to create the new volume. The new volume is now available, as shown in both Windows Explorer and the Server Manager Dashboard, as shown in Figure 3-52.

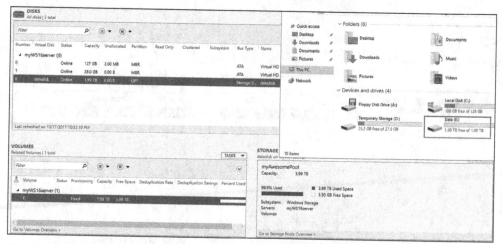

FIGURE 3-52 The new volume created from the storage pool and virtual disk

We can add and remove physical disks to an existing pool, and we can remove the virtual disk if needed without messing with the storage in the pool. However, the pool cannot be deleted until the virtual disk is removed.

Using storage pools instead of a traditional operating system striping brings many advantages in terms of manageability and performance. It is recommended that you use storage pools in both on-premises and Azure virtual machines.

Recover from failed storage

Hardware reliability has drastically improved over the last decade or so. With the improvements in drive, storage, and memory technologies, among others, not only has performance increased significantly, but their dependability has provided the needed confidence to run enterprise-level applications.

However, hardware is not perfect and will eventually fail. Reasons for failure range from anything between normal wear and tear to environmental factors and malicious behavior. As such, applications must be able to recover from such failures, including applications such as SQL Server.

And while hardware reliability and dependability have improved, and SQL Server continues to make improvements and enhancements, data loss is unacceptable, regardless of the layer it is caused by. As such, proper strategies need to be in place to be able to recover from the unexpected failure of hardware, especially disk and storage, and insure data integrity within SQL Server.

Recovering from failed storage constitutes a two-phase approach; first, the recovery of the storage system and bringing it back online, and second, the restoration of SQL Server and bringing its databases back online in a transactionally consistent state. This section discusses the second phase of recovering from failed storage, which focuses on ensuring that SQL Server and its database can recover from any failure.

Checking database corruption

A huge part of database recovery is proactively checking for database corruption long before corruption happens. Database corruption at a high level is defined as a problem associated with the storage of the actual data at the disk or IO sub-system level. In the majority of cases, corruption is due to problems due to hardware failures, either with the drives, controllers, or even software drivers.

A key tool in a proper recovery strategy is the DBCC CHECKDB function, which checks the logical and physical integrity of all the objects in a specified database. When recovering from any type of failure, including corruption caused by failed storage, you need to know where the corruption is in the database in order to fix it. Running CHECKDB returns a detailed report as to the overall health and integrity and highlight issues. Review it thoroughly to understand what the issues are and where the corruption is. CHECKDB provides the necessary information as to what the problem is, and in what object the corruption exists. A more detailed look at CHECKDB can be found later in Skill 3.2.

Database backups

The biggest part of recovering from failed storage is the ability to restore the databases to a proper functioning state with as little data loss as possible. This means having an appropriate backup and restore strategy that is frequently tested to ensure a recovery that is as smooth and painless as possible. The last thing you want is to find out in the middle of a production recovery situation that you have no backups or that your backups are worthless.

Backup and restore strategies should be customized to each particular environment, taking into consideration including available resources, and server and database workloads. A well-designed backup and restore strategy maximizes data availability while minimizing data loss.

A backup strategy defines the type and frequency of backups, taking into account the nature and speed of the hardware, how the backups are to be tested, and where and how the backups are to be stored.

As a rule of thumb, database backups should follow these best practices:

- **Full backups**   In most cases, a full database backup should be performed weekly. These can be performed online.
- **Differential**   Based on the most recent, previous full backup, a differential backup captures only the data that has changed since that full back.
- **Transaction log backups**   Transaction logs contain all of the recent activity and can be used to restore a database back to a specific point in time. They also can be performed online

- **System databases** System databases contain important details about logins, jobs, and, depending on your installation, SSIS and other critical information. As such, you might consider backing system databases up nightly or every other night.

A backup strategy is incomplete without backing up the system databases. The system databases contain a lot of information, such as system configuration and SQL Server job information. Depending on how frequent your database changes are, you might consider a daily or weekly backup frequency.

An optimal backup strategy depends on many factors that are specific to each environment, but at the minimum the following aspects should be considered:

- The frequency at which data changes.
- Size of the database and the amount of disk space a full backup takes.
- Are database changes concentrated on a small subset of tables or a broader part of the database?
- Your RPO/RTO requirements.

The frequency at which a database ought to be backed up should be based on your RPO and RTO requirements. RPO (Recovery Point Objective) is the point in time to which you can recover data, meaning, it is the acceptable amount of data loss. RTO (Recovery Time Objective) is how much time you have to bring up a system form the time a disaster occurs.

Your backups will depend on what your RPO is. For example, if your RPO is 15 minutes, you should take backups every 15 minutes or less. Determining your RPO will come down to where your business can restart and carry on. This information becomes the key component of your organization's risk appetite and helps in determining the amount of money your organization is willing to spend on resilience. Every backup strategy and recovery plan should be comprised of both a RPO and RTO.

An effective backup and restore strategy includes proper planning, implementation, and testing. A backup strategy is not effective unless you have successfully restored the databases and tested them in a restore situation.

An old IT adage states: "A DBA is only as good as their last backup." In order to recover from any failure, especially hardware, a good backup, and restore strategy is necessary, if not required. Once the storage is brought back online, following your restore strategy should get you back up and running.

The section "Verify Database Integrity" in Skill 3.2 discusses both the CHECKDB function and restoring a database to recover from corruption in more detail.

Skill 3.2: Perform database maintenance

Database maintenance is a critical aspect in keeping a database running and performing properly and smoothly. Regular data maintenance consists of performing a set of tasks with the intent of ensuring proper data performance, database availability, and resilience is maintained, appropriate security is in place to ensure the integrity of the data, and more. This skill deals with the performance maintenance aspects of a database and the tasks necessary to ensure proper database performance.

> **This skill covers how to:**
> - Monitor DMVs
> - Maintain indexes
> - Automate maintenance tasks
> - Update statistics
> - Verify database integrity
> - Recover from database corruption

Monitor DMVs

SQL Server comes with a set of DMVs (dynamic management views) to diagnose and troubleshoot performance problems. Technically, they are called DMOs (Dynamic Management Objects), which are either views or functions. In this section, the DMO views that focus on performance are categorized as follows:

- Database
- Execution
- Index and IO
- Transaction

Index and IO DMVs can be broken out into their own category, as seen in the Microsoft documentation, but for purposes here they are combined for simplicity. The following sections discuss the more commonly used DMVs.

Database

There are 10 DMVs that are specifically related to database performance information, plus another five that are specific to Azure SQL Database and SQL Data Warehouse. The three most commonly used DMVs to assist in database performance are listed here.

- **sys.dm_db_file_space_usage**   Returns information about the space used for each file in the database.

- **sys.dm_db_partition_stats**   Returns page and row count information for each partition in the selected database.

- **sys.dm_db_session_space_usage**   Returns the number of pages allocated and deallocated by each session for the database. This is applicable only to the tempdb database.

The following query uses the sys.dm_db_partition_stats DMV to return the size of the database in MB.

```
SELECT SUM(reserved_page_count)*8.0/1024 AS DBSize
FROM sys.dm_db_partition_stats;
GO
```

The sys.dm_db_partition_stats DMV provides information about the space used to store and manage row data and is therefore useful for also providing information on the size used by individual objects within the database. This information can be used to determine how quickly the database is growing and specifically how quickly objects are growing to determine if we have further partitions that need to be created to improve performance.

As mentioned, there are a few DMVs unique to Azure SQL Database and Data Warehouse, and the most commonly used three are listed below.

- **sys.dm_db_wait_stats**   Returns information about all the waits encountered.

- **sys.dm_db_resources_stats**   Returns CPU, I/O, and memory consumption information for an Azure SQL Database, one row for every 16 seconds.

- **sys.dm_db_operation_stats**   Returns information about operations performed on the database.

An interesting piece of information is that the SQL Database monitoring graph in the Azure portal obtains much of its information from these DMVs. One of the graphs in the portal shows DTU utilization, and DTUs are based on CPU, I/O, and memory. Thus, the DTU utilization metric in the monitoring graph uses the sys.dm_db_resources_stats DMV for much of its information.

Likewise, the information in the sys.dm_db_resources_stats DMV could be used to determine the percentage of DTU usage for the selected database.

```
SELECT end_time,
(SELECT Max(v)
FROM (VALUES (avg_cpu_percent), (avg_data_io_percent), (avg_log_write_percent)) AS
value(v)) AS [avg_DTU_percent]
FROM sys.dm_db_resource_stats;
```

Execution

There are over 40 DMVs that provide insight into execution-related activity within the database. However, only a handful are commonly used to troubleshoot database performance, which focus primarily on query execution and are listed below.

- **sys.dm_exec_query_stats** Provides aggregated performance statistics for cached query plans.

- **sys.dm_exec_session_wait_stats** Provides information about all the waits encountered by threads that executed for each session.

- **sys.dm_exec_sql_text** Shows the plain text of the SQL batch identified by the SQL_handle.

- **sys.dm_exec_query_plan** Shows the Showplan in XML format for the SQL batch provided in the sql_handle.

- **sys.dm_exec_requests** Returns information about every request currently executing within the SQL Server.

- **sys.dm_exec_sessions** Shows one row per authenticated session on SQL Server. This is a server-scoped view containing information about all active user connections and tasks.

- **sys.dm_exec_text_query_plan** Returns the query plan in text format for a T-SQL batch or a specific statement within the batch.

- **sys.dm_exec_connections** Displays detailed connection information for each established connection to the instance of SQL Server.

A couple of these can be put to use by using a query shown in Skill 3.1 that loops a few hundred times executing several SELECT statements and executing a couple of stored procedures.

```
DECLARE @counter int, @id int, @id2 int, @date_from DATETIME, @date_to DATETIME;
SET @counter = 1;
WHILE @counter < 501
    BEGIN
        SET @id = (SELECT CAST(RAND() * 1000 AS INT))
        SET @id2 = (SELECT CAST(RAND() * 100 AS INT))
        SET @date_from = '2013-01-01';
        SET @date_to = '2016-05-31';

        SELECT * FROM sales.orders where OrderID = @id
        SELECT * FROM sales.Invoices where OrderID = @id
        SELECT * FROM sales.Invoices where CustomerID = @id2

        SET @date_from = ((@date_from + (ABS(CAST(CAST( NewID() AS BINARY(8)) AS INT))
% CAST((@date_to - @date_from) AS INT))))
        SET @date_to = DATEADD(m, 1, @date_from)

        EXEC [Integration].[GetOrderUpdates] @date_from, @date_to
        EXEC [Website].[SearchForCustomers] 'GU', 100

        SET @counter = @counter + 1
    END;
GO
```

With the above query running in SQL Server Management Studio against the Wide-WorldImporters database, open another query window and execute the following T-SQL, which queries the sys.dm_exec_requests DMV to look for any pending requests that are pending. The DMV is joined to the sys.dm_exec_sql_text to find out the exact T-SQL statement that is awaiting execution.

```
SELECT er.session_id, er.status, er.blocking_session_id, er.wait_type, er.wait_time,
er.wait_resource,
er.transaction_id, dest.text
FROM sys.dm_exec_requests er
CROSS APPLY sys.dm_exec_sql_text(er.sql_handle) AS dest
WHERE er.status = N'suspended'
```

Executing this query shows that there is one request pending, as shown in Figure 3-53.

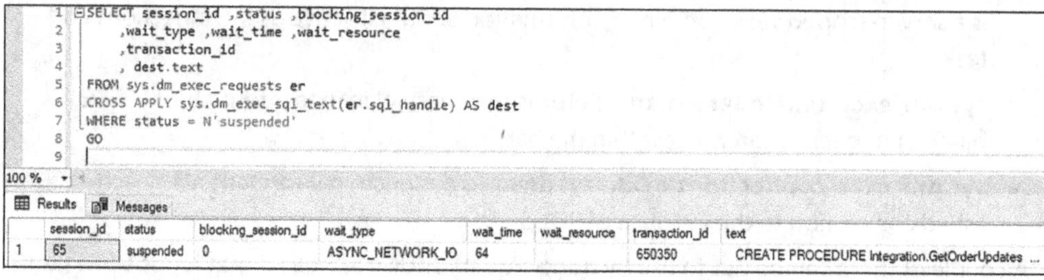

FIGURE 3-53 Using Dynamic Management View to show pending requests

What is also returned in the query results is the wait type that provides additional information as to why the statement is pending.

In addition to knowing what is being run in the database, it is good to know who is connected and what they are doing. To find this information out you can use the sys.dm_exec_session and sys.dm_exec_connections DMVs, as shown in the following query.

```
SELECT
ec.client_net_address,
es.program_name,
es.host_name,
COUNT(ec.session_id) AS connection_count
FROM    sys.dm_exec_sessions AS es
INNER JOIN sys.dm_exec_connections AS ec ON es.session_id = ec.session_id
GROUP BY ec.client_net_address , es.program_name , es.host_name
ORDER BY es.program_name, ec.client_net_address;
```

Executing this query returns the location from where the connection is coming from, the program name, and machine name, and the number of connections coming from the host machine, as shown in Figure 3-54.

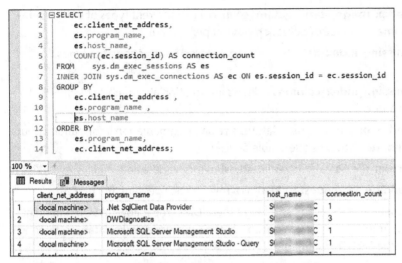

```
 1  ☐SELECT
 2      ec.client_net_address,
 3      es.program_name,
 4      es.host_name,
 5      COUNT(ec.session_id) AS connection_count
 6  FROM    sys.dm_exec_sessions AS es
 7  INNER JOIN sys.dm_exec_connections AS ec ON es.session_id = ec.session_id
 8  GROUP BY
 9      ec.client_net_address ,
10      es.program_name ,
11      es.host_name
12  ORDER BY
13      es.program_name,
14      ec.client_net_address;
```

100 %   ▾

▦ Results ▧ Messages

	client_net_address	program_name	host_name	connection_count
1	<local machine>	.Net SqlClient Data Provider	S▨▨▨▨C	1
2	<local machine>	DWDiagnostics	S▨▨▨▨C	3
3	<local machine>	Microsoft SQL Server Management Studio	S▨▨▨▨C	1
4	<local machine>	Microsoft SQL Server Management Studio - Query	S▨▨▨▨C	1

FIGURE 3-54 Viewing connections using Dynamic Management Views

Index and I/O

With a total of 13 index-related and I/O-related DMVs, it is not as many as the number of execution DMVs, but the 13 still provide great insight into database performance and how to address issues.

These index DMVs provide the insight into helping you provide the right balance between too many and too few indexes and finding the sweet spot for index performance. Fine-tuning indexes is an art and a delicate balance, and thus the reason that the index-related DMVs, along with the wait stat DMVs, are typically the most-used DMVs of any category.

Index-related DMVs help provide insight into creating and maintaining a proper indexing strategy, as well as answer critical indexing and performance tuning questions, such as what indexes exist but are never used or are no longer in use, and the opposite, what indexes are missing that would improve performance? These DMVs can also provide insight into how the current indexes are being used.

I/O-related indexes provide pivotal information into the physical reads and writes of the system, which is an expensive operation. SQL Server does not manage the read and writes directly but instead passes that responsibility off to the Windows I/O manager. While minimal physical I/O is unavoidable, the less, the better. Thus, the most effective way to minimize I/O is to write proper code and compliment it with the appropriate column indexes. Thus, utilizing the appropriate I/O and index DMVs helps provide the insight into how to tune the database.

The list below explains the commonly used index and I/O related DMVs to troubleshoot database performance.

- **sys.dm_db_index_usage_stats**   Returns counts of the different types of index operations and the time each type of operation was last performed.

- **sys.dm_db_missing_index_details**   Displays detailed information about missing indexes.

- **sys.dm_db_missing_index_columns**   Shows information about table columns that are missing an index.

- **sys.dm_db_index_physical_stats**   Returns size and fragmentation information about the data and indexes of the specified table or view.

- **sys.dm_io_virtual_file_stats**   Shows I/O statistics for the data and log files.

- **sys.dm_io_pending_io_requests**   Returns a row for each pending I/O request.

The following examples show how to use a few of these DMs. The following SQL statement queries a few columns from the Person.Person table in the AdventureWorks database, filtering one of the columns in the SELECT statement.

```
SELECT City, StateProvinceID, PostalCode
FROM Person.Address
WHERE StateProvinceID = 9;
GO
```

Once the above statement is executed, we can then run the following query that combines some of the DMVs listed above; sys.dm_db_missing_index_details, sys.dm_db_missing_index_columns, and one more called sys.dm_db_missing_index_groups. When a query is optimized by the query optimizer, missing index information is obtained and returned when querying the missing index DMVs.

```
SELECT mig.*, statement AS table_name, column_id, column_name, column_usage
FROM sys.dm_db_missing_index_details AS mid
CROSS APPLY sys.dm_db_missing_index_columns (mid.index_handle)
INNER JOIN sys.dm_db_missing_index_groups AS mig ON mig.index_handle = mid.index_handle
ORDER BY mig.index_group_handle, mig.index_handle, column_id;
GO
```

Running the above query shows that query performance could be improved by adding the missing indexes shown in Figure 3-55.

```
 1 ⊟SELECT City, StateProvinceID, PostalCode
 2   FROM Person.Address
 3   WHERE StateProvinceID = 9;
 4   GO
 5
 6 ⊟SELECT mig.*, statement AS table_name, column_id, column_name, column_usage
 7   FROM sys.dm_db_missing_index_details AS mid
 8   CROSS APPLY sys.dm_db_missing_index_columns (mid.index_handle)
 9   INNER JOIN sys.dm_db_missing_index_groups AS mig ON mig.index_handle = mid.index_handle
10   ORDER BY mig.index_group_handle, mig.index_handle, column_id;
11   GO
```

100 % ▼

🔲 Results | 📄 Messages

	index_group_handle	index_handle	table_name	column_id	column_name	column_usage
1	2	1	[AdventureWorks2014].[Person].[Address]	4	City	INCLUDE
2	2	1	[AdventureWorks2014].[Person].[Address]	5	StateProvinceID	EQUALITY
3	2	1	[AdventureWorks2014].[Person].[Address]	6	PostalCode	INCLUDE

FIGURE 3-55 Finding missing indexes using Dynamic Management View

Now, it should be mentioned that every index recommended by the missing index DMVs does not have to be added. In fact, best practice states that they should not be added without doing some level of investigation. Remember, over-indexing is also bad and can lead to bad performance because too many indexes can be just as bad as not enough indexes, or even worse. You'll find that SQL Server is a bit enthusiastic about suggesting "INCLUDE" columns, so the responsibility falls upon you to look at the results and apply those that pertain to your consistent workload. Also, don't be afraid to remove an index if you don't see the performance gains after applying it.

Transaction

SQL Server provides 11 DMVs aimed at locating and identifying the transactions that are causing locking and blocking issues and the sessions to which they belong. The most commonly used DMVs are listed below.

- **sys.dm_tran_locks** Shows information about currently active lock manager resources.
- **sys.dm_tran_database_transactions** Displays information about transactions at the database level.
- **sys.dm_tran_session_transactions** Shows related information for transactions and their associated sessions.
- **sys.dm_tran_active_transactions** Shows information about instance-level transactions.
- **sys.dm_tran_current_transactions** Displays a single row of state information of the transaction in the current session.

An easy demo to show the dm_tran_locks in action is simply create a locking situation. For example, in the tempdb database, create the following table with a few rows of data.

```
CREATE TABLE table_lock
(
  c1 int, c2 int
);
GO

CREATE INDEX table_lock_ci on table_lock(c1);
GO

INSERT INTO table_lock VALUES (1,1);
INSERT INTO table_lock VALUES (2,2);
INSERT INTO table_lock VALUES (3,3);
INSERT INTO table_lock VALUES (4,4);
INSERT INTO table_lock VALUES (5,5);
INSERT INTO table_lock VALUES (6,6);
GO
```

Next, in the same query window, execute the following T-SQL.

```
SET TRANSACTION ISOLATION LEVEL READ COMMITTED;

BEGIN TRAN
SELECT c1 FROM table_lock  WITH(holdlock, rowlock);
```

While the query is executing, open a second query window, type and execute the following:

```
BEGIN TRAN
UPDATE table_lock SET c1 = 5
```

What happens is that the UPDATE is locked from executing because the first session in the first query window has not been committed or rolled back. To see this, execute the following query in a third query windows:

```
SELECT resource_type, resource_associated_entity_id, request_status, request_
mode,request_session_id,
resource_description
FROM sys.dm_tran_locks
--WHERE resource_database_id = 2
ORDER BY request_session_id
```

Figure 3-56 shows the results of the query in which we can see a lock by the first session. This is signified by the request_mode type X, which means the holding session has an exclusive lock and access to the resource, in this case table_lock, and session 2 is waiting for the release of the lock.

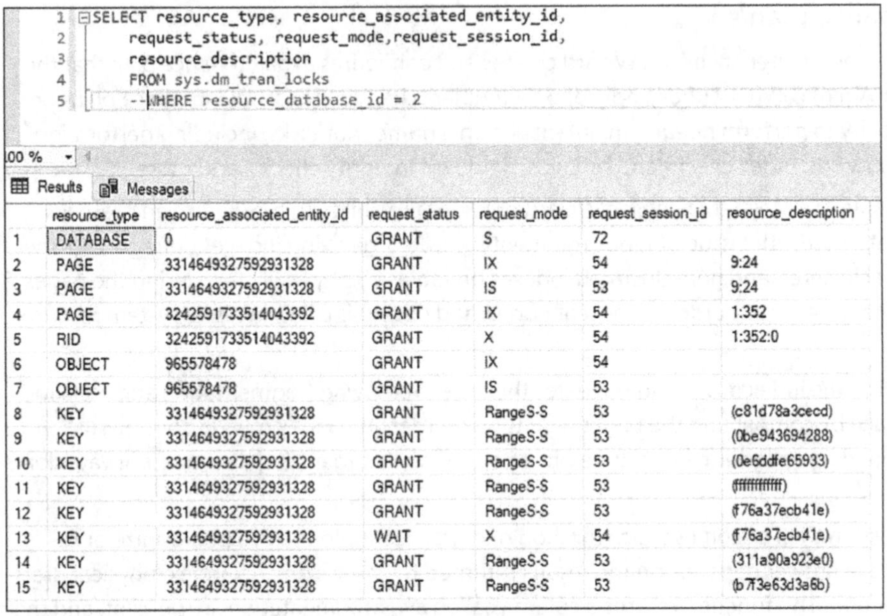

```
1  ☐SELECT resource_type, resource_associated_entity_id,
2        request_status, request_mode,request_session_id,
3        resource_description
4     FROM sys.dm_tran_locks
5     --WHERE resource_database_id = 2
```

100 % ▾ ◂

☷ Results ᯤ Messages

	resource_type	resource_associated_entity_id	request_status	request_mode	request_session_id	resource_description
1	DATABASE	0	GRANT	S	72	
2	PAGE	3314649327592931328	GRANT	IX	54	9:24
3	PAGE	3314649327592931328	GRANT	IS	53	9:24
4	PAGE	3242591733514043392	GRANT	IX	54	1:352
5	RID	3242591733514043392	GRANT	X	54	1:352:0
6	OBJECT	965578478	GRANT	IX	54	
7	OBJECT	965578478	GRANT	IS	53	
8	KEY	3314649327592931328	GRANT	RangeS-S	53	(c81d78a3cecd)
9	KEY	3314649327592931328	GRANT	RangeS-S	53	(0be943694288)
10	KEY	3314649327592931328	GRANT	RangeS-S	53	(0e6ddfe65933)
11	KEY	3314649327592931328	GRANT	RangeS-S	53	(ffffffffffff)
12	KEY	3314649327592931328	GRANT	RangeS-S	53	(f76a37ecb41e)
13	KEY	3314649327592931328	WAIT	X	54	(f76a37ecb41e)
14	KEY	3314649327592931328	GRANT	RangeS-S	53	(311a90a923e0)
15	KEY	3314649327592931328	GRANT	RangeS-S	53	(b73e63d3a6b)

FIGURE 3-56 Viewing locks using Dynamic Management Views

Maintain indexes

Index maintenance is vital for the welfare of your database and for the wellbeing of a smooth-performing database. Ignoring index maintenance or applying improper maintenance can significantly cripple database performance and lead to maintenance headaches down the road.

There are several aspects of maintaining indexes and several tools in which to perform the necessary maintenance tasks. The primary maintenance tasks include:

- Identifying and removing index fragmentation
- Identifying and creating missing indexes
- Identifying and removing unused indexes
- Identifying and updating outdated indexes and column statistics

It would be nice if there was a single tool that could accomplish everything in the list above, but there is not. Therefore, the above-mentioned tasks require the use of two main tools; the Maintenance Plan Wizard and the Database Engine Tuning Advisor. We'll begin with the Maintenance Plan Wizard.

Maintenance plan

The SQL Server Maintenance Plan Wizard creates and configures a maintenance plan that the SQL Server Agent can run either singly or on a regular schedule. These maintenance plans provide the ability to perform needed maintenance on a number of tasks, including performing database backups, index checks and rebuilds, database integrity checks, and more.

For indexes, the Maintenance Plan Wizard provides the ability to reorganize and rebuild indexes that address the issue of index fragmentation. Reorganizing indexes defragments the leaf level of clustered and non-clustered indexes on tables by physically reordering the pages to match the left-to-right order of the leaf nodes, and does this using minimal system resources.

Rebuilding the index drops and recreates the index, removing fragmentation and reclaiming disk space by compacting the pages, and then reorders the index rows in contiguous pages. Rebuilding an index can be done online or offline. Reorganizing an index is always done offline.

The question then becomes which method of defragmentation to use (reorganize or rebuild), and the answer depends on the results returned by the sys.dm_db_index_physical_stats system function. This function returns a column called avg_fragmentation_in_percent, and the basic rule of thumb suggests that if the value in this column is between five and 30, you can reorganize the index. Anything over a value of 30 necessitates a rebuild. Rebuilding indexes can be done online or offline, and reorganizing indexes is always executed online. It is recommended that index rebuilds be done online to achieve similar availability to that of index reorganization.

Very low levels of fragmentation (anything less than five percent) need not be addressed because the benefit of removing the fragmentation typically outweighs the cost of the reorganization or building of the index. However, five percent of a billion rows is still a lot, so statistics will come in to play in scenarios such as this to determine if a rebuild or reorg of an index is necessary.

For example, the following query calls the sys.dm_db_index_physical_stats system function, which takes a database and table name as parameters. In this example the WideWorldImports database and Sales.Invoice table is being passed to the function, as shown in the following code.

```
DECLARE @db_id SMALLINT;
DECLARE @object_id INT;

SET @db_id = DB_ID(N'WideWorldImporters');
SET @object_id = OBJECT_ID(N'WideWorldImporters.Sales.Invoices');

SELECT object_id, index_id, index_type_desc, index_depth, avg_fragmentation_in_percent,
fragment_count, avg_fragment_size_in_pages, page_count
```

```
FROM sys.dm_db_index_physical_stats(@db_id, @object_id, NULL, NULL , 'LIMITED')
ORDER BY avg_fragmentation_in_percent DESC;
```

Figure 3-57 shows the results of this query, which shows 10 indexes that exist on the table, eight of which have an average fragmentation count of over 85 percent, possibly making good candidates for an index rebuild or reorganization.

```
 1  ⊟DECLARE @db_id SMALLINT;
 2    DECLARE @object_id INT;
 3
 4    SET @db_id = DB_ID(N'WideWorldImporters');
 5    SET @object_id = OBJECT_ID(N'WideWorldImporters.Sales.Invoices');
 6
 7  ⊟SELECT object_id, index_id, index_type_desc, index_depth, avg_fragmentation_in_percent,
 8    fragment_count, avg_fragment_size_in_pages, page_count
 9    FROM sys.dm_db_index_physical_stats(@db_id, @object_id, NULL, NULL , 'LIMITED')
10    ORDER BY avg_fragmentation_in_percent DESC;
```

100 %

⊞ Results ⬛ Messages

	object_id	index_id	index_type_desc	index_depth	avg_fragmentation_in_percent	fragment_count	avg_fragment_size_in_pages	page_count
1	2018106230	3	NONCLUSTERED INDEX	2	98.6842105263158	152	1	152
2	2018106230	7	NONCLUSTERED INDEX	2	98.6842105263158	152	1	152
3	2018106230	4	NONCLUSTERED INDEX	2	98.3122362869198	234	1.01282051282051	237
4	2018106230	2	NONCLUSTERED INDEX	2	98.1707317073171	164	1	164
5	2018106230	6	NONCLUSTERED INDEX	2	98.1707317073171	164	1	164
6	2018106230	9	NONCLUSTERED INDEX	2	97.887323943662	142	1	142
7	2018106230	8	NONCLUSTERED INDEX	2	97.9411764705588	136	1	136
8	2018106230	1	CLUSTERED INDEX	3	85.5696425427012	9899	1.14738862511365	11358
9	2018106230	5	NONCLUSTERED INDEX	2	0.819672131147541	17	7.17647058823529	122
10	2018106230	10	NONCLUSTERED INDEX	3	0.460829493087558	57	7.6140350877193	434

FIGURE 3-57 Reviewing index fragmentation using Dynamic Management Views

The Maintenance Plan Wizard is used to rebuild and reorganize indexes on this table. To begin, open SQL Server Management Studio and expand the Management node, and then right-click the Maintenance Plan Wizard node, and select the Maintenance Plan Wizard option from the Context Menu, as shown in Figure 3-58.

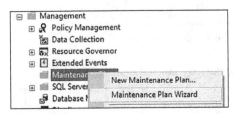

FIGURE 3-58 Starting the Maintenance Plan Wizard

On the Welcome page of the Maintenance Plan Wizard, click Next. The Welcome page simply summarizes the capabilities of the wizard. On the Select Plan Properties page of the wizard, enter a name for the maintenance plan and a description if you would like. Leave the other options as configured. The Run As option specifies what service account to run the maintenance plan. By default this is the SQL Server Agent account, and unless a specific account has been created for this purpose, there is no reason to change it.

We define the schedule later on, so leave this as is. The option to schedule a single schedule or separate schedules for the tasks is kind of out of place because at this point no tasks have been selected. So for now, leave it checked to run as a single schedule for the entire plan, and click Next.

The Select Maintenance Task page is used to select which tasks will be performed by the wizard. The Maintenance Plan Wizard provides the ability to reorganize and rebuild indexes, so select both of those, as shown in Figure 3-59, and then click next.

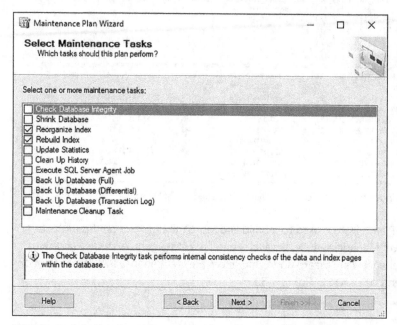

FIGURE 3-59 Selecting the maintenance tasks to include in the maintenance plan

The Maintenance Task Order page provides the option to change the order in which the tasks are executed. For these two tasks, this should not be ignored and the order in which these two tasks is executed is important.

Recall from the information above that the decision on whether to rebuild or reorganize is based on the percentage of the fragmentation, and the basic rule of thumb is that if the value in this column is between five and 30, you can reorganize the index. Anything over a value of 30 necessitates a rebuild. Thus, you will want to rebuild first as any index with a fragmentation with a percentage of over 30 percent will be caught and addressed first. Then, those indexes over five percent fragmentation are then addressed by the reorganize task, ignoring the other indexes that have just been rebuilt by the rebuild task, because their index fragmentation is now below the threshold.

Make sure the Rebuild Index task is listed first, as shown in Figure 3-60, and then click Next.

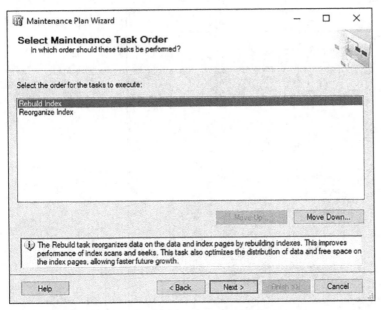

FIGURE 3-60 Setting the order of the maintenance tasks

The next two pages in the wizard are the configuration pages for the rebuild task and the reorganize task. Figure 3-61 shows the Rebuilt Index Task configuration page. On this page, select the databases you want this task to check, whether you want it to check tables, views, or both, and the specific table views to check.

The Default Free Space Per Page option drops the indexes on the tables in the database and re-creates them with the fill factor that was specified when the index was created. The Change Free Space Per Page option drops the indexes on the table and recreates them with a new, automatically calculated fill factor that reserves the specified amount of free space on the index pages. The higher the percentage, the more free space is reserved.

The Keep Index Online option allows users to access the underlying table or indexed data during the index operations, and the Sort Results In Tempdb option determines where the intermediate sort results are stored, which are generated during the index creation.

As discussed, leave the fragmentation and page count values where they are, and click Next.

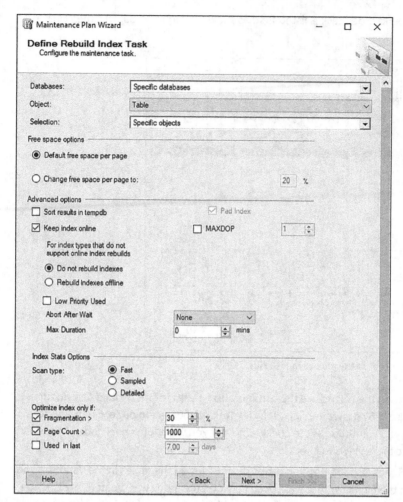

FIGURE 3-61 Configuring the rebuild index task

For the Reorganize task, shown in Figure 3-62, configure the databases and objects similar to the Rebuild task, and then configure the other options as needed. The Scan type defines how the system consumes resources while it gathers index statistics. You can choose between consuming less resources (Fast), or more resources (Detailed), depending on how much precision is needed for index statistics. The Optimize Index options are similar to the Rebuild tasks, but be sure to change the Fragmentation percentage to a value around 10, but no less than five, and then click Next.

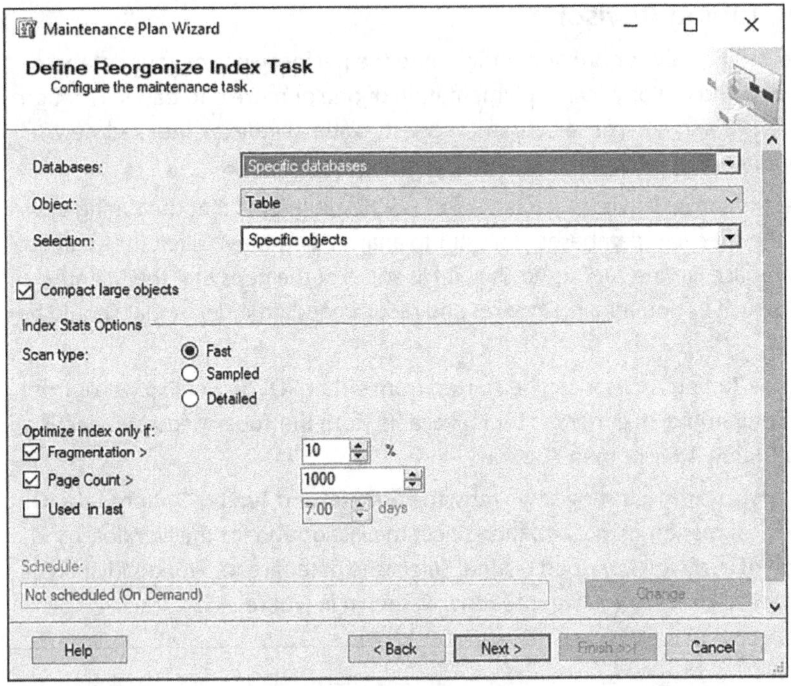

FIGURE 3-62 Configuring the reorganize index task

The Select Report Options page simply specifies the options for saving or distributing a report that details the results of the maintenance plan actions. The two options allow the report to be saved to a local file or to be emailed.

The Complete The Wizard page summarizes the configuration. Click Finish, which creates the maintenance plan, and add the tasks to the plan, and add any scheduling options. Because no recurring schedule was defined, you can right-click the maintenance plan and click Execute to run the plan. Creating a recurring schedule for the maintenance plans is discussed later in this skill.

There is one more point to mention before moving on. The values for the fragmentation percent and the page count thresholds are a starting point and these numbers should vary depending on your environment.

Database Engine Tuning Advisor

The Database Engine Tuning Advisor provides insight into the performance of your database by analyzing a workload and the physical implementation of one or more databases. Through a workload analysis, the tuning advisor selects and suggests optimal indexes, indexed views, and partitions without needing to understand the structure of the database.

The workload that the tuning advisor uses is a set of T-SQL statements that the tuning advisor executes against the specified databases you want to analyze and tune. Given the analytical capabilities of the Database Engine Tuning Advisor, it fills some of the gaps that the Maintenance Plan cannot do, such as find missing indexes and recommending indexes that should be removed.

The Database Engine Tuning Advisor can be started from either SQL Server Profiler or from SQL Server Management Studio. In either tool, it is available from the Tools menu by selecting the Database Engine Tuning Advisor menu option.

When the tuning advisor starts, it shows two tabs; the General and Tuning Options tabs. On the General tab, provide a session name, and then select the File option for the workload and browse to the location of a .sql for workload testing. Select the database for workload analysis, then select the database and tables you want to tune, as shown in Figure 3-63.

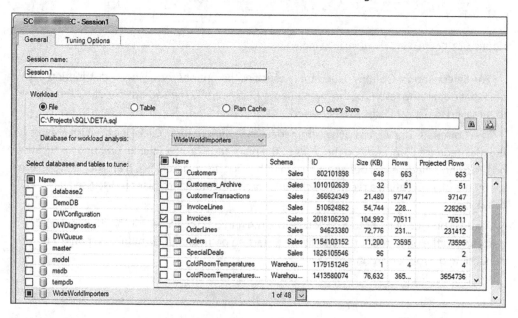

FIGURE 3-63 Configuring the General tab of the Database Engine Tuning Advisor

The .sql file selected for the workload analysis should contain one or more SELECT statements, which would represent a decent database workload.

The Tuning Options tab is used to configure the general tuning options. Typically, you won't need to change much on this page, depending on your SQL environment. For example, do you want the tuning advisor to check both indexes and indexed views, just indexes, or non-clustered indexes? Also, what partitioning strategy do you want to employ during analysis? Most times you won't need to make any changes, and in this example we just want to analyze the indexes, which is the default configuration setting, shown in Figure 3-64.

The Partitioning Strategy and Physical Design Structures section tell the Tuning Advisor to also look at, ecommend, and change characteristics of the database when looking at tuning options.

The Partitioning Strategy options tell the tuning advisor if and how to look at partitions when performing the analysis. If no partitioning is selected, it will not look at or recommend the use of partitions, whereas Full partitioning will provide recommendations for the use of partitions. The Aligned partitions will recommend partitions that are aligned with existing partitions of underlying tables or view.

The Physical Design Structures section tells the Tuning Advisor whether or not to keep or drop specific structures during analysis.

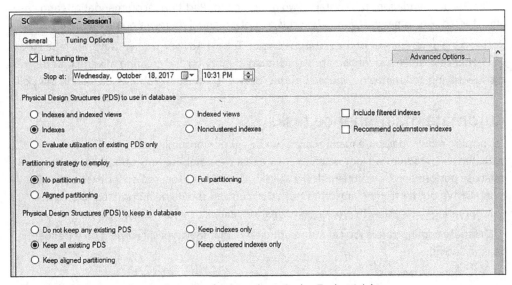

3-64 Configuring the Tuning Options tab of the Database Engine Tuning Advisor

Once the tuning session has been configured, click the Start Analysis button on the toolbar and the tuning advisor runs the script provided on the General tab to generate a workload and run an analysis of the indexes. By default, the Limit tuning time is checked and the amount of time the analysis runs is one hour. As the analysis is running, a Progress tab appears showing the progress of the analysis.

Once the analysis is complete, two additional tabs appear: Recommendations and Reports, as shown in Figure 3-65.

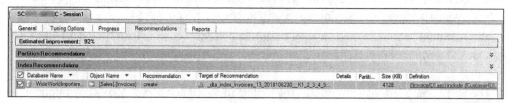

FIGURE 3-65 Reviewing the recommendations results

As you can see in Figure 3-65, the tuning analysis revealed that a missing index was identified on the Sales.Invoices table with a recommendation to create the missing index. Likewise, had an index been identified as unused or causing poor performance, that index would have been listed with a value of Drop in the Recommendation column of the results.

The Recommendations tab contains two grids, one for Partition recommendations and another for Index recommendations. The grids do not expand if there are no recommendations.

Given the deep analysis of the Database Engine Tuning Advisor, it solves several of the index maintenance problems identified above including identifying and creating missing indexes, and identifying and removing unused indexes. Updating statistics is addressed later in this skill.

Automate maintenance tasks

Performing regular database maintenance can be a time-consuming process. The skills discussed so far require vigilant watch to ensure that the database runs smoothly and proper database performance is maintained. The skills discussed have focused on indexes and monitoring DMVs, but there are many other tasks that can and should be automated to ensure a well-operating database with proper performance, reliability, and availability.

Database administrators look at automating tasks that they typically repeat on a frequent basis, including:

- Database backups
- Maintaining indexes
- Checking database integrity
- Managing database and disk space
- Updating statistics

There are several ways to automate many of these tasks, and the following sections discuss two of the more popular approaches: SQL Server Maintenance Plans and PowerShell.

Maintenance plans

SQL Server Maintenance Plans create a workflow of tasks aimed at keeping your database well maintained and optimized. Many of the tasks are grouped together based on functionality to improve task maintenance.

Maintenance plans can be created either by using the user interface in SQL Server Management Studio or via T-SQL. The user interface in SQL Server Management Studio provides the ability to create maintenance plans two ways:

- Maintenance Plan Wizard
- Maintenance Plan Design Surface

The Maintenance Plan Wizard provides a step-by-step, guided walk-through to create a plan that the SQL Server Agent can run manually or on scheduled basis. You have seen an example of this in this skill when creating a plan to rebuild and reorganize indexes.

The Maintenance Plan Design Surface also creates a maintenance plan but provides the ability to utilize an enhanced workflow and control the workflow steps.

To create a maintenance plan using the design surface, right-click the Maintenance Plans node in the Object Explorer Window in SQL Server Management Studio, and select New Maintenance Plan from the Context menu. In the New Maintenance Plan dialog, provide a name for the maintenance plan, and click OK.

A maintenance plan tab opens in the details section of SQL Server Management Studio, displaying the name and a subplan. A subplan is used where the tasks of the plan are defined, with each subplan able to hold a collection of tasks.

The design surface is similar to SQL Server Integration Services, where tasks are dragged onto the design surface from a toolbox. From the View menu in SQL Server Management Studio, select Toolbox to display the toolbox window that contains all of the maintenance plan tasks. From the Toolbox window, drag the Check Database Integrity Task and Back Up Database Task onto the design surface, as shown in Figure 3-66.

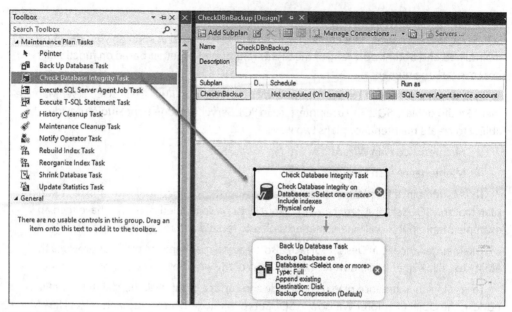

FIGURE 3-66 Configuring a maintenance plan in the design surface

Each task can be configured by double-clicking the specific task, and configuring the Task Configuration dialog. For example, double-clicking the Database Integrity Task displays the Check Database Integrity Task dialog through which the specific database you want to check is selected and integrity check options are selected. Configure both tasks by double-clicking each task and configuring as appropriate.

As mentioned, the Maintenance Plan Design Surface provides an enhanced workflow and more control over the steps in the workflow, which is not capable to do in the Maintenance Plan Wizard. Thus, additional workflow and decision tree options can be applied, as shown in Figure 3-67. In this example, if the Check Database Integrity Task fails, we don't want to back up the database, we only want it backed up if the integrity check succeeds. Rather, we would prefer another action be taken if the integrity check fails. As such, as shown in Figure 3-67, we can add another task to the design surface, such as the Notify Operator Task or Execute T-SQL Statement Task, and route to that task given the failure of the database integrity check.

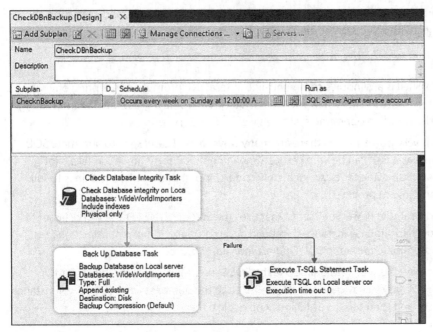

FIGURE 3-67 Configuring detailed task workflow

To schedule the maintenance plan, click the Job Schedule Properties button on the subplan and configure the frequency in which the plan will run in the Job Schedule Properties dialog. Click OK on the dialog, and then save the maintenance plan.

Once the maintenance plan is saved it appears underneath the Maintenance Plans node. Additionally, each subplan created appears in the Jobs node underneath the SQL Server Agent node, as shown in Figure 3-68.

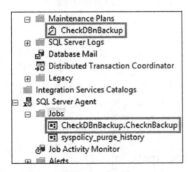

FIGURE 3-68 The maintenance plan and correlated job in object explorer

Keep in mind that each maintenance plan can have multiple subplans, and each subplan shows up as a job within the Jobs node.

PowerShell

Windows PowerShell is a Windows command-line, interactive prompt and scripting environment built on top of the .NET Framework and has quickly become a great tool for automating tasks of all kinds, including operating system as well as SQL Server.

PowerShell is very powerful and there are many ways to use PowerShell to automate SQL tasks. As versatile as it is, it can be very verbose, meaning that it sometimes can take a lot of code to accomplish some tasks. As such, only code-snippets are supplied and links to full source code samples are provided.

You can find a sample PowerShell script that uses the Standard .NET Framework classes to connect to a specific database instance to rebuild and reorganize indexes at *https://gallery. technet.microsoft.com/scriptcenter/SQL-Optimization-In-95d12ce6*.

Many of the examples you find online use the SQL Server Management Objects (SMO) because it makes it easy to navigate and iterate through the databases of a SQL Server instance and their objects, and then use the SMO index object like this:

```
$index.Rebuild()
$index.Reorganize()
```

The following code snipped provides a high-level sample of iterating the objects, checking their fragmentation level, and either rebuilding or re-indexing based on the results.

```
$v = [System.Reflection.Assembly]::LoadWithPartialName( 'Microsoft.SqlServer.SMO')
$smo = new-object ('Microsoft.SqlServer.Management.Smo.Server') $inst
$dbs = $smo.Databases

foreach ($db in $dbs) {
$tbs = $db.Tables
foreach ($tb in $tbs) {
$ixs = $tb.Indexes
foreach ($ix in $ixs) {

# Get the Fragmentation and page count information
$q = @"
SELECT avg_fragmentation_in_percent, page_count FROM sys.dm_db_index_physical_
stats($dbid, $tbid, $ixid, NULL, NULL)
"@

$res = invoke-sqlcmd -ServerInstance $inst -Database $dbname -Query $q
$frval = $res.avg_fragmentation_in_percent
$pgcnt = $res.page_count

if ($frval -gt 30 -and $pgcnt -gt 1000) {
$ix.Rebuild()
```

```
}
elseif ($frval -gt 10 -and $pgcnt -gt 1000) {
$ix.Reorganize()
}
}
}
}
```

Obviously this code snippet is not complete, but it provides insight on how you can use PowerShell to accomplish many of the maintenance tasks discussed. Once the PowerShell script is tested appropriately, it can be scheduled several ways, such as using the Windows scheduler, or through a SQL Server job.

Update statistics

The query optimizer uses statistics to create query plans to improve query performance. Most of the time, the query optimizer has already generated the necessary statistics for an optimal query plan, but there are times where additional statistics are necessary or the existing statistics need updating for a better query plan.

For the query optimizer, statistics contain information about the distribution of values in one or more columns of a table or indexed view. The query optimizer uses these statistics to estimate the cardinality, or number of rows, in the query result. The cardinality estimates are generated by the cardinality estimator and are used to create a high-quality query plan. If the cardinality estimates are off, resulting in poor statistics, the result could be the difference between a poor performing and resource-intensive index scan versus the better performing index seek.

Statistics can be updated several ways. In many environments, statistics are updated via a maintenance plan that provides a proactive approach to updating statistics. When creating a maintenance plan using the Maintenance Plan Wizard, select the Update Statistics option on the Select Maintenance Tasks page. The Define Update Statistics Task page then allows you to configure the maintenance task, shown in Figure 3-69.

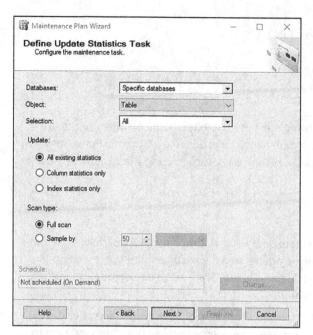

FIGURE 3-69 Configuring the update statistics task

Index statistics are created automatically when the index is created. Column statistics are created manually using the CREATE STATISTICS statement, or they are created automatically if the Auto Create Statistics option is set to True.

The Scan type defines the amount of data used to determine the statistic. The Full scan option costs more resource time, but ensures that the statistics are accurate. The Sample By option uses the percentage of the rows specified and extrapolates the rest, resulting in a faster update of the statistics but the statistics may not be accurate. As such, the Full scan is recommended, but updating statistics should be done off hours.

The query optimizer is quite smart. It determines when the statistics might be out of date and updates them as needed for a query plan. This option is on by default via a database-level setting, the Auto Update Statistics configuration setting, shown in Figure 3-70.

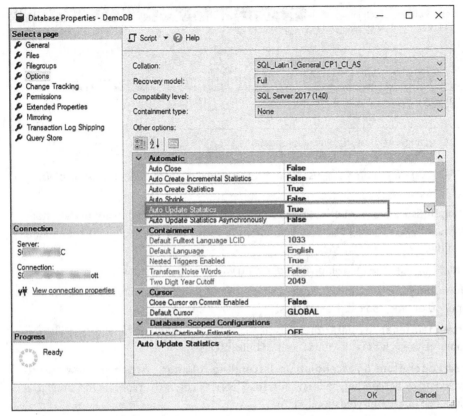

FIGURE 3-70 The auto update statics option in the Database Properties dialog

The question then becomes when to update statistics. If the query optimizer is so smart, why do statistics need to be updated via a DBA? As smart as the query optimizer is, it is not perfect. It does its best, but there are times when query plans can be improved, thus improving query performance, by updating statistics more frequently than the Auto Update Statistics setting dictates. Statistics become out of date after INSERT, UPDATE, DELETE, and MERGE operations change the data distribution in the table or indexed view, and the query optimizer determines their out of date by counting the number of data modifications since the latest statistics update, and comparing the number of modifications to the number of rows in the table or indexed view.

A great way to determine when statistics were last updated is by looking at the last_updated column in the sys.dm_db_stats_properties DMV, as shown in Figure 3-71.

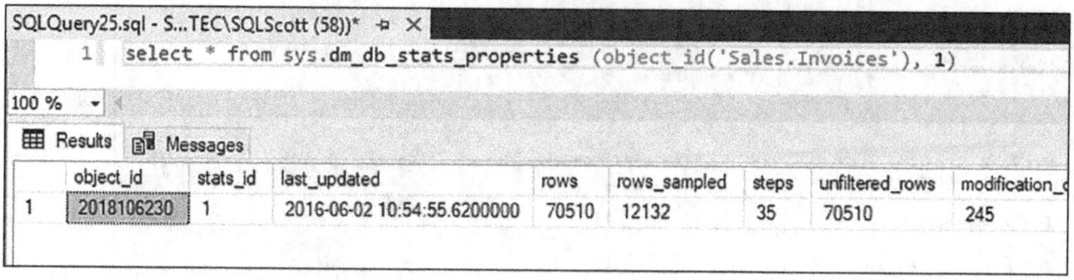

FIGURE 3-71 Checking when statistics were last updated

The STATS_DATE function is also useful as it returns similar information, but broken out by index.

Updating statistics causes queries to recompile, so it is recommended to not update statistics too frequently due to the performance tradeoff between improving query plans and query recompile time.

Therefore, consider the following when deciding when to update statistics:

- **Slow query performance** If queries have a slow or unpredictable response time over a period of time, look at the statistics.
- **After maintenance operations** Some maintenance operations change the distribution of data, such as table truncations or bulk inserts.
- **Insert operations on ascending or descending columns** Appending new rows to ascending or descending columns, such as IDENTITY columns, might be too small to trigger an automatic statistics update.

Updating statistics can also be updated using T-SQL. The following T-SQL statement updates the statistics for all the indexes on the Sales.Invoices table in the WideWorldImporters database.

```
UPDATE STATISTICS Sales.Invoices;
```

The following T-SQL statement updates the statistics for all the FK_Sales_Invoices_OrderID index on the Sales.Invoices table in the WideWorldImporters database.

```
UPDATE STATISTICS Sales.Invoices AK_Sales_Invoices_OrderID;
```

Updating statistics should not be overlooked. It should be a regular part of your maintenance plan strategy, simply because issues like bad parameter sniffing can be alleviated with better statistics

Verify database integrity

A few years ago a member of the Microsoft SQL Server product support team published a blog post and it stated that more than 95 percent of all corruption cases turned out to be caused by a platform issue, the layer below SQL Server. The primary cause was a firmware bug, or third-party driver, with the second most common cause being actual hardware failure. The idea is that many things can cause database corruption, such as damage to the hard drive, environmental factors and influences, normal hardware wear and tear, or bad data in general.

The question isn't if database corruption will happen, it's when. Database corruption will happen at some point. The focus is on the things you should be doing to proactively monitor for database corruption and how to address it when it does happen.

The following two sections discuss the options available to proactively monitor for database corruption and to check and verify database integrity.

Maintenance plan

This skill has covered SQL Server Maintenance plans quite a bit, and for good reason. They provide a proactive and quick way to get insight into the status of your database. Checking the integrity of your database is no different because a maintenance plan task exists that checks the integrity of your database.

The Check Database Integrity Task checks the allocation and structural integrity of all the objects in a specified database, or multiple database. Additionally, the task can check the integrity of all the index and table data pages.

When creating a maintenance plan using the Maintenance Plan Wizard, select the Check Database Integrity option on the Select Maintenance Tasks page. The Define Database Check Integrity Task page then allows you to configure the maintenance task, shown before in Figure 3-72.

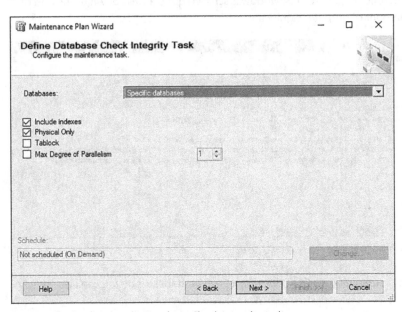

FIGURE 3-72 Configuring the Database Check Integrity task

Behind the scenes, the Check Database Integrity Task encapsulates the DBCC CHECKDB statement, providing a user-interface to configure, schedule, and run the DBCC CHECKDB statement.

The benefit of using a maintenance plan is that, as you learned earlier, you can include this plan as part of an overall workflow and take action based on the outcome of the task.

DBCC CHECKDB

The DBCC CHECKDB statement accomplishes the same functionality as the maintenance plan, with the difference being that you are running a T-SQL statement with the output being returned in the output window. The DBCC CHECKDB statement checks the logical and physical integrity of all the objects. It does this by also executing additional DBCC statements:

- **DBCC CHECKALLOC**   Checks the consistency of disk space allocation.
- **DBCC CHECKTABLE**   Checks the integrity of all the pages and structures that make up the table or indexed view.
- **DBCC CHECKCATALOG**   Checks the catalog consistency.

DBCC CHECKDB also validates the contents of every indexed view in the database and validates link-level consistency between table metadata and file system directories.

To run DBCC CHECKDB, execute the statement in a query window, as shown in Figure 3-73. As you can see, CHECKDB found 0 allocation errors and 0 consistency checks in the database. Also notice that the scrollbar in the results window is scrolled quite a ways down to the end of the output, so the amount of output is significant.

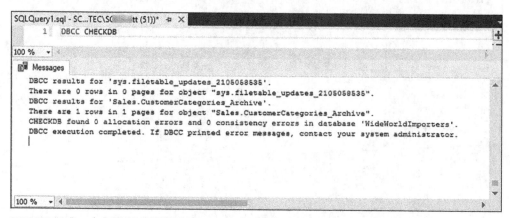

FIGURE 3-73 Running DBCC CHECKDB in a query window

The example above runs DBCC CHECKDB for the current database, but you can also specify the database to check:

```
DBCC CHECKDB ([WideWorldImporters])
```

There are certain benefits to checking database integrity using the DBCC CHECKDB statement because there are several parameters you can pass to the statement, such as the REPAIR_REBUILD parameter, which performs repairs that have no possibility of data loss, including repairing missing rows in non-clustered indexes, and rebuilding indexes.

One of the parameters that is available to use with DBCC CHECKDB is called REPAIR_ALLOW_DATA_LOSS. This option tells DBCC CHECKDB to try and repair all reported errors, even if it means data loss. As such, it is recommended that this be used only in a "worst case" scenario. The recommended approach is to restore the database from the last known good backup and not use this parameter.

The idea behind verifying database integrity is to detect database correction as early as possible. If database corruption goes undetected long enough it could, and probably will, lead to data loss. There is nothing you can do to prevent database corruption. As stated earlier, it's not a matter of if, but when. The goal is to detect it as soon as possible so corrective action can be taken, and DBCC CHECKDB is the best way to detect it, whether you run it via T-SQL or a maintenance plan.

The question you should be asking yourself is: How often should you validate database integrity and run consistency checks? To answer that question, you need to look at your environment. Is your I/O subsystem pretty flaky or is it the most reliable thing on the planet? Do you have solid backup strategy or no backup strategy at all? If you do take regular backups, how confident are you that you can recover from corruption with little to no downtime?

The answers to these questions depends on how often you should verify database integrity. You might be comfortable running consistency checks weekly if you have faith in your environment and are a rock star with your backups and backup strategy. If you are on the opposite end of the spectrum, you might want to consider changing your ways.

The good thing is that, regardless of whether or not you use T-SQL or the maintenance plan, you can schedule the consistency check easily to run on a regular schedule, and you should do so.

Recover from database corruption

Database corruption is inevitable. As mentioned previously, it is not a matter of if, but when. You have done your best to monitor and prevent database corruption, but it happened. They say that the best offense is a good defense, and this absolutely applies here. Recovering from database corruption is all about applying a defensive strategy to make recovery a winning situation.

Before discussing recovery, let's take a moment to talk about a good backup plan and strategy. The last thing you want is to find out in the middle of a production recovery situation that you have no backups or your backups are worthless.

As a rule of thumb, database backups should follow these best practices:

- **Full backups** In most cases, a full database backup should be performed weekly. These can be performed online.

- **Differential backups** Captures only the data that has changed since the most recent, full backup.

- **Transaction log backups** Transaction logs contain all the recent activity and can be used to restore a database back to a specific point in time. They also can be performed online. Backup frequency depends on activity.

- **System databases** Weekly for stable installations.

A backup strategy is incomplete without backing up the system databases. The system databases contain a lot of information, such as system configuration and SQL Server job information. Depending on how frequent your database changes are, you might consider a daily or weekly backup frequency.

Transaction log backups depend on how active your database is. A database with heavy transactions might look at backing up the transaction log every 10, 15, or 30 minutes. Less active database might look at backing up the transaction log every one or two hours.

Additionally, when backing up, consider using advanced features such as checksum to detect problems with the backup media itself. Checksum specifies that the backup operation verifies each page for checksum and torn page and generates a checksum for the entire backup.

Part of having a good backup strategy also consists of knowing where to back them up to. Make sure you are not storing your backups in the same physical location as the database files. If the physical drive goes bad, you can use other drives or remote locations that stored the backups to perform a restore.

Now that you have your backup strategy in place, the next step is to practice recovery operations. Just because backups were taken and the backup process succeeded doesn't mean that all is well. Without practicing and walking through the recovery process in its entirety you cannot be entirely sure of the integrity of the backups.

Therefore, have a test server on hand, or in the cloud, to frequently test your backups and your restore strategy, and follow a restore process that you would follow in a production, real-life situation. This minimizes any problems that occur during an actual corruption issue.

With all of that as a foundation, our attention should now focus on the steps necessary to recovery from a corrupted database.

The first step is to run CHECKDB and review the output results because you need to know where the corruption is. If you used a maintenance plan to run CHECKDB, write the output to a file so you have a copy. Review it thoroughly to understand what the issues are and where the corruption is. CHECKDB provides the necessary information to what the problem is, and in what object the corruption exists.

Depending where the corruption is will depend on what the steps are to recover. If the corruption exists in a non-clustered index for example, rebuilding the index just might solve the problem and you're on your way. To fix the index, you need to disable the index by running the ALTER INDEX statement. For example:

```
ALTER INDEX IX_Sales_OrderID ON Sales.Invoices DISABLE;
```

Next, rebuild the index by again using the ALTER INDEX statement, this time specifying to rebuild online.:

```
ALTER INDEX IX_Sales_OrderID ON Sales.Invoices REBUILD WITH ONLINE=ON;
```

This will go through the process of recreating the index and fix any corruption issues. Rerun the CHECKDB again to see if the corruption has been fixed.

If the corruption exists in a data table or other object, you will most likely be looking at restoring the database. You could potentially be looking at repairing the database, but at the cost of losing data, so a repair option should not be considered at this point in the recovery process.

To recover through a database restore, the first step is to make a tail-log backup. A tail-log backup captures any transaction log records that were written to the transaction log since the last time it was backed up.

To back up the tail of the transaction log, right-click the corrupted database and from the context menu select Tasks -> Back Up. In the Back Up Database dialog, set the Backup type to Transaction Log, then on the Media Options page in the Reliability section make sure the Verify Backup When Finished And Perform Checksum Before Writing Media options are checked. Then in the Transaction log section, check the Back Up The Tail Of The Log, as shown in Figure 3-74.

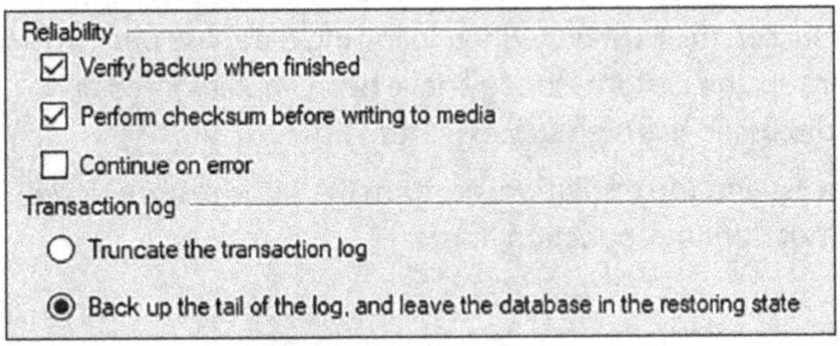

FIGURE 3-74 Configuration options for restoring the tail of the transaction log

If you have followed a best-practices backup strategy and have full and transaction log backups, the next step is to review your backups to identify when the corruption occurred. Again, this is where a best-practices restore strategy, and a test server, comes into play.

Take the most recent full backup and restore it on the test server, running CheckDB on it, and then repeating the process with the next previous full backup until you find the backup that was made before the corruption occurred. At this point, depending on the error returned by CHECKDB and the object on which the corruption exists, the option might exist to restore a page or filegroup which will be faster and in a lot of cases be performed while the database is still online.

Page and File/Filegroup objects can be restored by right-clicking the corrupted database and select Restore > Page or File And FileGroups, as shown in Figure 3-75.

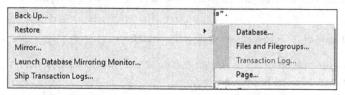

FIGURE 3-75 The menu option to restore a specific data page

The goal of the page restore is to restore one or more damaged pages without restoring the whole database. Pages that are candidates for restore have been marked as "suspect" and the Restore Page dialog helps restore those from backupsets. SQL Server maintains an internal table called the Suspect_Pages table, which is used for maintaining information about suspect pages, and provides information that helps decide whether a restore is necessary. This table resides in the msdb database.

If the corruption is beyond the ability to restore a page or filegroup, a full database restore is needed. Again, on a test server, review your backups to identify when the corruption occurred and find the backup that was made before the corruption occurred. Then, restore all of the transaction log backups, then finally the tail-log backup.

Run CHECKDB again to ensure the corruption does not exist and the problem has been properly and efficiently solved. Again, the CHECKDB repair option should be used as a last option if the restore process was not successful. However, when following database back up best practices and an appropriate backup and restore strategy have been implemented and practiced, restoring the database as discussed has high success rates.

Once you are confident in the process and the resolution, perform the same restore options on the production server, preferably not during production hours.

With the database back online and operating normally, it would be beneficial to take some time to explore potential reasons of what initially caused the corruption. Could the corruption have been avoided, and if so, how? Take this time to do a thorough inspection of both hardware and software to uncover the reason for the corruption. For example, you can look at the page with a hex editor and possibly fix the problem, or hack-attach the suspect database, which is re-attaching a damaged database if it has been accidentally detached.

The point to take away here is that database corruption happens but it can be reduced greatly by having a solid back up strategy along with regular overall health monitoring.

Thought experiment

In this thought experiment, apply what you've learned about in this Chapter. You will find the answers to these questions in the next section.

You are a consultant to the Contoso Corporation. Contoso is an enterprise-level company that has a customer facing ordering system. The number of orders continues to grow and the size of the database is growing exponentially. The size of the database is reaching 400 GB, and much of that is old historical data, but the amount of new data grows rapidly on a daily basis and users have reported slower response times in the application.

Company policy states that records should be kept for a period of time, but Contoso's CIO states that storage cost is becoming an issue. In addition, the CIO has asked the DBAs to look at the performance issue and they have applied several indexes without any change in performance. The CIO has also reported that their current hardware is getting old and several hardware issues on the SQL Server box has appeared and he is unsure if they have a proper recovery plan in place.

1. What can Contoso due to address the storage cost issue while still keeping their cold data?
2. How should Contoso address their application performance problems?
3. What should Contoso's recovery approach be?
4. How should Contoso approach be in defining a maintenance strategy?

Thought experiment answers

This section provides the solution to the thought experiment. Each answer explains why the answer is correct.

1. Contoso should use Stretch Database to migrate all their historical data to Azure. This will require no application changes, free up disk space locally, and still meet security and company policy.
2. In addition to reviewing existing code, Contoso should use many of the dynamic management views as well as the Database Engine Tuning Advisor to help identify missing

indexes and remove unused indexes. Contoso should also look at query statistics. Contoso should also look at and validate existing hardware infrastructure.

3. Contoso should ensure that an appropriate backup and recovery strategy is in place for their environment. Contoso should regularly test this strategy in a test environment to ensure a successful strategy.

4. Contoso should define and implement a maintenance schedule which includes verifying database integrity and performing index maintenance and updating statistics.

Chapter summary

- The SMB 3.0 protocol included optimizations that SQL Server can take advantage of, including significant performance enhancements and improvements.
- The SMB 3.0 protocol comes with Windows Server 2012 and later versions.
- The Stretch Database feature was added to SQL Server 2016 to provide cost efficient storage of cold data.
- Stretch Database can be implemented without any changes to the application.
- The remote table for Stretch Database can be optimized with a performance tier like any other Azure SQL database.
- An Azure storage account comes with blob, table, queue, and file storage services.
- The Azure file share service, part of an Azure storage account, provide the ability to create fully managed file shares that are accessible via the SMB protocol.
- Azure file shares can be mounted both on-premises and in the cloud.
- Azure SQL Database service tiers provide flexibility in changing performance and storage levels based on database workload.
- Azure SQL Database service tiers can be changed to meet the workload demands with little to no downtime.
- SQL Server includes many dynamic management views through which to track and review wait statistics.
- SQL Server tracks wait for information to help troubleshoot and track down performance issues.
- Storage pools, introduced in Windows Server 2012, allow the grouping of physical disks into a resource pool.
- Virtual disks, called storage spaces, can be created from the resources within a storage pool.
- Index maintenance is a critical part of database maintenance to ensure a well-performing database.
- Index maintenance includes removing index fragmentation, identifying missing indexes, and removing unused indexes.

- Maintenance tasks can be used to monitor and maintain many aspects of SQL Server, including indexes, statistics, and database integrity.
- Database integrity should be performed often on a regular schedule.
- A proper backup and restore strategy should be created, maintained, and tested to be able to recover from database corruption.

Index

A

AAD. *See* Azure Active Directory
access policies 215–216
Active Directory Federation Services (ADFS) 23
Active Directory Integrated 25
Active Directory Password Authentication 25
Active Directory Universal Authentication 25
ACUs. *See* Azure Compute Units
adaptive joins
  batch mode 9
Add-AzureRmSqlServerKeyVaultKey cmdlet 139
ADFS. *See* Active Directory Federation Services
agent jobs 37
Agile methodology 72–73
alerts 163–164, 166–171
  associating with operators 169–170
  creating 166, 170
  events generating 166
  severity of 166–167, 171
  strategy for 171
Alerts and Operators nodes 163–164
ALTER DATABASE statement 138, 174
ALTER INDEX statement 271
Always Encrypted
  benefits of 106
  configuration of 106–123
  implementing 120–124
  keys 106, 110–112, 116, 119, 123
  management considerations 123–124
  permissions 113–114
AlwaysOn Availability Groups 36, 70, 85–87
application logs 166
application permissions 107
ARM. *See* Azure Resource Manager
ASR. *See* Azure Site Recovery

ASYNC_NETWORK_IO wait type 224
auditing
  in Azure SQL Database 16–17
authentication 23
  Always Encrypted 107
  multi-factor 23
  Windows Authentication 24, 25
authenticators 127
automatic failover 22–23
automatic tuning 7–9
automation
  of database maintenance tasks 258–263
availability
  management of 36–38
Availability Groups (AGs) 36–38
  AlwaysOn 36, 70, 85–87
availability sets 91–92
Azure
  availability sets in 91–92
  backup and restore of 81–84
  disks in 48–49
  storage account 81–82
  virtual machines. *See* virtual machines (VMs)
Azure Active Directory (AAD) 22–25
Azure Blob service 212–216
Azure Command Line Interface (CLI) 11, 13, 208
  firewall rules 102–103
  setting firewall rules using 15
Azure Compute Units (ACUs) 43
Azure Files 191
Azure Key Vault 80, 107, 111–112, 115, 118, 120
Azure Portal 5, 29, 208
  firewall rules 97–99
Azure PowerShell
  firewall rules 100–101
  installation 14–15

D

T

About the authors

JOSEPH D'ANTONI is a Senior Consultant and Microsoft Data Platform MVP with over 20 years of experience working in both Fortune 500 and smaller firms. He is a Principal Consultant for Denny Cherry & Associates and lives in Malvern, PA. He is a frequent speaker at major tech events like Microsoft Ignite, PASS Summit, and Enterprise Data World. He blogs about all topics technology at joeydantoni.com. He holds a BS in Computer Information Systems from Louisiana Tech Univers

SCOTT KLEIN CTO of Cloud and Devices with nearly two decades of experience working with Microsoft SQL Server. Prior to becoming CTO, Scott spent six years at Microsoft, traveling the globe as a technical evangelist training and speaking about SQL Server and Microsoft's Azure data services. Scott's recent focus has been on advanced analytics, including big data and IoT, providing real-world training to help bring intelligence to your data. Scott has authored several books, his latest focuses on using Microsoft's IoT suite to process and analyze data. Scott is continuously striving and looking for ways to help developers and companies grok the wonderful world of data.

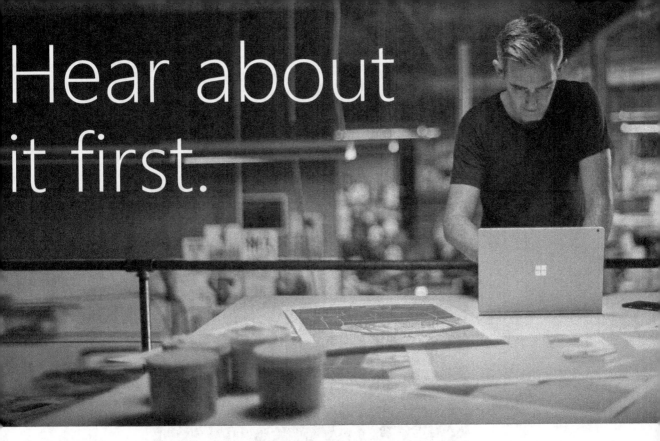

Hear about it first.

Get the latest news from Microsoft Press sent to your inbox.

- New and upcoming books
- Special offers
- Free eBooks
- How-to articles

Sign up today at MicrosoftPressStore.com/Newsletters

 Microsoft

Now that you've read the book...

Tell us what you think!

Was it useful?
Did it teach you what you wanted to learn?
Was there room for improvement?

Let us know at https://aka.ms/tellpress

Your feedback goes directly to the staff at Microsoft Press,
and we read every one of your responses. Thanks in advance!

 Microsoft